CW00405655

Scotland Textile Industry

Business and Investment

Opportunities Handbook

Just The facts101

Textbook Key Facts

by **Cram101**
Textbook NOT Included

Table of Contents

Just The Facts101

Exam Prep for

Scotland Textile Industry Business and Investment Opportunities Handbook

Just The Facts101 Exam Prep is your link from
the texbook and lecture to your exams.

**Just The Facts101 Exam Preps are unauthorized and comprehensive reviews
of your textbooks.**

Just The Facts101 Exam Prep

eAIN 449031

Foundations of Business

A business, also known as an enterprise, agency or a firm, is an entity involved in the provision of goods and/or services to consumers. Businesses are prevalent in capitalist economies, where most of them are privately owned and provide goods and services to customers in exchange for other goods, services, or money.

:: Graphic design ::

An _____ is an artifact that depicts visual perception, such as a photograph or other two-dimensional picture, that resembles a subject—usually a physical object—and thus provides a depiction of it. In the context of signal processing, an _____ is a distributed amplitude of color.

Exam Probability: **Medium**

1. *Answer choices:*

- a. Jade Magnet
- b. Image
- c. Iris printer
- d. Trial graphics

Guidance: level 1

:: Decision theory ::

Within economics the concept of _____ is used to model worth or value, but its usage has evolved significantly over time. The term was introduced initially as a measure of pleasure or satisfaction within the theory of utilitarianism by moral philosophers such as Jeremy Bentham and John Stuart Mill. But the term has been adapted and reapplied within neoclassical economics, which dominates modern economic theory, as a _____ function that represents a consumer's preference ordering over a choice set. As such, it is devoid of its original interpretation as a measurement of the pleasure or satisfaction obtained by the consumer from that choice.

Exam Probability: **Medium**

2. *Answer choices:*
(see index for correct answer)

- a. Dominance-based rough set approach
- b. Stochastic dominance
- c. Decision-theoretic rough sets
- d. Consensus decision-making

Guidance: level 1

:: Financial statements ::

In financial accounting, a _____ or statement of financial position or statement of financial condition is a summary of the financial balances of an individual or organization, whether it be a sole proprietorship, a business partnership, a corporation, private limited company or other organization such as Government or not-for-profit entity. Assets, liabilities and ownership equity are listed as of a specific date, such as the end of its financial year. A _____ is often described as a "snapshot of a company's financial condition". Of the four basic financial statements, the _____ is the only statement which applies to a single point in time of a business' calendar year.

Exam Probability: **Medium**

3. *Answer choices:*
(see index for correct answer)

- a. Balance sheet
- b. Clean surplus accounting
- c. PnL Explained

- d. Financial statement

Guidance: level 1

:: Human resource management ::

_____ encompasses values and behaviors that contribute to the unique social and psychological environment of a business. The _____ influences the way people interact, the context within which knowledge is created, the resistance they will have towards certain changes, and ultimately the way they share knowledge. _____ represents the collective values, beliefs and principles of organizational members and is a product of factors such as history, product, market, technology, strategy, type of employees, management style, and national culture; culture includes the organization's vision, values, norms, systems, symbols, language, assumptions, environment, location, beliefs and habits.

Exam Probability: **Low**

4. *Answer choices:*
(see index for correct answer)

- a. Functional job analysis
- b. CEO succession
- c. Organizational culture
- d. Trust fall

Guidance: level 1

:: Accounting software ::

_____ is any item or verifiable record that is generally accepted as payment for goods and services and repayment of debts, such as taxes, in a particular country or socio-economic context. The main functions of _____ are distinguished as: a medium of exchange, a unit of account, a store of value and sometimes, a standard of deferred payment. Any item or verifiable record that fulfils these functions can be considered as _____ .

Exam Probability: **High**

5. *Answer choices:*
(see index for correct answer)

- a. DHPOS
- b. Time tracking software
- c. Money
- d. Invoiceit

Guidance: level 1

:: ::

_____ is the means to see, hear, or become aware of something or someone through our fundamental senses. The term _____ derives from the Latin word perceptio, and is the organization, identification, and interpretation of sensory information in order to represent and understand the presented information, or the environment.

Exam Probability: **Low**

6. *Answer choices:*
(see index for correct answer)

- a. interpersonal communication
- b. Perception
- c. information systems assessment
- d. corporate values

Guidance: level 1

:: Rhetoric ::

_____ is the pattern of narrative development that aims to make vivid a place, object, character, or group. _____ is one of four rhetorical modes , along with exposition, argumentation, and narration. In practice it would be difficult to write literature that drew on just one of the four basic modes.

Exam Probability: **Low**

7. *Answer choices:*
(see index for correct answer)

- a. Essentially contested concept
- b. Description
- c. Amplification
- d. Pronuntiatio

Guidance: level 1

In business and finance, _____ is a system of organizations, people, activities, information, and resources involved inmoving a product or service from supplier to customer. _____ activities involve the transformation of natural resources, raw materials, and components into a finished product that is delivered to the end customer. In sophisticated _____ systems, used products may re-enter the _____ at any point where residual value is recyclable. _____ s link value chains.

Exam Probability: **Medium**

8. *Answer choices:*
(see index for correct answer)

- a. Final assembly schedule
- b. Supply chain
- c. Widget
- d. inventory management

Guidance: level 1

:: Unemployment ::

In economics, a _____ is a business cycle contraction when there is a general decline in economic activity. Macroeconomic indicators such as GDP , investment spending, capacity utilization, household income, business profits, and inflation fall, while bankruptcies and the unemployment rate rise. In the United Kingdom, it is defined as a negative economic growth for two consecutive quarters.

Exam Probability: **High**

9. *Answer choices:*
(see index for correct answer)

- a. Recession
- b. Reserve army of labour
- c. Waithood
- d. Texas Workforce Commission

Guidance: level 1

:: Supply chain management ::

_____ is the process of finding and agreeing to terms, and acquiring goods, services, or works from an external source, often via a tendering or competitive bidding process. _____ is used to ensure the buyer receives goods, services, or works at the best possible price when aspects such as quality, quantity, time, and location are compared. Corporations and public bodies often define processes intended to promote fair and open competition for their business while minimizing risks such as exposure to fraud and collusion.

Exam Probability: **High**

10. *Answer choices:*
(see index for correct answer)

- a. XIO Strategies
- b. Mobile asset management
- c. Chain of responsibility
- d. Procurement

Guidance: level 1

:: Business models ::

A _____ is "an autonomous association of persons united voluntarily to meet their common economic, social, and cultural needs and aspirations through a jointly-owned and democratically-controlled enterprise". _____ s may include.

Exam Probability: **Medium**

11. *Answer choices:*
(see index for correct answer)

- a. Market game
- b. Pay to play
- c. Cooperative
- d. What if chart

Guidance: level 1

:: Macroeconomics ::

_____ is the increase in the inflation-adjusted market value of the goods and services produced by an economy over time. It is conventionally measured as the percent rate of increase in real gross domestic product, or real GDP.

Exam Probability: **Medium**

12. *Answer choices:*
(see index for correct answer)

- a. Cumulative process
- b. Induced innovation
- c. Economic growth
- d. Asset-based economy

Guidance: level 1

:: Corporate crime ::

_____ LLP, based in Chicago, was an American holding company. Formerly one of the "Big Five" accounting firms , the firm had provided auditing, tax, and consulting services to large corporations. By 2001, it had become one of the world's largest multinational companies.

Exam Probability: **Medium**

13. *Answer choices:*
(see index for correct answer)

- a. New England Compounding Center
- b. NatWest Three
- c. Corporate Manslaughter and Corporate Homicide Act 2007
- d. FirstEnergy

Guidance: level 1

:: Business ::

_____ is a trade policy that does not restrict imports or exports; it can also be understood as the free market idea applied to international trade. In government, _____ is predominantly advocated by political parties that hold liberal economic positions while economically left-wing and nationalist political parties generally support protectionism, the opposite of _____ .

Exam Probability: **High**

14. *Answer choices:*
(see index for correct answer)

- a. Door-to-door
- b. For-profit charity
- c. Atmospherics
- d. Free trade

Guidance: level 1

:: Monopoly (economics) ::

A _____ is a form of intellectual property that gives its owner the legal right to exclude others from making, using, selling, and importing an invention for a limited period of years, in exchange for publishing an enabling public disclosure of the invention. In most countries _____ rights fall under civil law and the _____ holder needs to sue someone infringing the _____ in order to enforce his or her rights. In some industries _____ s are an essential form of competitive advantage; in others they are irrelevant.

Exam Probability: **High**

15. *Answer choices:*
(see index for correct answer)

- a. Barriers to exit
- b. Contestable market
- c. Regulatory economics
- d. Patent

Guidance: level 1

:: ::

_____ refers to a business or organization attempting to acquire goods or services to accomplish its goals. Although there are several organizations that attempt to set standards in the _____ process, processes can vary greatly between organizations. Typically the word " _____ " is not used interchangeably with the word "procurement", since procurement typically includes expediting, supplier quality, and transportation and logistics in addition to _____ .

Exam Probability: **Low**

16. *Answer choices:*

(see index for correct answer)

- a. personal values
- b. Purchasing
- c. similarity-attraction theory
- d. levels of analysis

Guidance: level 1

:: Information technology ::

_____ is the use of computers to store, retrieve, transmit, and manipulate data, or information, often in the context of a business or other enterprise. IT is considered to be a subset of information and communications technology . An _____ system is generally an information system, a communications system or, more specifically speaking, a computer system – including all hardware, software and peripheral equipment – operated by a limited group of users.

Exam Probability: **High**

17. *Answer choices:*

(see index for correct answer)

- a. IT industry competitiveness index
- b. CIO-plus
- c. CineGrid
- d. Information technology

Guidance: level 1

:: Management accounting ::

In economics, _____ s, indirect costs or overheads are business expenses that are not dependent on the level of goods or services produced by the business. They tend to be time-related, such as interest or rents being paid per month, and are often referred to as overhead costs. This is in contrast to variable costs, which are volume-related and unknown at the beginning of the accounting year. For a simple example, such as a bakery, the monthly rent for the baking facilities, and the monthly payments for the security system and basic phone line are _____ s, as they do not change according to how much bread the bakery produces and sells. On the other hand, the wage costs of the bakery are variable, as the bakery will have to hire more workers if the production of bread increases. Economists reckon _____ as a entry barrier for new entrepreneurs.

Exam Probability: **Medium**

18. *Answer choices:*
(see index for correct answer)

- a. activity based costing
- b. Semi-variable cost
- c. Fixed cost
- d. Institute of Cost and Management Accountants of Bangladesh

Guidance: level 1

:: Consumer theory ::

A _____ is a technical term in psychology, economics and philosophy usually used in relation to choosing between alternatives. For example, someone prefers A over B if they would rather choose A than B.

Exam Probability: **Medium**

19. *Answer choices:*
(see index for correct answer)

- a. Quality bias
- b. Revealed preference
- c. Preference
- d. Compensated demand

Guidance: level 1

:: ::

_____ is the collection of techniques, skills, methods, and processes used in the production of goods or services or in the accomplishment of objectives, such as scientific investigation. _____ can be the knowledge of techniques, processes, and the like, or it can be embedded in machines to allow for operation without detailed knowledge of their workings. Systems applying _____ by taking an input, changing it according to the system's use, and then producing an outcome are referred to as _____ systems or technological systems.

Exam Probability: **Medium**

20. *Answer choices:*
(see index for correct answer)

- a. open system
- b. corporate values
- c. functional perspective
- d. empathy

Guidance: level 1

:: Training ::

_____ is teaching, or developing in oneself or others, any skills and knowledge that relate to specific useful competencies. _____ has specific goals of improving one's capability, capacity, productivity and performance. It forms the core of apprenticeships and provides the backbone of content at institutes of technology . In addition to the basic _____ required for a trade, occupation or profession, observers of the labor-market recognize as of 2008 the need to continue _____ beyond initial qualifications: to maintain, upgrade and update skills throughout working life. People within many professions and occupations may refer to this sort of _____ as professional development.

Exam Probability: **Medium**

21. *Answer choices:*
(see index for correct answer)

- a. Large Group Capacitation
- b. Screencast
- c. Training

- d. Endurance training

Guidance: level 1

:: Mereology ::

_____ , in the abstract, is what belongs to or with something, whether as an attribute or as a component of said thing. In the context of this article, it is one or more components , whether physical or incorporeal, of a person's estate; or so belonging to, as in being owned by, a person or jointly a group of people or a legal entity like a corporation or even a society. Depending on the nature of the _____ , an owner of _____ has the right to consume, alter, share, redefine, rent, mortgage, pawn, sell, exchange, transfer, give away or destroy it, or to exclude others from doing these things, as well as to perhaps abandon it; whereas regardless of the nature of the _____ , the owner thereof has the right to properly use it , or at the very least exclusively keep it.

Exam Probability: **High**

22. *Answer choices:*
(see index for correct answer)

- a. Mereological essentialism
- b. Property
- c. Simple
- d. Mereotopology

Guidance: level 1

:: Stochastic processes ::

_____ is a system of rules that are created and enforced through social or governmental institutions to regulate behavior. It has been defined both as "the Science of Justice" and "the Art of Justice". _____ is a system that regulates and ensures that individuals or a community adhere to the will of the state. State-enforced _____ s can be made by a collective legislature or by a single legislator, resulting in statutes, by the executive through decrees and regulations, or established by judges through precedent, normally in common _____ jurisdictions. Private individuals can create legally binding contracts, including arbitration agreements that may elect to accept alternative arbitration to the normal court process. The formation of _____ s themselves may be influenced by a constitution, written or tacit, and the rights encoded therein. The _____ shapes politics, economics, history and society in various ways and serves as a mediator of relations between people.

Exam Probability: **High**

23. *Answer choices:*
(see index for correct answer)

- a. Cheeger bound
- b. Law
- c. Jump process
- d. G/G/1 queue

Guidance: level 1

:: Financial markets ::

A _____ is a financial market in which long-term debt or equity-backed securities are bought and sold. _____ s channel the wealth of savers to those who can put it to long-term productive use, such as companies or governments making long-term investments. Financial regulators like the Bank of England and the U.S. Securities and Exchange Commission oversee _____ s to protect investors against fraud, among other duties.

Exam Probability: **High**

24. *Answer choices:*
(see index for correct answer)

- a. Global Industry Classification Standard
- b. Exchange of futures for swaps

- c. Clearing balance requirement
- d. Capital market

Guidance: level 1

:: Credit cards ::

The _____ Company, also known as Amex, is an American multinational financial services corporation headquartered in Three World Financial Center in New York City. The company was founded in 1850 and is one of the 30 components of the Dow Jones Industrial Average. The company is best known for its charge card, credit card, and traveler's cheque businesses.

Exam Probability: **Medium**

25. *Answer choices:*
(see index for correct answer)

- a. Card scheme
- b. Bankcard
- c. American Express
- d. MasterCard

Guidance: level 1

:: ::

_____ is a means of protection from financial loss. It is a form of risk management, primarily used to hedge against the risk of a contingent or uncertain loss

Exam Probability: **High**

26. *Answer choices:*
(see index for correct answer)

- a. hierarchical
- b. levels of analysis
- c. surface-level diversity
- d. open system

Guidance: level 1

:: Employment ::

The _____ is an individual's metaphorical "journey" through learning, work and other aspects of life. There are a number of ways to define _____ and the term is used in a variety of ways.

Exam Probability: **Low**

27. *Answer choices:*
(see index for correct answer)

- a. Active ageing
- b. Career
- c. Suspension
- d. Effective altruism

Guidance: level 1

:: E-commerce ::

_____ is the activity of buying or selling of products on online services or over the Internet. Electronic commerce draws on technologies such as mobile commerce, electronic funds transfer, supply chain management, Internet marketing, online transaction processing, electronic data interchange , inventory management systems, and automated data collection systems.

Exam Probability: **Low**

28. *Answer choices:*
(see index for correct answer)

- a. Electronic sell-through
- b. Global Product Classification
- c. Zingiri
- d. E-commerce

Guidance: level 1

:: Human resource management ::

_____ is the corporate management term for the act of reorganizing the legal, ownership, operational, or other structures of a company for the purpose of making it more profitable, or better organized for its present needs. Other reasons for _____ include a change of ownership or ownership structure, demerger, or a response to a crisis or major change in the business such as bankruptcy, repositioning, or buyout. _____ may also be described as corporate _____ , debt _____ and financial _____ .

Exam Probability: **Low**

29. *Answer choices:*
(see index for correct answer)

- a. Dr. Marri Channa Reddy Human Resource Development Institute of Andhra Pradesh
- b. Individual development plan
- c. Restructuring
- d. Emotional labor

Guidance: level 1

:: Critical thinking ::

In psychology, _____ is regarded as the cognitive process resulting in the selection of a belief or a course of action among several alternative possibilities. Every _____ process produces a final choice, which may or may not prompt action.

Exam Probability: **High**

30. *Answer choices:*
(see index for correct answer)

- a. Proof
- b. Decision-making
- c. Explanation
- d. SEE-I

Guidance: level 1

:: Financial risk ::

_____ is a type of risk faced by investors, corporations, and governments that political decisions, events, or conditions will significantly affect the profitability of a business actor or the expected value of a given economic action. _____ can be understood and managed with reasoned foresight and investment.

Exam Probability: **High**

31. *Answer choices:*
(see index for correct answer)

- a. Solvency cone
- b. Dividend policy
- c. Country risk
- d. Political risk

Guidance: level 1

:: ::

_____ is a marketing communication that employs an openly sponsored, non-personal message to promote or sell a product, service or idea. Sponsors of _____ are typically businesses wishing to promote their products or services. _____ is differentiated from public relations in that an advertiser pays for and has control over the message. It differs from personal selling in that the message is non-personal, i.e., not directed to a particular individual. _____ is communicated through various mass media, including traditional media such as newspapers, magazines, television, radio, outdoor _____ or direct mail; and new media such as search results, blogs, social media, websites or text messages. The actual presentation of the message in a medium is referred to as an advertisement, or "ad" or advert for short.

Exam Probability: **Medium**

32. *Answer choices:*
(see index for correct answer)

- a. information systems assessment
- b. functional perspective
- c. Advertising
- d. interpersonal communication

Guidance: level 1

An _____ is generally a room or other area where an organization's employees perform administrative work in order to support and realize objects and goals of the organization. The word " _____ " may also denote a position within an organization with specific duties attached to it ; the latter is in fact an earlier usage, _____ as place originally referring to the location of one's duty. When used as an adjective, the term " _____ " may refer to business-related tasks. In law, a company or organization has _____ s in any place where it has an official presence, even if that presence consists of a storage silo rather than an establishment with desk-and-chair. An _____ is also an architectural and design phenomenon: ranging from a small _____ such as a bench in the corner of a small business of extremely small size , through entire floors of buildings, up to and including massive buildings dedicated entirely to one company. In modern terms an _____ is usually the location where white-collar workers carry out their functions. As per James Stephenson, " _____ is that part of business enterprise which is devoted to the direction and co-ordination of its various activities."

Exam Probability: **Medium**

33. *Answer choices:*
(see index for correct answer)

- a. Office
- b. Fish! Philosophy
- c. Activity management
- d. Inter departmental communication

Guidance: level 1

:: Strategic alliances ::

A _____ is an agreement between two or more parties to pursue a set of agreed upon objectives needed while remaining independent organizations. A _____ will usually fall short of a legal partnership entity, agency, or corporate affiliate relationship. Typically, two companies form a _____ when each possesses one or more business assets or have expertise that will help the other by enhancing their businesses. _____ s can develop in outsourcing relationships where the parties desire to achieve long-term win-win benefits and innovation based on mutually desired outcomes.

Exam Probability: **High**

34. *Answer choices:*

- a. Management contract
- b. Bridge Alliance
- c. International joint venture
- d. Defensive termination

Guidance: level 1

:: Management occupations ::

_____ ship is the process of designing, launching and running a new business, which is often initially a small business. The people who create these businesses are called _____ s.

Exam Probability: **Medium**

35. *Answer choices:*

- a. Comprador
- b. Apparatchik
- c. Entrepreneur
- d. Directeur sportif

Guidance: level 1

:: Management ::

In organizational studies, _____ is the efficient and effective development of an organization's resources when they are needed. Such resources may include financial resources, inventory, human skills, production resources, or information technology and natural resources.

Exam Probability: **Medium**

36. *Answer choices:*
(see index for correct answer)

- a. Staff management
- b. Target culture
- c. Resource management
- d. Board of governors

Guidance: level 1

:: Generally Accepted Accounting Principles ::

An _____ or profit and loss account is one of the financial statements of a company and shows the company's revenues and expenses during a particular period.

Exam Probability: **Low**

37. *Answer choices:*
(see index for correct answer)

- a. Financial position of the United States
- b. Income statement
- c. Cash method of accounting
- d. Chinese accounting standards

Guidance: level 1

:: Costs ::

In microeconomic theory, the _____, or alternative cost, of making a particular choice is the value of the most valuable choice out of those that were not taken. In other words, opportunity that will require sacrifices.

Exam Probability: **Medium**

- a. Direct labor cost
- b. Direct materials cost
- c. Repugnancy costs
- d. Cost curve

Guidance: level 1

:: Logistics ::

_____ is generally the detailed organization and implementation of a complex operation. In a general business sense, _____ is the management of the flow of things between the point of origin and the point of consumption in order to meet requirements of customers or corporations. The resources managed in _____ may include tangible goods such as materials, equipment, and supplies, as well as food and other consumable items. The _____ of physical items usually involves the integration of information flow, materials handling, production, packaging, inventory, transportation, warehousing, and often security.

Exam Probability: **Low**

39. *Answer choices:*

(see index for correct answer)

- a. Spetstyazhavtotrans
- b. Logistics
- c. Waybill
- d. ISO/IEC 18000-3

Guidance: level 1

:: Stock market ::

_____ is freedom from, or resilience against, potential harm caused by others. Beneficiaries of _____ may be of persons and social groups, objects and institutions, ecosystems or any other entity or phenomenon vulnerable to unwanted change by its environment.

Exam Probability: **Low**

40. *Answer choices:*

(see index for correct answer)

- a. Abnormal return
- b. Profit warning
- c. Box spread
- d. H share

Guidance: level 1

:: International trade ::

The law or principle of _____ holds that under free trade, an agent will produce more of and consume less of a good for which they have a _____ . _____ is the economic reality describing the work gains from trade for individuals, firms, or nations, which arise from differences in their factor endowments or technological progress. In an economic model, agents have a _____ over others in producing a particular good if they can produce that good at a lower relative opportunity cost or autarky price, i.e. at a lower relative marginal cost prior to trade. One shouldn't compare the monetary costs of production or even the resource costs of production. Instead, one must compare the opportunity costs of producing goods across countries.

Exam Probability: **Medium**

41. *Answer choices:*
(see index for correct answer)

- a. Spice trade
- b. Comparative advantage
- c. Silk Road
- d. Bureau de change

Guidance: level 1

:: Manufacturing ::

A _____ is an object used to extend the ability of an individual to modify features of the surrounding environment. Although many animals use simple _____ s, only human beings, whose use of stone _____ s dates back hundreds of millennia, use _____ s to make other _____ s. The set of _____ s needed to perform different tasks that are part of the same activity is called gear or equipment.

42. *Answer choices:*

(see index for correct answer)

- a. Advanced planning and scheduling
- b. Distributed manufacturing
- c. Lean manufacturing
- d. Taguchi methods

Guidance: level 1

:: Goods ::

In most contexts, the concept of _____ denotes the conduct that should be preferred when posed with a choice between possible actions. _____ is generally considered to be the opposite of evil, and is of interest in the study of morality, ethics, religion and philosophy. The specific meaning and etymology of the term and its associated translations among ancient and contemporary languages show substantial variation in its inflection and meaning depending on circumstances of place, history, religious, or philosophical context.

43. *Answer choices:*

(see index for correct answer)

- a. Inferior good
- b. Good
- c. Substitute good
- d. Intermediate good

Guidance: level 1

:: Shareholders ::

A _____ is a payment made by a corporation to its shareholders, usually as a distribution of profits. When a corporation earns a profit or surplus, the corporation is able to re-invest the profit in the business and pay a proportion of the profit as a _____ to shareholders. Distribution to shareholders may be in cash or, if the corporation has a _____ reinvestment plan, the amount can be paid by the issue of further shares or share repurchase. When _____ s are paid, shareholders typically must pay income taxes, and the corporation does not receive a corporate income tax deduction for the _____ payments.

Exam Probability: **Medium**

44. *Answer choices:*
(see index for correct answer)

- a. Shotgun clause
- b. Institutional Shareholder Services
- c. Say on pay
- d. Poison pill

Guidance: level 1

:: ::

_____ is an abstract concept of management of complex systems according to a set of rules and trends. In systems theory, these types of rules exist in various fields of biology and society, but the term has slightly different meanings according to context. For example.

Exam Probability: **Medium**

45. *Answer choices:*
(see index for correct answer)

- a. process perspective
- b. Regulation
- c. personal values
- d. co-culture

Guidance: level 1

:: Business ::

A _____ is a mathematical object used to count, measure, and label. The original examples are the natural _____ s 1, 2, 3, 4, and so forth. A written symbol like "5" that represents a _____ is called a numeral. A numeral system is an organized way to write and manipulate this type of symbol, for example the Hindu–Arabic numeral system allows combinations of numerical digits like "5" and "0" to represent larger _____ s like 50. A numeral in linguistics can refer to a symbol like 5, the words or phrase that names a _____ , like "five hundred", or other words that mean a specific _____ , like "dozen". In addition to their use in counting and measuring, numerals are often used for labels , for ordering , and for codes . In common usage, _____ may refer to a symbol, a word or phrase, or the mathematical object.

Exam Probability: **Medium**

46. *Answer choices:*

- a. Number
- b. EPG Model
- c. First party leads
- d. Disappointment

Guidance: level 1

:: Bribery ::

_____ is the act of giving or receiving something of value in exchange for some kind of influence or action in return, that the recipient would otherwise not offer. _____ is defined by Black's Law Dictionary as the offering, giving, receiving, or soliciting of any item of value to influence the actions of an official or other person in charge of a public or legal duty. Essentially, _____ is offering to do something for someone for the expressed purpose of receiving something in exchange. Gifts of money or other items of value which are otherwise available to everyone on an equivalent basis, and not for dishonest purposes, is not _____ . Offering a discount or a refund to all purchasers is a legal rebate and is not _____ . For example, it is legal for an employee of a Public Utilities Commission involved in electric rate regulation to accept a rebate on electric service that reduces their cost for electricity, when the rebate is available to other residential electric customers. Giving the rebate to influence them to look favorably on the electric utility's rate increase applications, however, would be considered _____ .

Exam Probability: **Medium**

47. *Answer choices:*
(see index for correct answer)

- a. Holyland Case
- b. Cunningham scandal
- c. Bribery
- d. Kickback

Guidance: level 1

:: Poker strategy ::

_____ is any measure taken to guard a thing against damage caused by outside forces. _____ can be provided to physical objects, including organisms, to systems, and to intangible things like civil and political rights. Although the mechanisms for providing _____ vary widely, the basic meaning of the term remains the same. This is illustrated by an explanation found in a manual on electrical wiring.

Exam Probability: **Low**

48. *Answer choices:*
(see index for correct answer)

- a. Steal
- b. Position
- c. Check-raise
- d. Slow play

Guidance: level 1

:: Business ::

The seller, or the provider of the goods or services, completes a sale in response to an acquisition, appropriation, requisition or a direct interaction with the buyer at the point of sale. There is a passing of title of the item, and the settlement of a price, in which agreement is reached on a price for which transfer of ownership of the item will occur. The seller, not the purchaser typically executes the sale and it may be completed prior to the obligation of payment. In the case of indirect interaction, a person who sells goods or service on behalf of the owner is known as a salesman or saleswoman or salesperson, but this often refers to someone _____ goods in a store/shop, in which case other terms are also common, including salesclerk, shop assistant, and retail clerk.

Exam Probability: **High**

49. *Answer choices:*
(see index for correct answer)

- a. Business sector
- b. Ian McLeod
- c. Selling
- d. Ametek

Guidance: level 1

:: ::

_____ is the administration of an organization, whether it is a business, a not-for-profit organization, or government body. _____ includes the activities of setting the strategy of an organization and coordinating the efforts of its employees to accomplish its objectives through the application of available resources, such as financial, natural, technological, and human resources. The term " _____ " may also refer to those people who manage an organization.

50. *Answer choices:*
(see index for correct answer)

- a. information systems assessment
- b. Character
- c. Management
- d. interpersonal communication

Guidance: level 1

:: Critical thinking ::

An _____ is a set of statements usually constructed to describe a set of facts which clarifies the causes, context, and consequences of those facts. This description of the facts et cetera may establish rules or laws, and may clarify the existing rules or laws in relation to any objects, or phenomena examined. The components of an _____ can be implicit, and interwoven with one another.

Exam Probability: **Medium**

51. *Answer choices:*
(see index for correct answer)

- a. Explanation
- b. Succinctness
- c. Inquiry
- d. Inquiry: Critical Thinking Across the Disciplines

Guidance: level 1

:: Consumer theory ::

_____ is the quantity of a good that consumers are willing and able to purchase at various prices during a given period of time.

Exam Probability: **Medium**

52. *Answer choices:*
(see index for correct answer)

- a. Demand
- b. Quality bias
- c. Time-based pricing

- d. Cross elasticity of demand

Guidance: level 1

:: Customs duties ::

A _____ is a tax on imports or exports between sovereign states. It is a form of regulation of foreign trade and a policy that taxes foreign products to encourage or safeguard domestic industry. _____ s are the simplest and oldest instrument of trade policy. Traditionally, states have used them as a source of income. Now, they are among the most widely used instruments of protection, along with import and export quotas.

Exam Probability: **Medium**

53. *Answer choices:*
(see index for correct answer)

- a. Tariff-rate quota
- b. Canada Corn Act
- c. Tariff
- d. Import Surtaxes

Guidance: level 1

:: Business ethics ::

_____ is a type of harassment technique that relates to a sexual nature and the unwelcome or inappropriate promise of rewards in exchange for sexual favors. _____ includes a range of actions from mild transgressions to sexual abuse or assault. Harassment can occur in many different social settings such as the workplace, the home, school, churches, etc. Harassers or victims may be of any gender.

Exam Probability: **Low**

54. *Answer choices:*
(see index for correct answer)

- a. Terror-free investing
- b. Surface Transportation Assistance Act
- c. McJob
- d. Ethical consumerism

Guidance: level 1

In business, a _____ is the attribute that allows an organization to outperform its competitors. A _____ may include access to natural resources, such as high-grade ores or a low-cost power source, highly skilled labor, geographic location, high entry barriers, and access to new technology.

Exam Probability: **High**

55. *Answer choices:*
(see index for correct answer)

- a. Logistics support analysis
- b. Business economics
- c. Office management
- d. Competitive advantage

Guidance: level 1

In accounting, _____ is the income that a business have from its normal business activities, usually from the sale of goods and services to customers. _____ is also referred to as sales or turnover.Some companies receive _____ from interest, royalties, or other fees. _____ may refer to business income in general, or it may refer to the amount, in a monetary unit, earned during a period of time, as in "Last year, Company X had _____ of $42 million". Profits or net income generally imply total _____ minus total expenses in a given period. In accounting, in the balance statement it is a subsection of the Equity section and _____ increases equity, it is often referred to as the "top line" due to its position on the income statement at the very top. This is to be contrasted with the "bottom line" which denotes net income .

Exam Probability: **Medium**

56. *Answer choices:*
(see index for correct answer)

- a. Revenue
- b. Revenue recognition
- c. Cash method of accounting
- d. Standard Business Reporting

:: Treaties ::

An _____ is a relationship among people, groups, or states that have joined together for mutual benefit or to achieve some common purpose, whether or not explicit agreement has been worked out among them. Members of an _____ are called allies. _____ s form in many settings, including political _____ s, military _____ s, and business _____ s. When the term is used in the context of war or armed struggle, such associations may also be called allied powers, especially when discussing World War I or World War II.

Exam Probability: **Medium**

57. *Answer choices:*
(see index for correct answer)

- a. Reservation
- b. Alliance
- c. Clausula rebus sic stantibus
- d. Multilateral treaty

:: Social security ::

_____ is "any government system that provides monetary assistance to people with an inadequate or no income." In the United States, this is usually called welfare or a social safety net, especially when talking about Canada and European countries.

Exam Probability: **Medium**

58. *Answer choices:*
(see index for correct answer)

- a. Total Social Security Accounts
- b. Bituah Leumi
- c. Mahatma Gandhi Pravasi Suraksha Yojana
- d. Social insurance

_____ is the practice of initiating, planning, executing, controlling, and closing the work of a team to achieve specific goals and meet specific success criteria at the specified time.

Exam Probability: **High**

59. *Answer choices:*
(see index for correct answer)

- a. Twelve leverage points
- b. Energy monitoring and targeting
- c. Meeting
- d. Project management

Guidance: level 1

Management

Management is the administration of an organization, whether it is a business, a not-for-profit organization, or government body. Management includes the activities of setting the strategy of an organization and coordinating the efforts of its employees (or of volunteers) to accomplish its objectives through the application of available resources, such as financial, natural, technological, and human resources.

:: ::

_____ , in its broadest context, includes both the attainment of that which is just and the philosophical discussion of that which is just. The concept of _____ is based on numerous fields, and many differing viewpoints and perspectives including the concepts of moral correctness based on ethics, rationality, law, religion, equity and fairness. Often, the general discussion of _____ is divided into the realm of social _____ as found in philosophy, theology and religion, and, procedural _____ as found in the study and application of the law.

Exam Probability: **Low**

1. *Answer choices:*
(see index for correct answer)

- a. co-culture
- b. deep-level diversity
- c. hierarchical
- d. imperative

Guidance: level 1

:: Management ::

A _____ is a formal written document containing business goals, the methods on how these goals can be attained, and the time frame within which these goals need to be achieved. It also describes the nature of the business, background information on the organization, the organization's financial projections, and the strategies it intends to implement to achieve the stated targets. In its entirety, this document serves as a road map that provides direction to the business.

Exam Probability: **High**

2. *Answer choices:*

- a. Scenario planning
- b. Business rule
- c. Event to knowledge
- d. Reval

Guidance: level 1

:: Income ::

In business and accounting, net income is an entity's income minus cost of goods sold, expenses and taxes for an accounting period. It is computed as the residual of all revenues and gains over all expenses and losses for the period, and has also been defined as the net increase in shareholders' equity that results from a company's operations. In the context of the presentation of financial statements, the IFRS Foundation defines net income as synonymous with profit and loss. The difference between revenue and the cost of making a product or providing a service, before deducting overheads, payroll, taxation, and interest payments. This is different from operating income .

Exam Probability: **Medium**

3. *Answer choices:*

- a. Real income
- b. Income earner
- c. Bottom line
- d. Return of investment

Guidance: level 1

_____ is a kind of action that occur as two or more objects have an effect upon one another. The idea of a two-way effect is essential in the concept of _____ , as opposed to a one-way causal effect. A closely related term is interconnectivity, which deals with the _____ s of _____ s within systems: combinations of many simple _____ s can lead to surprising emergent phenomena. _____ has different tailored meanings in various sciences. Changes can also involve _____ .

Exam Probability: **Low**

4. *Answer choices:*

(see index for correct answer)

- a. open system
- b. functional perspective
- c. cultural
- d. Interaction

Guidance: level 1

:: Human resource management ::

_____ are the people who make up the workforce of an organization, business sector, or economy. "Human capital" is sometimes used synonymously with " _____ ", although human capital typically refers to a narrower effect . Likewise, other terms sometimes used include manpower, talent, labor, personnel, or simply people.

Exam Probability: **High**

5. *Answer choices:*

(see index for correct answer)

- a. Human resource consulting
- b. Management development
- c. Human resources
- d. Cultural capital

Guidance: level 1

:: Management ::

A _____ is a method or technique that has been generally accepted as superior to any alternatives because it produces results that are superior to those achieved by other means or because it has become a standard way of doing things, e.g., a standard way of complying with legal or ethical requirements.

Exam Probability: **Medium**

6. *Answer choices:*

- a. Meeting
- b. Completed Staff Work
- c. Visual learning
- d. Best practice

Guidance: level 1

:; Human resource management ..

An organizational chart is a diagram that shows the structure of an organization and the relationships and relative ranks of its parts and positions/jobs. The term is also used for similar diagrams, for example ones showing the different elements of a field of knowledge or a group of languages.

Exam Probability: **Low**

7. *Answer choices:*

- a. Co-determination
- b. Organization chart
- c. The war for talent
- d. Employee value proposition

Guidance: level 1

:: Materials ::

A _____ , also known as a feedstock, unprocessed material, or primary commodity, is a basic material that is used to produce goods, finished products, energy, or intermediate materials which are feedstock for future finished products. As feedstock, the term connotes these materials are bottleneck assets and are highly important with regard to producing other products. An example of this is crude oil, which is a _____ and a feedstock used in the production of industrial chemicals, fuels, plastics, and pharmaceutical goods; lumber is a _____ used to produce a variety of products including all types of furniture. The term " _____ " denotes materials in minimally processed or unprocessed in states; e.g., raw latex, crude oil, cotton, coal, raw biomass, iron ore, air, logs, or water i.e. "...any product of agriculture, forestry, fishing and any other mineral that is in its natural form or which has undergone the transformation required to prepare it for internationally marketing in substantial volumes."

Exam Probability: **Low**

8. *Answer choices:*
(see index for correct answer)

- a. Aerospace materials
- b. Tensometer
- c. Materials World
- d. Raw material

Guidance: level 1

:: Critical thinking ::

An _____ is someone who has a prolonged or intense experience through practice and education in a particular field. Informally, an _____ is someone widely recognized as a reliable source of technique or skill whose faculty for judging or deciding rightly, justly, or wisely is accorded authority and status by peers or the public in a specific well-distinguished domain. An _____ , more generally, is a person with extensive knowledge or ability based on research, experience, or occupation and in a particular area of study. _____ s are called in for advice on their respective subject, but they do not always agree on the particulars of a field of study. An _____ can be believed, by virtue of credential, training, education, profession, publication or experience, to have special knowledge of a subject beyond that of the average person, sufficient that others may officially rely upon the individual's opinion. Historically, an _____ was referred to as a sage . The individual was usually a profound thinker distinguished for wisdom and sound judgment.

Exam Probability: **High**

9. *Answer choices:*
(see index for correct answer)

- a. Association for Informal Logic and Critical Thinking
- b. Fallacy
- c. Inquiry
- d. Rhetoric

Guidance: level 1

:: Management ::

The _____ is a strategy performance management tool – a semi-standard structured report, that can be used by managers to keep track of the execution of activities by the staff within their control and to monitor the consequences arising from these actions.

Exam Probability: **Low**

10. *Answer choices:*
(see index for correct answer)

- a. Logistics support analysis
- b. Balanced scorecard
- c. Enterprise decision management

- d. Job rotation

Guidance: level 1

:: Business models ::

A _____ , _____ company or daughter company is a company that is owned or controlled by another company, which is called the parent company, parent, or holding company. The _____ can be a company, corporation, or limited liability company. In some cases it is a government or state-owned enterprise. In some cases, particularly in the music and book publishing industries, subsidiaries are referred to as imprints.

Exam Probability: **Low**

11. *Answer choices:*
(see index for correct answer)

- a. 70/20/10 Model
- b. Subsidiary
- c. Business-agile enterprise
- d. Revenue model

Guidance: level 1

:: Problem solving ::

In other words, _____ is a situation where a group of people meet to generate new ideas and solutions around a specific domain of interest by removing inhibitions. People are able to think more freely and they suggest as many spontaneous new ideas as possible. All the ideas are noted down and those ideas are not criticized and after _____ session the ideas are evaluated. The term was popularized by Alex Faickney Osborn in the 1953 book Applied Imagination.

Exam Probability: **High**

12. *Answer choices:*
(see index for correct answer)

- a. Rhetorical reason
- b. Brainstorming
- c. Social heuristics
- d. Nursing process

:: Product management ::

_____ s, also known as Shewhart charts or process-behavior charts, are a statistical process control tool used to determine if a manufacturing or business process is in a state of control.

Exam Probability: **Medium**

13. *Answer choices:*
(see index for correct answer)

- a. Trademark
- b. Dwinell-Wright Company
- c. Control chart
- d. Product manager

:: Management ::

In business, a _____ is the attribute that allows an organization to outperform its competitors. A _____ may include access to natural resources, such as high-grade ores or a low-cost power source, highly skilled labor, geographic location, high entry barriers, and access to new technology.

Exam Probability: **Low**

14. *Answer choices:*
(see index for correct answer)

- a. Competitive advantage
- b. Corporate recovery
- c. Relevance paradox
- d. Design leadership

:: Human resource management ::

_____ is the strategic approach to the effective management of people in an organization so that they help the business to gain a competitive advantage. It is designed to maximize employee performance in service of an employer's strategic objectives. HR is primarily concerned with the management of people within organizations, focusing on policies and on systems. HR departments are responsible for overseeing employee-benefits design, employee recruitment, training and development, performance appraisal, and Reward management . HR also concerns itself with organizational change and industrial relations, that is, the balancing of organizational practices with requirements arising from collective bargaining and from governmental laws.

Exam Probability: **High**

15. *Answer choices:*
(see index for correct answer)

- a. Aspiring Minds
- b. war for talent
- c. Incentive program
- d. Human resource management

Guidance: level 1

:: Human resource management ::

A _____ is a group of people with different functional expertise working toward a common goal. It may include people from finance, marketing, operations, and human resources departments. Typically, it includes employees from all levels of an organization. Members may also come from outside an organization .

Exam Probability: **High**

16. *Answer choices:*
(see index for correct answer)

- a. Cultural capital
- b. Employee retention
- c. Induction programme
- d. Human relations movement

Guidance: level 1

:: Business ethics ::

_____ is a type of harassment technique that relates to a sexual nature and the unwelcome or inappropriate promise of rewards in exchange for sexual favors. _____ includes a range of actions from mild transgressions to sexual abuse or assault. Harassment can occur in many different social settings such as the workplace, the home, school, churches, etc. Harassers or victims may be of any gender.

Exam Probability: **Medium**

17. *Answer choices:*
(see index for correct answer)

- a. Center for Adult Development
- b. Business Ethics Quarterly
- c. Corporate social entrepreneurship
- d. Sexual harassment

Guidance: level 1

:: Strategic management ::

_____ is a strategic planning technique used to help a person or organization identify strengths, weaknesses, opportunities, and threats related to business competition or project planning. It is intended to specify the objectives of the business venture or project and identify the internal and external factors that are favorable and unfavorable to achieving those objectives. Users of a _____ often ask and answer questions to generate meaningful information for each category to make the tool useful and identify their competitive advantage. SWOT has been described as the tried-and-true tool of strategic analysis.

Exam Probability: **Low**

18. *Answer choices:*
(see index for correct answer)

- a. BSC SWOT
- b. SWOT analysis
- c. strategy implementation
- d. Journal of Contingencies and Crisis Management

Guidance: level 1

Automatic _____ in continuous production processes is a combination of control engineering and chemical engineering disciplines that uses industrial control systems to achieve a production level of consistency, economy and safety which could not be achieved purely by human manual control. It is implemented widely in industries such as oil refining, pulp and paper manufacturing, chemical processing and power generating plants.

Exam Probability: **Low**

19. *Answer choices:*
(see index for correct answer)

- a. Fiberglass molding
- b. Production function
- c. Process control
- d. Job production

Guidance: level 1

:: Lean manufacturing ::

A continual improvement process, also often called a _____ process , is an ongoing effort to improve products, services, or processes. These efforts can seek "incremental" improvement over time or "breakthrough" improvement all at once. Delivery processes are constantly evaluated and improved in the light of their efficiency, effectiveness and flexibility.

Exam Probability: **Low**

20. *Answer choices:*
(see index for correct answer)

- a. Lean laboratory
- b. Continuous improvement
- c. Muri
- d. Production leveling

Guidance: level 1

:: Human resource management ::

_____ involves improving the effectiveness of organizations and the individuals and teams within them. Training may be viewed as related to immediate changes in organizational effectiveness via organized instruction, while development is related to the progress of longer-term organizational and employee goals. While _____ technically have differing definitions, the two are oftentimes used interchangeably and/or together. _____ has historically been a topic within applied psychology but has within the last two decades become closely associated with human resources management, talent management, human resources development, instructional design, human factors, and knowledge management.

Exam Probability: **High**

21. *Answer choices:*

(see index for correct answer)

- a. Training and development
- b. Talent management
- c. Reward management
- d. Cultural capital

Guidance: level 1

:: ::

A _____ is a leader's method of providing direction, implementing plans, and motivating people. Various authors have proposed identifying many different _____ s as exhibited by leaders in the political, business or other fields. Studies on _____ are conducted in the military field, expressing an approach that stresses a holistic view of leadership, including how a leader's physical presence determines how others perceive that leader. The factors of physical presence in this context include military bearing, physical fitness, confidence, and resilience. The leader's intellectual capacity helps to conceptualize solutions and to acquire knowledge to do the job. A leader's conceptual abilities apply agility, judgment, innovation, interpersonal tact, and domain knowledge. Domain knowledge encompasses tactical and technical knowledge as well as cultural and geopolitical awareness. Daniel Goleman in his article "Leadership that Gets Results" talks about six styles of leadership.

Exam Probability: **Medium**

22. *Answer choices:*
(see index for correct answer)

- a. Leadership style
- b. imperative
- c. levels of analysis
- d. process perspective

Guidance: level 1

:: Time management ::

_____ is the process of planning and exercising conscious control of time spent on specific activities, especially to increase effectiveness, efficiency, and productivity. It involves a juggling act of various demands upon a person relating to work, social life, family, hobbies, personal interests and commitments with the finiteness of time. Using time effectively gives the person "choice" on spending/managing activities at their own time and expediency.

Exam Probability: **High**

23. *Answer choices:*
(see index for correct answer)

- a. HabitRPG
- b. waiting room
- c. Sufficient unto the day is the evil thereof
- d. Maestro concept

Guidance: level 1

:: Information science ::

_____ is the resolution of uncertainty; it is that which answers the question of "what an entity is" and thus defines both its essence and nature of its characteristics. _____ relates to both data and knowledge, as data is meaningful _____ representing values attributed to parameters, and knowledge signifies understanding of a concept. _____ is uncoupled from an observer, which is an entity that can access _____ and thus discern what it specifies; _____ exists beyond an event horizon for example. In the case of knowledge, the _____ itself requires a cognitive observer to be obtained.

24. *Answer choices:*

- a. Information
- b. Blaise Cronin
- c. Evolutionary informatics
- d. Jason Farradane

Guidance: level 1

:: Production and manufacturing ::

_____ is a theory of management that analyzes and synthesizes workflows. Its main objective is improving economic efficiency, especially labor productivity. It was one of the earliest attempts to apply science to the engineering of processes and to management. _____ is sometimes known as Taylorism after its founder, Frederick Winslow Taylor.

25. *Answer choices:*

- a. Fixed position assembly
- b. Corrective and preventive action
- c. Production equipment control
- d. Scientific management

Guidance: level 1

:: ::

The _____ officer or just _____ , is the most senior corporate, executive, or administrative officer in charge of managing an organization especially an independent legal entity such as a company or nonprofit institution. CEOs lead a range of organizations, including public and private corporations, non-profit organizations and even some government organizations . The CEO of a corporation or company typically reports to the board of directors and is charged with maximizing the value of the entity, which may include maximizing the share price, market share, revenues or another element. In the non-profit and government sector, CEOs typically aim at achieving outcomes related to the organization's mission, such as reducing poverty, increasing literacy, etc.

Exam Probability: **Low**

26. *Answer choices:*

(see index for correct answer)

- a. hierarchical perspective
- b. Chief executive
- c. empathy
- d. co-culture

Guidance: level 1

:: ::

_____ is the practice of protecting the natural environment by individuals, organizations and governments. Its objectives are to conserve natural resources and the existing natural environment and, where possible, to repair damage and reverse trends.

Exam Probability: **Low**

27. *Answer choices:*

(see index for correct answer)

- a. levels of analysis
- b. Environmental protection
- c. personal values
- d. imperative

Guidance: level 1

A _____ or business method is a collection of related, structured activities or tasks by people or equipment which in a specific sequence produce a service or product for a particular customer or customers. _____ es occur at all organizational levels and may or may not be visible to the customers. A _____ may often be visualized as a flowchart of a sequence of activities with interleaving decision points or as a process matrix of a sequence of activities with relevance rules based on data in the process. The benefits of using _____ es include improved customer satisfaction and improved agility for reacting to rapid market change. Process-oriented organizations break down the barriers of structural departments and try to avoid functional silos.

Exam Probability: **Medium**

28. *Answer choices:*

(see index for correct answer)

- a. A Guide to the Business Analysis Body of Knowledge
- b. Process mining
- c. Business process
- d. Business operations

Guidance: level 1

:: ::

_____ or standardisation is the process of implementing and developing technical standards based on the consensus of different parties that include firms, users, interest groups, standards organizations and governments. _____ can help maximize compatibility, interoperability, safety, repeatability, or quality. It can also facilitate commoditization of formerly custom processes. In social sciences, including economics, the idea of _____ is close to the solution for a coordination problem, a situation in which all parties can realize mutual gains, but only by making mutually consistent decisions. This view includes the case of "spontaneous _____ processes", to produce de facto standards.

Exam Probability: **Low**

29. *Answer choices:*

- a. surface-level diversity
- b. Standardization
- c. co-culture
- d. empathy

Guidance: level 1

:: Labor rights ::

A _____ is a wrong or hardship suffered, real or supposed, which forms legitimate grounds of complaint. In the past, the word meant the infliction or cause of hardship.

Exam Probability: **Medium**

30. *Answer choices:*

- a. Kate Mullany House
- b. Labor rights
- c. Grievance
- d. China Labour Bulletin

Guidance: level 1

:: Survey methodology ::

An _____ is a conversation where questions are asked and answers are given. In common parlance, the word " _____ " refers to a one-on-one conversation between an _____ er and an _____ ee. The _____ er asks questions to which the _____ ee responds, usually so information may be transferred from _____ ee to _____ er . Sometimes, information can be transferred in both directions. It is a communication, unlike a speech, which produces a one-way flow of information.

Exam Probability: **Low**

31. *Answer choices:*

- a. Data editing
- b. Survey research
- c. Administrative error

- d. Coverage error

Guidance: level 1

:: ::

_____ is the process of two or more people or organizations working together to complete a task or achieve a goal. _____ is similar to cooperation. Most _____ requires leadership, although the form of leadership can be social within a decentralized and egalitarian group. Teams that work collaboratively often access greater resources, recognition and rewards when facing competition for finite resources.

Exam Probability: **High**

32. *Answer choices:*
(see index for correct answer)

- a. Character
- b. Collaboration
- c. information systems assessment
- d. process perspective

Guidance: level 1

:: Game theory ::

To _____ is to make a deal between different parties where each party gives up part of their demand. In arguments, _____ is a concept of finding agreement through communication, through a mutual acceptance of terms—often involving variations from an original goal or desires.

Exam Probability: **High**

33. *Answer choices:*
(see index for correct answer)

- a. Solution concept
- b. Social software
- c. Compromise
- d. The Intuitive Criterion

Guidance: level 1

_____ is a category of property that includes intangible creations of the human intellect. _____ encompasses two types of rights: industrial property rights and copyright. It was not until the 19th century that the term " _____ " began to be used, and not until the late 20th century that it became commonplace in the majority of the world.

Exam Probability: **Medium**

34. *Answer choices:*
(see index for correct answer)

- a. Intellectual property
- b. Quasi-rent
- c. Economies of scope
- d. Contestable market

Guidance: level 1

Some scenarios associate "this kind of planning" with learning "life skills".Schedules are necessary, or at least useful, in situations where individuals need to know what time they must be at a specific location to receive a specific service, and where people need to accomplish a set of goals within a set time period.

Exam Probability: **High**

35. *Answer choices:*
(see index for correct answer)

- a. interpersonal communication
- b. Sarbanes-Oxley act of 2002
- c. deep-level diversity
- d. Scheduling

Guidance: level 1

_____ is the amount of time someone works beyond normal working hours. The term is also used for the pay received for this time. Normal hours may be determined in several ways.

36. *Answer choices:*
(see index for correct answer)

- a. open system
- b. Overtime
- c. process perspective
- d. hierarchical perspective

Guidance: level 1

:: ::

In organizational behavior and industrial/organizational psychology, proactivity or _____ behavior by individuals refers to anticipatory, change-oriented and self-initiated behavior in situations. _____ behavior involves acting in advance of a future situation, rather than just reacting. It means taking control and making things happen rather than just adjusting to a situation or waiting for something to happen. _____ employees generally do not need to be asked to act, nor do they require detailed instructions.

37. *Answer choices:*
(see index for correct answer)

- a. cultural
- b. Proactive
- c. similarity-attraction theory
- d. interpersonal communication

Guidance: level 1

:: Training ::

_____ is teaching, or developing in oneself or others, any skills and knowledge that relate to specific useful competencies. _____ has specific goals of improving one's capability, capacity, productivity and performance. It forms the core of apprenticeships and provides the backbone of content at institutes of technology . In addition to the basic _____ required for a trade, occupation or profession, observers of the labor-market recognize as of 2008 the need to continue _____ beyond initial qualifications: to maintain, upgrade and update skills throughout working life. People within many professions and occupations may refer to this sort of _____ as professional development.

Exam Probability: **Medium**

38. *Answer choices:*
(see index for correct answer)

- a. Hypoventilation training
- b. Arts Party
- c. Endurance training
- d. Training

Guidance: level 1

:: Management ::

_____ is a method of quality control which employs statistical methods to monitor and control a process. This helps to ensure that the process operates efficiently, producing more specification-conforming products with less waste . SPC can be applied to any process where the "conforming product" output can be measured. Key tools used in SPC include run charts, control charts, a focus on continuous improvement, and the design of experiments. An example of a process where SPC is applied is manufacturing lines.

Exam Probability: **Low**

39. *Answer choices:*
(see index for correct answer)

- a. Environmental stewardship
- b. Law practice management
- c. Value proposition
- d. Change advisory board

Guidance: level 1

_____ is the pattern of narrative development that aims to make vivid a place, object, character, or group. _____ is one of four rhetorical modes , along with exposition, argumentation, and narration. In practice it would be difficult to write literature that drew on just one of the four basic modes.

Exam Probability: **Medium**

40. *Answer choices:*
(see index for correct answer)

- a. Exophora
- b. Description
- c. Brutus
- d. Scare quotes

Guidance: level 1

A _____ is a building for storing goods. _____ s are used by manufacturers, importers, exporters, wholesalers, transport businesses, customs, etc. They are usually large plain buildings in industrial parks on the outskirts of cities, towns or villages.

Exam Probability: **Medium**

41. *Answer choices:*
(see index for correct answer)

- a. Rytec Corporation
- b. Warehouse
- c. OMAC
- d. Machine coordinate system

Guidance: level 1

:: ::

A _____ is a problem offering two possibilities, neither of which is unambiguously acceptable or preferable. The possibilities are termed the horns of the _____ , a clichéd usage, but distinguishing the _____ from other kinds of predicament as a matter of usage.

Exam Probability: **Low**

42. *Answer choices:*
(see index for correct answer)

- a. empathy
- b. Dilemma
- c. interpersonal communication
- d. open system

Guidance: level 1

:: Behavior modification ::

In psychotherapy and mental health, _____ has a positive sense of empowering individuals, or a negative sense of encouraging dysfunctional behavior.

Exam Probability: **High**

43. *Answer choices:*
(see index for correct answer)

- a. Enabling
- b. behavioural change

Guidance: level 1

:: Production economics ::

_____ is the creation of a whole that is greater than the simple sum of its parts. The term _____ comes from the Attic Greek word sea synergia from synergos, , meaning "working together".

Exam Probability: **High**

44. *Answer choices:*
(see index for correct answer)

- a. Value and Capital
- b. Capitalist mode of production
- c. Synergy
- d. Isocost

Guidance: level 1

:: Employment discrimination ::

A _____ is a metaphor used to represent an invisible barrier that keeps a given demographic from rising beyond a certain level in a hierarchy.

Exam Probability: **Medium**

45. *Answer choices:*
(see index for correct answer)

- a. Glass ceiling
- b. Marriage bars
- c. Employment discrimination
- d. MacBride Principles

Guidance: level 1

:: Human resource management ::

_____ , executive management, upper management, or a management team is generally a team of individuals at the highest level of management of an organization who have the day-to-day tasks of managing that organization — sometimes a company or a corporation.

Exam Probability: **Medium**

46. *Answer choices:*
(see index for correct answer)

- a. Employee retention
- b. Open plan
- c. Trust fall
- d. Job enlargement

Guidance: level 1

:: International relations ::

A _____ is any event that is going to lead to an unstable and dangerous situation affecting an individual, group, community, or whole society. Crises are deemed to be negative changes in the security, economic, political, societal, or environmental affairs, especially when they occur abruptly, with little or no warning. More loosely, it is a term meaning "a testing time" or an "emergency event".

Exam Probability: **Medium**

47. *Answer choices:*

- a. Crisis
- b. Gambling for resurrection
- c. Freedom deficit
- d. Emerging power

Guidance: level 1

:: Business models ::

_____ es are privately owned corporations, partnerships, or sole proprietorships that have fewer employees and/or less annual revenue than a regular-sized business or corporation. Businesses are defined as "small" in terms of being able to apply for government support and qualify for preferential tax policy varies depending on the country and industry.

_____ es range from fifteen employees under the Australian Fair Work Act 2009, fifty employees according to the definition used by the European Union, and fewer than five hundred employees to qualify for many U.S. _____ Administration programs. While _____ es can also be classified according to other methods, such as annual revenues, shipments, sales, assets, or by annual gross or net revenue or net profits, the number of employees is one of the most widely used measures.

Exam Probability: **Low**

48. *Answer choices:*

- a. Utility computing
- b. Small business
- c. Organizational architecture
- d. Premium business model

:: Lean manufacturing ::

_____ is the Sino-Japanese word for "improvement". In business, _____ refers to activities that continuously improve all functions and involve all employees from the CEO to the assembly line workers. It also applies to processes, such as purchasing and logistics, that cross organizational boundaries into the supply chain. It has been applied in healthcare, psychotherapy, life-coaching, government, and banking.

Exam Probability: **Medium**

49. *Answer choices:*
<small>(see index for correct answer)</small>

- a. Lean enterprise
- b. Kaizen
- c. 5S
- d. The Machine That Changed the World

:: ::

An _____ is the production of goods or related services within an economy. The major source of revenue of a group or company is the indicator of its relevant _____ . When a large group has multiple sources of revenue generation, it is considered to be working in different industries. Manufacturing _____ became a key sector of production and labour in European and North American countries during the Industrial Revolution, upsetting previous mercantile and feudal economies. This came through many successive rapid advances in technology, such as the production of steel and coal.

Exam Probability: **High**

50. *Answer choices:*
<small>(see index for correct answer)</small>

- a. levels of analysis
- b. similarity-attraction theory
- c. Character

- d. Industry

:: ::

A _____ is monetary compensation paid by an employer to an employee in exchange for work done. Payment may be calculated as a fixed amount for each task completed , or at an hourly or daily rate , or based on an easily measured quantity of work done.

Exam Probability: **High**

51. *Answer choices:*
(see index for correct answer)

- a. information systems assessment
- b. Wage
- c. personal values
- d. hierarchical perspective

:: Industrial Revolution ::

The _____ , now also known as the First _____ , was the transition to new manufacturing processes in Europe and the US, in the period from about 1760 to sometime between 1820 and 1840. This transition included going from hand production methods to machines, new chemical manufacturing and iron production processes, the increasing use of steam power and water power, the development of machine tools and the rise of the mechanized factory system. The _____ also led to an unprecedented rise in the rate of population growth.

Exam Probability: **Low**

52. *Answer choices:*
(see index for correct answer)

- a. Thomas Walmsley and Sons
- b. Industrial Revolution
- c. Coalbrookdale
- d. Great Migration of Canada

A _____ is a type of job aid used to reduce failure by compensating for potential limits of human memory and attention. It helps to ensure consistency and completeness in carrying out a task. A basic example is the "to do list". A more advanced _____ would be a schedule, which lays out tasks to be done according to time of day or other factors. A primary task in _____ is documentation of the task and auditing against the documentation.

Exam Probability: **Low**

53. *Answer choices:*
(see index for correct answer)

- a. corporate values
- b. process perspective
- c. Checklist
- d. personal values

Guidance: level 1

:: Human resource management ::

_____ is a core function of human resource management and it is related to the specification of contents, methods and relationship of jobs in order to satisfy technological and organizational requirements as well as the social and personal requirements of the job holder or the employee. Its principles are geared towards how the nature of a person's job affects their attitudes and behavior at work, particularly relating to characteristics such as skill variety and autonomy. The aim of a _____ is to improve job satisfaction, to improve through-put, to improve quality and to reduce employee problems .

Exam Probability: **High**

54. *Answer choices:*
(see index for correct answer)

- a. Contractor management
- b. Job design
- c. Parallel running
- d. Cultural capital

Guidance: level 1

A _____ is a short statement of why an organization exists, what its overall goal is, identifying the goal of its operations: what kind of product or service it provides, its primary customers or market, and its geographical region of operation. It may include a short statement of such fundamental matters as the organization's values or philosophies, a business's main competitive advantages, or a desired future state—the "vision".

Exam Probability: **High**

55. *Answer choices:*
(see index for correct answer)

- a. Personal selling
- b. Strategic partner
- c. Mission statement
- d. centralization

Guidance: level 1

An _____ is a private network accessible only to an organization's staff. Often, a wide range of information and services are available on an organization's internal _____ that are unavailable to the public, unlike the Internet. A company-wide _____ can constitute an important focal point of internal communication and collaboration, and provide a single starting point to access internal and external resources. In its simplest form, an _____ is established with the technologies for local area networks and wide area networks . Many modern _____ s have search engines, user profiles, blogs, mobile apps with notifications, and events planning within their infrastructure.

Exam Probability: **High**

56. *Answer choices:*
(see index for correct answer)

- a. Phoenix Labs
- b. Intranet portal
- c. Cypherpunks
- d. Intranet

:: Planning ::

_____ is a high level plan to achieve one or more goals under conditions of uncertainty. In the sense of the "art of the general," which included several subsets of skills including tactics, siegecraft, logistics etc., the term came into use in the 6th century C.E. in East Roman terminology, and was translated into Western vernacular languages only in the 18th century. From then until the 20th century, the word "_____" came to denote "a comprehensive way to try to pursue political ends, including the threat or actual use of force, in a dialectic of wills" in a military conflict, in which both adversaries interact.

Exam Probability: **High**

57. *Answer choices:*
(see index for correct answer)

- a. Resource-Task Network
- b. Parish plan
- c. Concept driven strategy
- d. Strategy

:: Personality tests ::

The Myers–Briggs Type Indicator is an introspective self-report questionnaire with the purpose of indicating differing psychological preferences in how people perceive the world around them and make decisions. . Though the test superficially resembles some psychological theories it is commonly classified as pseudoscience, especially as pertains to its supposed predictive abilities.

Exam Probability: **High**

58. *Answer choices:*
(see index for correct answer)

- a. Johari window
- b. Myers-Briggs Type Indicator
- c. Keirsey Temperament Sorter

- d. Myers-Briggs type

Guidance: level 1

:: Behaviorism ::

In behavioral psychology, _____ is a consequence applied that will strengthen an organism's future behavior whenever that behavior is preceded by a specific antecedent stimulus. This strengthening effect may be measured as a higher frequency of behavior , longer duration , greater magnitude , or shorter latency . There are two types of _____ , known as positive _____ and negative _____ ; positive is where by a reward is offered on expression of the wanted behaviour and negative is taking away an undesirable element in the persons environment whenever the desired behaviour is achieved.

Exam Probability: **Low**

59. *Answer choices:*
(see index for correct answer)

- a. Reinforcement
- b. Systematic desensitization
- c. contingency management
- d. Programmed instruction

Guidance: level 1

Business law

Corporate law (also known as business law) is the body of law governing the rights, relations, and conduct of persons, companies, organizations and businesses. It refers to the legal practice relating to, or the theory of corporations. Corporate law often describes the law relating to matters which derive directly from the life-cycle of a corporation. It thus encompasses the formation, funding, governance, and death of a corporation.

:: Progressive Era in the United States ::

The Clayton Antitrust Act of 1914 , was a part of United States antitrust law with the goal of adding further substance to the U.S. antitrust law regime; the _____ sought to prevent anticompetitive practices in their incipiency. That regime started with the Sherman Antitrust Act of 1890, the first Federal law outlawing practices considered harmful to consumers . The _____ specified particular prohibited conduct, the three-level enforcement scheme, the exemptions, and the remedial measures.

Exam Probability: **Low**

1. *Answer choices:*
(see index for correct answer)

- a. Mann Act
- b. Clayton Act
- c. pragmatism

Guidance: level 1

:: Ethically disputed business practices ::

_____ is the trading of a public company's stock or other securities by individuals with access to nonpublic information about the company. In various countries, some kinds of trading based on insider information is illegal. This is because it is seen as unfair to other investors who do not have access to the information, as the investor with insider information could potentially make larger profits than a typical investor could make. The rules governing _____ are complex and vary significantly from country to country. The extent of enforcement also varies from one country to another. The definition of insider in one jurisdiction can be broad, and may cover not only insiders themselves but also any persons related to them, such as brokers, associates and even family members. A person who becomes aware of non-public information and trades on that basis may be guilty of a crime.

Exam Probability: **High**

2. *Answer choices:*
(see index for correct answer)

- a. Sugging
- b. Persuasive technology
- c. Spamming
- d. Nokku kooli

Guidance: level 1

:: Business law ::

The term is used to designate a range of diverse, if often kindred, concepts. These have historically been addressed in a number of discrete disciplines, notably mathematics, physics, chemistry, ethics, aesthetics, ontology, and theology.

Exam Probability: **Low**

3. *Answer choices:*
(see index for correct answer)

- a. Ease of doing business index
- b. Commercial law
- c. Valuation using the Market Penetration Model
- d. Perfection

Guidance: level 1

:: Insurance law ::

_____ exists when an insured person derives a financial or other kind of benefit from the continuous existence, without repairment or damage, of the insured object . A person has an _____ in something when loss of or damage to that thing would cause the person to suffer a financial or other kind of loss.Normally, _____ is established by ownership, possession, or direct relationship. For example, people have _____ s in their own homes and vehicles, but not in their neighbors` homes and vehicles, and almost certainly not those of strangers.

Exam Probability: **High**

4. *Answer choices:*
(see index for correct answer)

- a. Insurable interest
- b. Aleatory contract
- c. QC clause
- d. Australian insurance law

Guidance: level 1

:: False advertising law ::

The Lanham Act is the primary federal trademark statute of law in the United States. The Act prohibits a number of activities, including trademark infringement, trademark dilution, and false advertising.

Exam Probability: **Low**

5. *Answer choices:*
(see index for correct answer)

- a. Rebecca Tushnet
- b. Lanham Act

Guidance: level 1

:: Contract law ::

A _____ , unlike a void contract, is a valid contract which may be either affirmed or rejected at the option of one of the parties. At most, one party to the contract is bound. The unbound party may repudiate the contract, at which time the contract becomes void.

Exam Probability: **Low**

6. *Answer choices:*
(see index for correct answer)

- a. United States contract law
- b. Last shot
- c. Expectation damages
- d. Baseball business rules

Guidance: level 1

:: Contract law ::

In contract law, _____ is an excuse for the nonperformance of duties under a contract, based on a change in circumstances , the nonoccurrence of which was an underlying assumption of the contract, that makes performance of the contract literally impossible.

Exam Probability: **Medium**

7. *Answer choices:*
(see index for correct answer)

- a. Rescission
- b. Choice of law clause
- c. Impossibility
- d. Unenforceable

Guidance: level 1

:: Legal doctrines and principles ::

_____ is a defense in the law of torts, which bars or reduces a plaintiff's right to recovery against a negligent tortfeasor if the defendant can demonstrate that the plaintiff voluntarily and knowingly assumed the risks at issue inherent to the dangerous activity in which he was participating at the time of his or her injury.

Exam Probability: **High**

8. *Answer choices:*
(see index for correct answer)

- a. Exclusionary rule
- b. Abstention doctrine
- c. Assumption of risk
- d. Act of state

Guidance: level 1

:: ::

Competition arises whenever at least two parties strive for a goal which cannot be shared: where one's gain is the other's loss .

Exam Probability: **Low**

9. *Answer choices:*
(see index for correct answer)

- a. hierarchical
- b. corporate values
- c. Competitor
- d. co-culture

Guidance: level 1

:: Commercial item transport and distribution ::

A _____ is a commitment or expectation to perform some action in general or if certain circumstances arise. A _____ may arise from a system of ethics or morality, especially in an honor culture. Many duties are created by law, sometimes including a codified punishment or liability for non-performance. Performing one's _____ may require some sacrifice of self-interest.

Exam Probability: **High**

10. *Answer choices:*
(see index for correct answer)

- a. Food distribution
- b. EUR-pallet
- c. Tanker
- d. Bonded warehouse

Guidance: level 1

:: ::

_____ is the assignment of any responsibility or authority to another person to carry out specific activities. It is one of the core concepts of management leadership. However, the person who delegated the work remains accountable for the outcome of the delegated work. _____ empowers a subordinate to make decisions, i.e. it is a shifting of decision-making authority from one organizational level to a lower one. _____ , if properly done, is not fabrication. The opposite of effective _____ is micromanagement, where a manager provides too much input, direction, and review of delegated work. In general, _____ is good and can save money and time, help in building skills, and motivate people. On the other hand, poor _____ might cause frustration and confusion to all the involved parties. Some agents, however, do not favour a _____ and consider the power of making a decision rather burdensome.

Exam Probability: **Low**

11. *Answer choices:*
(see index for correct answer)

- a. hierarchical perspective
- b. open system
- c. Delegation

- d. Character

Guidance: level 1

:: Contract law ::

_____ , also called an anticipatory breach, is a term in the law of contracts that describes a declaration by the promising party to a contract that he or she does not intend to live up to his or her obligations under the contract.

Exam Probability: **High**

12. *Answer choices:*
(see index for correct answer)

- a. Anticipatory repudiation
- b. Per minas
- c. Perfect tender
- d. Oral contract

Guidance: level 1

:: Decision theory ::

Within economics the concept of _____ is used to model worth or value, but its usage has evolved significantly over time. The term was introduced initially as a measure of pleasure or satisfaction within the theory of utilitarianism by moral philosophers such as Jeremy Bentham and John Stuart Mill. But the term has been adapted and reapplied within neoclassical economics, which dominates modern economic theory, as a _____ function that represents a consumer's preference ordering over a choice set. As such, it is devoid of its original interpretation as a measurement of the pleasure or satisfaction obtained by the consumer from that choice.

Exam Probability: **Low**

13. *Answer choices:*
(see index for correct answer)

- a. Pignistic probability
- b. Normative model of decision-making
- c. Utility
- d. ELECTRE

:: Working time ::

Labour law is the area of law most commonly relating to the relationship between trade unions, employers and the government.

Exam Probability: **High**

14. *Answer choices:*

(see index for correct answer)

- a. Forty-Hour Week Convention, 1935
- b. Clyde Engineering Co Ltd v Cowburn
- c. Juliet Schor
- d. Employment law

Guidance: level 1

:: International trade ::

_____ involves the transfer of goods or services from one person or entity to another, often in exchange for money. A system or network that allows _____ is called a market.

Exam Probability: **Medium**

15. *Answer choices:*

(see index for correct answer)

- a. Foreign Agricultural Service
- b. SinoLatin Capital
- c. Modalities
- d. Trade

Guidance: level 1

:: Competition regulators ::

The _____ is an independent agency of the United States government, established in 1914 by the _____ Act. Its principal mission is the promotion of consumer protection and the elimination and prevention of anticompetitive business practices, such as coercive monopoly. It is headquartered in the _____ Building in Washington, D.C.

Exam Probability: **Low**

16. *Answer choices:*

(see index for correct answer)

- a. Jersey Competition Regulatory Authority
- b. Competition and Markets Authority
- c. Industrial Commission
- d. Federal Cartel Office

Guidance: level 1

:: ::

_____ or accountancy is the measurement, processing, and communication of financial information about economic entities such as businesses and corporations. The modern field was established by the Italian mathematician Luca Pacioli in 1494. _____ , which has been called the "language of business", measures the results of an organization's economic activities and conveys this information to a variety of users, including investors, creditors, management, and regulators. Practitioners of _____ are known as accountants. The terms " _____ " and "financial reporting" are often used as synonyms.

Exam Probability: **High**

17. *Answer choices:*

(see index for correct answer)

- a. information systems assessment
- b. co-culture
- c. Character
- d. empathy

Guidance: level 1

:: ::

_____ is a judicial device in common law legal systems whereby a court may prevent, or "estop" a person from making assertions or from going back on his or her word; the person being sanctioned is "estopped". _____ may prevent someone from bringing a particular claim. Legal doctrines of _____ are based in both common law and equity.

Exam Probability: **Medium**

18. *Answer choices:*

(see index for correct answer)

- a. cultural
- b. open system
- c. deep-level diversity
- d. corporate values

Guidance: level 1

:: ::

The _____ of 1977 is a United States federal law known primarily for two of its main provisions: one that addresses accounting transparency requirements under the Securities Exchange Act of 1934 and another concerning bribery of foreign officials. The Act was amended in 1988 and in 1998, and has been subject to continued congressional concerns, namely whether its enforcement discourages U.S. companies from investing abroad.

Exam Probability: **High**

19. *Answer choices:*

(see index for correct answer)

- a. levels of analysis
- b. hierarchical perspective
- c. Foreign Corrupt Practices Act
- d. process perspective

Guidance: level 1

:: ::

In law, a _____ is the formal finding of fact made by a jury on matters or questions submitted to the jury by a judge. In a bench trial, the judge's decision near the end of the trial is simply referred to as a finding. In England and Wales, a coroner's findings are called _____ s .

Exam Probability: **Low**

20. *Answer choices:*
(see index for correct answer)

- a. hierarchical perspective
- b. Verdict
- c. deep-level diversity
- d. information systems assessment

Guidance: level 1

:: ::

_____ is the body of law that governs the activities of administrative agencies of government. Government agency action can include rule making, adjudication, or the enforcement of a specific regulatory agenda. _____ is considered a branch of public law. As a body of law, _____ deals with the decision-making of the administrative units of government that are part of a national regulatory scheme in such areas as police law, international trade, manufacturing, the environment, taxation, broadcasting, immigration and transport. _____ expanded greatly during the twentieth century, as legislative bodies worldwide created more government agencies to regulate the social, economic and political spheres of human interaction.

Exam Probability: **Medium**

21. *Answer choices:*
(see index for correct answer)

- a. similarity-attraction theory
- b. hierarchical perspective
- c. Character
- d. Administrative law

Guidance: level 1

:: ::

A _____ is a request to do something, most commonly addressed to a government official or public entity. _____ s to a deity are a form of prayer called supplication.

Exam Probability: **Medium**

22. *Answer choices:*
(see index for correct answer)

- a. Petition
- b. co-culture
- c. deep-level diversity
- d. open system

Guidance: level 1

:: ::

_____ Corporation was an American energy, commodities, and services company based in Houston, Texas. It was founded in 1985 as a merger between Houston Natural Gas and InterNorth, both relatively small regional companies. Before its bankruptcy on December 3, 2001, _____ employed approximately 29,000 staff and was a major electricity, natural gas, communications and pulp and paper company, with claimed revenues of nearly $101 billion during 2000. Fortune named _____ "America's Most Innovative Company" for six consecutive years.

Exam Probability: **Medium**

23. *Answer choices:*
(see index for correct answer)

- a. process perspective
- b. functional perspective
- c. deep-level diversity
- d. interpersonal communication

Guidance: level 1

:: Business law ::

A _____ is a group of people who jointly supervise the activities of an organization, which can be either a for-profit business, nonprofit organization, or a government agency. Such a board's powers, duties, and responsibilities are determined by government regulations and the organization's own constitution and bylaws. These authorities may specify the number of members of the board, how they are to be chosen, and how often they are to meet.

Exam Probability: **Medium**

24. *Answer choices:*
(see index for correct answer)

- a. Limited liability
- b. Practicing without a license
- c. Ordinary course of business
- d. Relational contract

Guidance: level 1

:: ::

An _____ is a criminal accusation that a person has committed a crime. In jurisdictions that use the concept of felonies, the most serious criminal offence is a felony; jurisdictions that do not use the felonies concept often use that of an indictable offence, an offence that requires an _____ .

Exam Probability: **Medium**

25. *Answer choices:*
(see index for correct answer)

- a. hierarchical
- b. Sarbanes-Oxley act of 2002
- c. Indictment
- d. Character

Guidance: level 1

:: ::

In contract law, rescission is an equitable remedy which allows a contractual party to cancel the contract. Parties may _____ if they are the victims of a vitiating factor, such as misrepresentation, mistake, duress, or undue influence. Rescission is the unwinding of a transaction. This is done to bring the parties, as far as possible, back to the position in which they were before they entered into a contract .

Exam Probability: **Medium**

26. *Answer choices:*
(see index for correct answer)

- a. hierarchical perspective
- b. Rescind
- c. surface-level diversity
- d. corporate values

Guidance: level 1

:: ::

_____ s and acquisitions are transactions in which the ownership of companies, other business organizations, or their operating units are transferred or consolidated with other entities. As an aspect of strategic management, M&A can allow enterprises to grow or downsize, and change the nature of their business or competitive position.

Exam Probability: **Low**

27. *Answer choices:*
(see index for correct answer)

- a. surface-level diversity
- b. interpersonal communication
- c. similarity-attraction theory
- d. Merger

Guidance: level 1

:: Equity (law) ::

An assignment is a legal term used in the context of the law of contract and of property. In both instances, assignment is the process whereby a person, the assignor, transfers rights or benefits to another, the _____ . An assignment may not transfer a duty, burden or detriment without the express agreement of the _____ . The right or benefit being assigned may be a gift or it may be paid for with a contractual consideration such as money.

Exam Probability: **Medium**

28. *Answer choices:*
(see index for correct answer)

- a. assignor
- b. Equitable conversion

Guidance: level 1

:: Patent law ::

A _____ is generally any statement intended to specify or delimit the scope of rights and obligations that may be exercised and enforced by parties in a legally recognized relationship. In contrast to other terms for legally operative language, the term _____ usually implies situations that involve some level of uncertainty, waiver, or risk.

Exam Probability: **High**

29. *Answer choices:*
(see index for correct answer)

- a. Patentability
- b. Patent monetization
- c. Patent infringement
- d. Disclaimer

Guidance: level 1

:: ::

An _____ is a written sworn statement of fact voluntarily made by an affiant or deponent under an oath or affirmation administered by a person authorized to do so by law. Such statement is witnessed as to the authenticity of the affiant's signature by a taker of oaths, such as a notary public or commissioner of oaths. An _____ is a type of verified statement or showing, or in other words, it contains a verification, meaning it is under oath or penalty of perjury, and this serves as evidence to its veracity and is required for court proceedings.

Exam Probability: **Low**

30. *Answer choices:*
(see index for correct answer)

- a. cultural
- b. hierarchical
- c. information systems assessment
- d. Affidavit

Guidance: level 1

:: Manufactured goods ::

A _____ or final good is any commodity that is produced or consumed by the consumer to satisfy current wants or needs. _____ s are ultimately consumed, rather than used in the production of another good. For example, a microwave oven or a bicycle that is sold to a consumer is a final good or _____ , but the components that are sold to be used in those goods are intermediate goods. For example, textiles or transistors can be used to make some further goods.

Exam Probability: **Medium**

31. *Answer choices:*
(see index for correct answer)

- a. Consumer Good
- b. Tarpaulin
- c. Household goods
- d. Product ecosystem theory

Guidance: level 1

:: ::

_____ is the practice of protecting the natural environment by individuals, organizations and governments. Its objectives are to conserve natural resources and the existing natural environment and, where possible, to repair damage and reverse trends.

Exam Probability: **Low**

32. *Answer choices:*
(see index for correct answer)

- a. open system
- b. information systems assessment
- c. cultural
- d. Environmental Protection

Guidance: level 1

:: ::

_____ is property that is movable. In common law systems, _____ may also be called chattels or personalty. In civil law systems, _____ is often called movable property or movables – any property that can be moved from one location to another.

Exam Probability: **Low**

33. *Answer choices:*
(see index for correct answer)

- a. Personal property
- b. empathy
- c. cultural
- d. functional perspective

Guidance: level 1

:: ::

The _____ is the highest court within the hierarchy of courts in many legal jurisdictions. Other descriptions for such courts include court of last resort, apex court, and high court of appeal. Broadly speaking, the decisions of a _____ are not subject to further review by any other court. _____ s typically function primarily as appellate courts, hearing appeals from decisions of lower trial courts, or from intermediate-level appellate courts.

Exam Probability: **Medium**

34. *Answer choices:*
(see index for correct answer)

- a. imperative
- b. surface-level diversity
- c. Character
- d. Supreme Court

Guidance: level 1

:: Clauses of the United States Constitution ::

The _____ describes an enumerated power listed in the United States Constitution . The clause states that the United States Congress shall have power "To regulate Commerce with foreign Nations, and among the several States, and with the Indian Tribes." Courts and commentators have tended to discuss each of these three areas of commerce as a separate power granted to Congress. It is common to see the individual components of the _____ referred to under specific terms: the Foreign _____ , the Interstate _____ , and the Indian _____ .

Exam Probability: **High**

35. *Answer choices:*
(see index for correct answer)

- a. Double Jeopardy Clause
- b. Full Faith and Credit Clause
- c. Full faith and credit

Guidance: level 1

:: ::

In regulatory jurisdictions that provide for it , _____ is a group of laws and organizations designed to ensure the rights of consumers as well as fair trade, competition and accurate information in the marketplace. The laws are designed to prevent the businesses that engage in fraud or specified unfair practices from gaining an advantage over competitors. They may also provides additional protection for those most vulnerable in society. _____ laws are a form of government regulation that aim to protect the rights of consumers. For example, a government may require businesses to disclose detailed information about products—particularly in areas where safety or public health is an issue, such as food.

Exam Probability: **Medium**

36. *Answer choices:*
(see index for correct answer)

- a. cultural
- b. similarity-attraction theory
- c. hierarchical perspective
- d. interpersonal communication

Guidance: level 1

:: Intention ::

_____ is the mental element of a person's intention to commit a crime; or knowledge that one's action or lack of action would cause a crime to be committed. It is a necessary element of many crimes.

Exam Probability: **Low**

37. *Answer choices:*
(see index for correct answer)

- a. Mens rea
- b. bona fide

Guidance: level 1

:: ::

In common law legal systems, _____ is a principle or rule established in a previous legal case that is either binding on or persuasive for a court or other tribunal when deciding subsequent cases with similar issues or facts. Common-law legal systems place great value on deciding cases according to consistent principled rules, so that similar facts will yield similar and predictable outcomes, and observance of _____ is the mechanism by which that goal is attained. The principle by which judges are bound to _____ s is known as stare decisis. Common-law _____ is a third kind of law, on equal footing with statutory law and delegated legislation or regulatory law

.

Exam Probability: **Medium**

38. *Answer choices:*
(see index for correct answer)

- a. Precedent
- b. empathy
- c. imperative
- d. surface-level diversity

Guidance: level 1

:: Business law ::

A _____ is an arrangement where parties, known as partners, agree to cooperate to advance their mutual interests. The partners in a _____ may be individuals, businesses, interest-based organizations, schools, governments or combinations. Organizations may partner to increase the likelihood of each achieving their mission and to amplify their reach. A _____ may result in issuing and holding equity or may be only governed by a contract.

Exam Probability: **Low**

39. *Answer choices:*
(see index for correct answer)

- a. Tax patent
- b. Security interest
- c. Arbitration clause
- d. Consignment agreement

Guidance: level 1

_____ is the principled guide to action taken by the administrative executive branches of the state with regard to a class of issues, in a manner consistent with law and institutional customs.

Exam Probability: **Medium**

40. *Answer choices:*
(see index for correct answer)

- a. empathy
- b. Character
- c. interpersonal communication
- d. information systems assessment

Guidance: level 1

:: Business law ::

In the United States, the United Kingdom, Australia, Canada and South Africa, _____ relates to the doctrines of the law of agency. It is relevant particularly in corporate law and constitutional law. _____ refers to a situation where a reasonable third party would understand that an agent had authority to act. This means a principal is bound by the agent's actions, even if the agent had no actual authority, whether express or implied. It raises an estoppel because the third party is given an assurance, which he relies on and would be inequitable for the principal to deny the authority given. _____ can legally be found, even if actual authority has not been given.

Exam Probability: **Medium**

41. *Answer choices:*
(see index for correct answer)

- a. Business valuation
- b. Retained interest
- c. Turnkey
- d. Bulk transfer

Guidance: level 1

:: Marketing ::

_____ or stock is the goods and materials that a business holds for the ultimate goal of resale .

42. *Answer choices:*
(see index for correct answer)

- a. Inventory
- b. Marketing intelligence
- c. Movie packaging
- d. Non-price competition

Guidance: level 1

:: ::

A _____ , in law, is a set of facts sufficient to justify a right to sue to obtain money, property, or the enforcement of a right against another party. The term also refers to the legal theory upon which a plaintiff brings suit . The legal document which carries a claim is often called a `statement of claim` in English law, or a `complaint` in U.S. federal practice and in many U.S. states. It can be any communication notifying the party to whom it is addressed of an alleged fault which resulted in damages, often expressed in amount of money the receiving party should pay/reimburse.

43. *Answer choices:*
(see index for correct answer)

- a. Sarbanes-Oxley act of 2002
- b. deep-level diversity
- c. Cause of action
- d. hierarchical

Guidance: level 1

:: Contract law ::

Offer and acceptance analysis is a traditional approach in contract law. The offer and acceptance formula, developed in the 19th century, identifies a moment of formation when the parties are of one mind. This classical approach to contract formation has been modified by developments in the law of estoppel, misleading conduct, misrepresentation and unjust enrichment.

Exam Probability: **Medium**

44. *Answer choices:*
(see index for correct answer)

- a. Prenuptial agreement
- b. Illegal agreement
- c. Unjust enrichment
- d. Offeror

Guidance: level 1

:: ::

The _____ is the central philosophical concept in the deontological moral philosophy of Immanuel Kant. Introduced in Kant's 1785 Groundwork of the Metaphysics of Morals, it may be defined as a way of evaluating motivations for action.

Exam Probability: **Low**

45. *Answer choices:*
(see index for correct answer)

- a. surface-level diversity
- b. Categorical imperative
- c. deep-level diversity
- d. co-culture

Guidance: level 1

:: Real estate ::

_____ , real estate, realty, or immovable property In English common law refers to landed properties belonging to some person. It include all structures, crops, buildings, machinery, wells, dams, ponds, mines, canals, and roads, among other things. The term is historic, arising from the now-discontinued form of action, which distinguish between _____ disputes and personal property disputes. Personal property was, and continues to refer to all properties that are not real properties.

46. *Answer choices:*
(see index for correct answer)

- a. Real-estate lock box
- b. Real property
- c. Crown land
- d. Monotenure

Guidance: level 1

:: Contract law ::

_____ is the act of recall or annulment. It is the cancelling of an act, the recalling of a grant or privilege, or the making void of some deed previously existing.

47. *Answer choices:*
(see index for correct answer)

- a. Contractual term
- b. Condition subsequent
- c. Morals clause
- d. Revocation

Guidance: level 1

:: Business ::

_____ is a trade policy that does not restrict imports or exports; it can also be understood as the free market idea applied to international trade. In government, _____ is predominantly advocated by political parties that hold liberal economic positions while economically left-wing and nationalist political parties generally support protectionism, the opposite of _____ .

Exam Probability: **Medium**

48. *Answer choices:*
(see index for correct answer)

- a. Equality impact assessment
- b. Organizational life cycle
- c. Free trade
- d. Local multiplier effect

Guidance: level 1

:: ::

Competition law is a law that promotes or seeks to maintain market competition by regulating anti-competitive conduct by companies. Competition law is implemented through public and private enforcement. Competition law is known as " _____ law" in the United States for historical reasons, and as "anti-monopoly law" in China and Russia. In previous years it has been known as trade practices law in the United Kingdom and Australia. In the European Union, it is referred to as both _____ and competition law.

Exam Probability: **High**

49. *Answer choices:*
(see index for correct answer)

- a. corporate values
- b. hierarchical perspective
- c. Antitrust
- d. deep-level diversity

Guidance: level 1

:: Business models ::

A _____ , _____ company or daughter company is a company that is owned or controlled by another company, which is called the parent company, parent, or holding company. The _____ can be a company, corporation, or limited liability company. In some cases it is a government or state-owned enterprise. In some cases, particularly in the music and book publishing industries, subsidiaries are referred to as imprints.

Exam Probability: **Low**

50. *Answer choices:*
(see index for correct answer)

- a. Independent business
- b. Business Model Canvas
- c. Subsidiary
- d. Parent company

Guidance: level 1

:: ::

The _____ of 1973, , is a federal law, codified as 29 U.S.C. § 701 et seq. The principal sponsor of the bill was Rep. John Brademas [IN-3]. The _____ of 1973 replaces the Vocational _____ of 1973, to extend and revise the authorization of grants to States for vocational rehabilitation services, with special emphasis on services to those with the most severe disabilities, to expand special Federal responsibilities and research and training programs with respect to individuals with disabilities, to establish special responsibilities in the Secretary of Health, Education, and Welfare for coordination of all programs with respect to individuals with disabilities within the Department of Health, Education, and Welfare, and for other purposes.

Exam Probability: **Low**

51. *Answer choices:*
(see index for correct answer)

- a. Rehabilitation Act
- b. similarity-attraction theory
- c. corporate values
- d. hierarchical perspective

Guidance: level 1

A _____ is any person who contracts to acquire an asset in return for some form of consideration.

Exam Probability: **Low**

52. *Answer choices:*
(see index for correct answer)

- a. Buyer
- b. imperative
- c. information systems assessment
- d. Sarbanes-Oxley act of 2002

Guidance: level 1

:: Decision theory ::

A _____ is a deliberate system of principles to guide decisions and achieve rational outcomes. A _____ is a statement of intent, and is implemented as a procedure or protocol. Policies are generally adopted by a governance body within an organization. Policies can assist in both subjective and objective decision making. Policies to assist in subjective decision making usually assist senior management with decisions that must be based on the relative merits of a number of factors, and as a result are often hard to test objectively, e.g. work-life balance _____ . In contrast policies to assist in objective decision making are usually operational in nature and can be objectively tested, e.g. password _____ .

Exam Probability: **High**

53. *Answer choices:*
(see index for correct answer)

- a. Normative model of decision-making
- b. TOPSIS
- c. Outcome primacy
- d. Dominance-based rough set approach

Guidance: level 1

A _____ is monetary compensation paid by an employer to an employee in exchange for work done. Payment may be calculated as a fixed amount for each task completed , or at an hourly or daily rate , or based on an easily measured quantity of work done.

Exam Probability: **Low**

54. *Answer choices:*
(see index for correct answer)

- a. personal values
- b. information systems assessment
- c. Wage
- d. hierarchical perspective

Guidance: level 1

:: Treaties ::

A _____ is an agreement under international law entered into by actors in international law, namely sovereign states and international organizations. A _____ may also be known as an agreement, protocol, covenant, convention, pact, or exchange of letters, among other terms. Regardless of terminology, all of these forms of agreements are, under international law, equally considered treaties and the rules are the same.

Exam Probability: **Medium**

55. *Answer choices:*
(see index for correct answer)

- a. Treaty
- b. Bilateral treaty
- c. Alliance
- d. Subsidiary alliance

Guidance: level 1

:: Contract law ::

An _____ is a contract that has not yet been fully performed or fully executed. It is a contract in which both sides still have important performance remaining. However, an obligation to pay money, even if such obligation is material, does not usually make a contract executory. An obligation is material if a breach of contract would result from the failure to satisfy the obligation. A contract that has been fully performed by one party but not by the other party is not an _____ .

Exam Probability: **High**

56. *Answer choices:*
(see index for correct answer)

- a. Severability
- b. Cohabitation agreement
- c. Executory contract
- d. Domicilium citandi et executandi

Guidance: level 1

:: ::

A _____ , in common law jurisdictions, is a civil wrong that causes a claimant to suffer loss or harm resulting in legal liability for the person who commits the _____ ious act. It can include the intentional infliction of emotional distress, negligence, financial losses, injuries, invasion of privacy, and many other things.

Exam Probability: **Low**

57. *Answer choices:*
(see index for correct answer)

- a. hierarchical
- b. hierarchical perspective
- c. Tort
- d. deep-level diversity

Guidance: level 1

:: ::

In law, a _____ is a coming together of parties to a dispute, to present information in a tribunal, a formal setting with the authority to adjudicate claims or disputes. One form of tribunal is a court. The tribunal, which may occur before a judge, jury, or other designated trier of fact, aims to achieve a resolution to their dispute.

Exam Probability: **Medium**

58. *Answer choices:*
(see index for correct answer)

- a. imperative
- b. similarity-attraction theory
- c. Trial
- d. interpersonal communication

Guidance: level 1

:: Corporate finance ::

_____ is a contract law concept about the purchase of the release from a debt obligation. It is one of the methods by which parties to a contract may terminate their agreement. The release is completed by the transfer of valuable consideration that must not be the actual performance of the obligation itself. The accord is the agreement to discharge the obligation and the satisfaction is the legal "consideration" which binds the parties to the agreement. A valid accord does not discharge the prior contract; instead it suspends the right to enforce it in accordance with the terms of the accord contract, in which satisfaction, or performance of the contract will discharge both contracts. If the creditor breaches the accord, then the debtor will be able to bring up the existence of the accord in order to enjoin any action against him.

Exam Probability: **Medium**

59. *Answer choices:*
(see index for correct answer)

- a. Tender offer
- b. Initial license offering
- c. Special purpose entity
- d. Accord and satisfaction

Guidance: level 1

Finance

Finance is a field that is concerned with the allocation (investment) of assets and liabilities over space and time, often under conditions of risk or uncertainty. Finance can also be defined as the science of money management. Participants in the market aim to price assets based on their risk level, fundamental value, and their expected rate of return. Finance can be split into three sub-categories: public finance, corporate finance and personal finance.

:: ::

Pharmaceutical _____ is the creation of a particular pharmaceutical product to fit the unique need of a patient. To do this, _____ pharmacists combine or process appropriate ingredients using various tools.

Exam Probability: **Medium**

1. *Answer choices:*
(see index for correct answer)

- a. hierarchical
- b. interpersonal communication
- c. open system
- d. empathy

Guidance: level 1

:: Pension funds ::

_____ s typically have large amounts of money to invest and are the major investors in listed and private companies. They are especially important to the stock market where large institutional investors dominate. The largest 300 _____ s collectively hold about $6 trillion in assets. In January 2008, The Economist reported that Morgan Stanley estimates that _____ s worldwide hold over US$20 trillion in assets, the largest for any category of investor ahead of mutual funds, insurance companies, currency reserves, sovereign wealth funds, hedge funds, or private equity.

Exam Probability: **High**

2. *Answer choices:*
(see index for correct answer)

- a. Pension buyout
- b. Pension fund
- c. Texas Municipal Retirement System

Guidance: level 1

:: ::

_____ is the process of making predictions of the future based on past and present data and most commonly by analysis of trends. A commonplace example might be estimation of some variable of interest at some specified future date. Prediction is a similar, but more general term. Both might refer to formal statistical methods employing time series, cross-sectional or longitudinal data, or alternatively to less formal judgmental methods. Usage can differ between areas of application: for example, in hydrology the terms "forecast" and " _____ " are sometimes reserved for estimates of values at certain specific future times, while the term "prediction" is used for more general estimates, such as the number of times floods will occur over a long period.

Exam Probability: **High**

3. *Answer choices:*
(see index for correct answer)

- a. information systems assessment
- b. Forecasting
- c. imperative
- d. cultural

:: Debt ::

_____ , in finance and economics, is payment from a borrower or deposit-taking financial institution to a lender or depositor of an amount above repayment of the principal sum , at a particular rate. It is distinct from a fee which the borrower may pay the lender or some third party. It is also distinct from dividend which is paid by a company to its shareholders from its profit or reserve, but not at a particular rate decided beforehand, rather on a pro rata basis as a share in the reward gained by risk taking entrepreneurs when the revenue earned exceeds the total costs.

Exam Probability: **Medium**

4. *Answer choices:*
(see index for correct answer)

- a. Charge-off
- b. Christians Against Poverty
- c. Crown debt
- d. Student debt

:: Mathematical finance ::

_____ is the value of an asset at a specific date. It measures the nominal future sum of money that a given sum of money is "worth" at a specified time in the future assuming a certain interest rate, or more generally, rate of return; it is the present value multiplied by the accumulation function.The value does not include corrections for inflation or other factors that affect the true value of money in the future. This is used in time value of money calculations.

Exam Probability: **High**

5. *Answer choices:*
(see index for correct answer)

- a. Perpetuity
- b. Future value
- c. Weighted average return on assets
- d. Present value

:: Financial markets ::

A _____ is a financial market in which long-term debt or equity-backed securities are bought and sold. _____ s channel the wealth of savers to those who can put it to long-term productive use, such as companies or governments making long-term investments. Financial regulators like the Bank of England and the U.S. Securities and Exchange Commission oversee _____ s to protect investors against fraud, among other duties.

Exam Probability: **High**

6. *Answer choices:*
(see index for correct answer)

- a. Flight-to-quality
- b. Advanced Computerized Execution System
- c. Capital market
- d. Hot money

:: bad_topic ::

_____ refers to systematic approach to the governance and realization of value from the things that a group or entity is responsible for, over their whole life cycles. It may apply both to tangible assets and to intangible assets . _____ is a systematic process of developing, operating, maintaining, upgrading, and disposing of assets in the most cost-effective manner .

Exam Probability: **Medium**

7. *Answer choices:*
(see index for correct answer)

- a. Web advertising
- b. MBNA Corporation
- c. Caremark Rx
- d. Asset management

An _____ is a series of payments made at equal intervals. Examples of annuities are regular deposits to a savings account, monthly home mortgage payments, monthly insurance payments and pension payments. Annuities can be classified by the frequency of payment dates. The payments may be made weekly, monthly, quarterly, yearly, or at any other regular interval of time.

Exam Probability: **Low**

8. *Answer choices:*
(see index for correct answer)

- a. Social protection
- b. Beadsman
- c. Mandatory retirement
- d. Annuity

Guidance: level 1

An _____ , for United States federal income tax, is a closely held corporation that makes a valid election to be taxed under Subchapter S of Chapter 1 of the Internal Revenue Code. In general, _____ s do not pay any income taxes. Instead, the corporation's income or losses are divided among and passed through to its shareholders. The shareholders must then report the income or loss on their own individual income tax returns.

Exam Probability: **High**

9. *Answer choices:*
(see index for correct answer)

- a. deep-level diversity
- b. process perspective
- c. S corporation
- d. Sarbanes-Oxley act of 2002

Guidance: level 1

The _____ Corporation is an American multinational investment bank and financial services company based in Charlotte, North Carolina with central hubs in New York City, London, Hong Kong, Minneapolis, and Toronto. _____ was formed through NationsBank's acquisition of BankAmerica in 1998. It is the second largest banking institution in the United States, after JP Morgan Chase. As a part of the Big Four, it services approximately 10.73% of all American bank deposits, in direct competition with Citigroup, Wells Fargo, and JPMorgan Chase. Its primary financial services revolve around commercial banking, wealth management, and investment banking.

Exam Probability: **Low**

10. *Answer choices:*
(see index for correct answer)

- a. The Royal Bank of Scotland
- b. UniCredit
- c. Mizuho Financial Group
- d. Bank of America

Guidance: level 1

:: E-commerce ::

A _____ is a plastic payment card that can be used instead of cash when making purchases. It is similar to a credit card, but unlike a credit card, the money is immediately transferred directly from the cardholder's bank account when performing a transaction.

Exam Probability: **Medium**

11. *Answer choices:*
(see index for correct answer)

- a. Wanelo
- b. TRANZ 330
- c. GS1 US
- d. Debit card

Guidance: level 1

:: ::

_____ is a marketing communication that employs an openly sponsored, non-personal message to promote or sell a product, service or idea. Sponsors of _____ are typically businesses wishing to promote their products or services. _____ is differentiated from public relations in that an advertiser pays for and has control over the message. It differs from personal selling in that the message is non-personal, i.e., not directed to a particular individual. _____ is communicated through various mass media, including traditional media such as newspapers, magazines, television, radio, outdoor _____ or direct mail; and new media such as search results, blogs, social media, websites or text messages. The actual presentation of the message in a medium is referred to as an advertisement, or "ad" or advert for short.

Exam Probability: **Medium**

12. *Answer choices:*
(see index for correct answer)

- a. process perspective
- b. Sarbanes-Oxley act of 2002
- c. interpersonal communication
- d. levels of analysis

Guidance: level 1

:: ::

_____ officially refers to an administrative area of the Principality of Monaco, specifically the ward of _____/Spélugues, where the _____ Casino is located. Informally the name also refers to a larger district, the _____ Quarter , which besides _____/Spélugues also includes the wards of La Rousse/Saint Roman, Larvotto/Bas Moulins, and Saint Michel. The permanent population of the ward of _____ is about 3,500, while that of the quarter is about 15,000. Monaco has four traditional quarters. From west to east they are: Fontvieille , Monaco-Ville , La Condamine, and _____ .

Exam Probability: **Medium**

13. *Answer choices:*
(see index for correct answer)

- a. imperative
- b. Sarbanes-Oxley act of 2002
- c. Monte Carlo

- d. information systems assessment

:: Expense ::

_____ relates to the cost of borrowing money. It is the price that a lender charges a borrower for the use of the lender's money. On the income statement, _____ can represent the cost of borrowing money from banks, bond investors, and other sources. _____ is different from operating expense and CAPEX, for it relates to the capital structure of a company, and it is usually tax-deductible.

Exam Probability: **Medium**

14. *Answer choices:*
(see index for correct answer)

- a. Operating expense
- b. Accretion expense
- c. Freight expense
- d. Stock option expensing

:: ::

A _____ is the process of presenting a topic to an audience. It is typically a demonstration, introduction, lecture, or speech meant to inform, persuade, inspire, motivate, or to build good will or to present a new idea or product. The term can also be used for a formal or ritualized introduction or offering, as with the _____ of a debutante. _____ s in certain formats are also known as keynote address.

Exam Probability: **Low**

15. *Answer choices:*
(see index for correct answer)

- a. Presentation
- b. empathy
- c. process perspective
- d. interpersonal communication

_____ involves decision making. It can include judging the merits of multiple options and selecting one or more of them. One can make a _____ between imagined options or between real options followed by the corresponding action. For example, a traveler might choose a route for a journey based on the preference of arriving at a given destination as soon as possible. The preferred route can then follow from information such as the length of each of the possible routes, traffic conditions, etc. The arrival at a _____ can include more complex motivators such as cognition, instinct, and feeling.

Exam Probability: **Medium**

16. *Answer choices:*
(see index for correct answer)

- a. Choice
- b. deep-level diversity
- c. information systems assessment
- d. imperative

Guidance: level 1

:: Financial ratios ::

The _____ is a financial ratio indicating the relative proportion of shareholders' equity and debt used to finance a company's assets. Closely related to leveraging, the ratio is also known as risk, gearing or leverage. The two components are often taken from the firm's balance sheet or statement of financial position , but the ratio may also be calculated using market values for both, if the company's debt and equity are publicly traded, or using a combination of book value for debt and market value for equity financially.

Exam Probability: **High**

17. *Answer choices:*
(see index for correct answer)

- a. Sustainable growth rate
- b. Jaws ratio
- c. Theoretical ex-rights price
- d. Debt-to-equity ratio

Guidance: level 1

In accounting/accountancy, _____ are journal entries usually made at the end of an accounting period to allocate income and expenditure to the period in which they actually occurred. The revenue recognition principle is the basis of making _____ that pertain to unearned and accrued revenues under accrual-basis accounting. They are sometimes called Balance Day adjustments because they are made on balance day.

Exam Probability: **High**

18. *Answer choices:*
(see index for correct answer)

- a. Fair value accounting
- b. Statement of financial position
- c. Capital appreciation
- d. Checkoff

Guidance: level 1

:: Stock market ::

A _____ or stock divide increases the number of shares in a company. The price is adjusted such that the before and after market capitalization of the company remains the same and dilution does not occur. Options and warrants are included.

Exam Probability: **Medium**

19. *Answer choices:*
(see index for correct answer)

- a. Shadow stock
- b. Tech Buzz
- c. P chip
- d. Stock split

Guidance: level 1

:: Mereology ::

_____ , in the abstract, is what belongs to or with something, whether as an attribute or as a component of said thing. In the context of this article, it is one or more components , whether physical or incorporeal, of a person's estate; or so belonging to, as in being owned by, a person or jointly a group of people or a legal entity like a corporation or even a society. Depending on the nature of the _____ , an owner of _____ has the right to consume, alter, share, redefine, rent, mortgage, pawn, sell, exchange, transfer, give away or destroy it, or to exclude others from doing these things, as well as to perhaps abandon it; whereas regardless of the nature of the _____ , the owner thereof has the right to properly use it , or at the very least exclusively keep it.

Exam Probability: **High**

20. *Answer choices:*
(see index for correct answer)

- a. Property
- b. Mereological essentialism
- c. Simple
- d. Mereotopology

Guidance: level 1

:: Business law ::

A _____ is a group of people who jointly supervise the activities of an organization, which can be either a for-profit business, nonprofit organization, or a government agency. Such a board's powers, duties, and responsibilities are determined by government regulations and the organization's own constitution and bylaws. These authorities may specify the number of members of the board, how they are to be chosen, and how often they are to meet.

Exam Probability: **High**

21. *Answer choices:*
(see index for correct answer)

- a. Process agent
- b. Limited liability
- c. Board of directors
- d. License

:: Interest ::

In finance, _____ is the interest on a bond or loan that has accumulated since the principal investment, or since the previous coupon payment if there has been one already.

Exam Probability: **Medium**

22. *Answer choices:*
(see index for correct answer)

- a. Riba
- b. Abstinence theory of interest
- c. Accrued interest
- d. Discretionary deposit

:: Expense ::

A company`s _____, or As a result, the computation of the _____ is considerably more complex. Tax law may provide for different treatment of items of income and expenses as a result of tax policy. The differences may be of permanent or temporary nature. Permanent items are in the form of non taxable income and non taxable expenses. Things such as expenses considered not deductible by taxing authorities , the range of tax rates applicable to various levels of income, different tax rates in different jurisdictions, multiple layers of tax on income, and other issues.

Exam Probability: **Medium**

23. *Answer choices:*
(see index for correct answer)

- a. Tax expense
- b. Momentem
- c. Corporate travel
- d. Business overhead expense disability insurance

:: Cash flow ::

_____ s are narrowly interconnected with the concepts of value, interest rate and liquidity. A _____ that shall happen on a future day tN can be transformed into a _____ of the same value in t0.

24. *Answer choices:*
(see index for correct answer)

- a. Discounted cash flow
- b. Factoring
- c. Free cash flow
- d. Cash flow

Guidance: level 1

:: Business economics ::

A _____ is a term used primarily in cost accounting to describe something to which costs are assigned. Common examples of _____ s are: product lines, geographic territories, customers, departments or anything else for which management would like to quantify cost.

25. *Answer choices:*
(see index for correct answer)

- a. Cost object
- b. Function cost analysis
- c. Center for Business and Economic Research
- d. Model audit

Guidance: level 1

:: ::

_____ is an eight-block-long street running roughly northwest to southeast from Broadway to South Street, at the East River, in the Financial District of Lower Manhattan in New York City. Over time, the term has become a metonym for the financial markets of the United States as a whole, the American financial services industry , or New York–based financial interests.

26. *Answer choices:*
(see index for correct answer)

- a. cultural
- b. surface-level diversity
- c. Wall Street
- d. personal values

Guidance: level 1

:: Decision theory ::

A _____ is a deliberate system of principles to guide decisions and achieve rational outcomes. A _____ is a statement of intent, and is implemented as a procedure or protocol. Policies are generally adopted by a governance body within an organization. Policies can assist in both subjective and objective decision making. Policies to assist in subjective decision making usually assist senior management with decisions that must be based on the relative merits of a number of factors, and as a result are often hard to test objectively, e.g. work-life balance _____ . In contrast policies to assist in objective decision making are usually operational in nature and can be objectively tested, e.g. password _____ .

27. *Answer choices:*
(see index for correct answer)

- a. Policy
- b. Rete algorithm
- c. Decision-matrix method
- d. Subjective expected utility

Guidance: level 1

:: Marketing ::

A _____ is something that is necessary for an organism to live a healthy life. _____ s are distinguished from wants in that, in the case of a _____ , a deficiency causes a clear adverse outcome: a dysfunction or death. In other words, a _____ is something required for a safe, stable and healthy life while a want is a desire, wish or aspiration. When _____ s or wants are backed by purchasing power, they have the potential to become economic demands.

Exam Probability: **High**

28. *Answer choices:*
(see index for correct answer)

- a. Need
- b. Call to action
- c. elaboration likelihood
- d. Customer acquisition management

Guidance: level 1

:: Accounting terminology ::

_____ or capital expense is the money a company spends to buy, maintain, or improve its fixed assets, such as buildings, vehicles, equipment, or land. It is considered a _____ when the asset is newly purchased or when money is used towards extending the useful life of an existing asset, such as repairing the roof.

Exam Probability: **Medium**

29. *Answer choices:*
(see index for correct answer)

- a. Cash flow management
- b. Capital appreciation
- c. Internal auditing
- d. Capital expenditure

Guidance: level 1

:: ::

_____ focuses on ratios, equities and debts. It is useful for portfolio management,distribution of dividend,capital raising,hedging and looking after fluctuations in foreign currency and product cycles.Financial managers are the people who will do research and based on the research, decide what sort of capital to obtain in order to fund the company's assets as well as maximizing the value of the firm for all the stakeholders. It also refers to the efficient and effective management of money in such a manner as to accomplish the objectives of the organization. It is the specialized function directly associated with the top management. The significance of this function is not seen in the `Line` but also in the capacity of the `Staff` in overall of a company. It has been defined differently by different experts in the field.

Exam Probability: **High**

30. *Answer choices:*
(see index for correct answer)

- a. hierarchical perspective
- b. cultural
- c. Financial management
- d. corporate values

Guidance: level 1

:: Valuation (finance) ::

_____ refers to an assessment of the viability, stability, and profitability of a business, sub-business or project.

Exam Probability: **High**

31. *Answer choices:*
(see index for correct answer)

- a. Cyclically adjusted price-to-earnings ratio
- b. Diminution in value
- c. Channel check
- d. Financial analysis

Guidance: level 1

:: Financial markets ::

_____ s are monetary contracts between parties. They can be created, traded, modified and settled. They can be cash , evidence of an ownership interest in an entity , or a contractual right to receive or deliver cash .

Exam Probability: **High**

32. *Answer choices:*
(see index for correct answer)

- a. Spot contract
- b. Financial instrument
- c. Market depth
- d. Convertible arbitrage

Guidance: level 1

:: Accounting source documents ::

A _____ or account statement is a summary of financial transactions which have occurred over a given period on a bank account held by a person or business with a financial institution.

Exam Probability: **High**

33. *Answer choices:*
(see index for correct answer)

- a. Bank statement
- b. Parcel audit
- c. Credit memorandum
- d. Air waybill

Guidance: level 1

:: Basic financial concepts ::

In finance, maturity or _____ refers to the final payment date of a loan or other financial instrument, at which point the principal is due to be paid.

Exam Probability: **High**

34. *Answer choices:*

- a. Maturity date
- b. Present value of costs
- c. Short interest
- d. Leverage cycle

Guidance: level 1

:: Commerce ::

Continuation of an entity as a _____ is presumed as the basis for financial reporting unless and until the entity's liquidation becomes imminent. Preparation of financial statements under this presumption is commonly referred to as the _____ basis of accounting. If and when an entity's liquidation becomes imminent, financial statements are prepared under the liquidation basis of accounting .

Exam Probability: **High**

35. *Answer choices:*

- a. White Elephant Sale
- b. Bill of sale
- c. RFM
- d. Church sale

Guidance: level 1

:: Management accounting ::

_____ is the process of recording, classifying, analyzing, summarizing, and allocating costs associated with a process,after that developing various courses of action to control the costs. Its goal is to advise the management on how to optimize business practices and processes based on cost efficiency and capability. _____ provides the detailed cost information that management needs to control current operations and plan for the future.

Exam Probability: **Low**

36. *Answer choices:*

- a. Target income sales

- b. Cost driver
- c. Cost accounting
- d. Institute of Certified Management Accountants

:: Generally Accepted Accounting Principles ::

A _____ or reacquired stock is stock which is bought back by the issuing company, reducing the amount of outstanding stock on the open market .

Exam Probability: **Low**

37. *Answer choices:*
(see index for correct answer)

- a. net realisable value
- b. Treasury stock
- c. Deferral
- d. Construction in progress

:: ::

Business is the activity of making one`s living or making money by producing or buying and selling products . Simply put, it is "any activity or enterprise entered into for profit. It does not mean it is a company, a corporation, partnership, or have any such formal organization, but it can range from a street peddler to General Motors."

Exam Probability: **Low**

38. *Answer choices:*
(see index for correct answer)

- a. information systems assessment
- b. co-culture
- c. Firm
- d. process perspective

:: Inventory ::

In business and accounting/accountancy, _____ or continuous inventory describes systems of inventory where information on inventory quantity and availability is updated on a continuous basis as a function of doing business. Generally this is accomplished by connecting the inventory system with order entry and in retail the point of sale system. In this case, book inventory would be exactly the same as, or almost the same, as the real inventory.

Exam Probability: **High**

39. *Answer choices:*
(see index for correct answer)

- a. Perpetual inventory
- b. Lower of cost or market
- c. Phantom inventory
- d. Average cost method

Guidance: level 1

:: Manufacturing ::

_____ s are goods that have completed the manufacturing process but have not yet been sold or distributed to the end user.

Exam Probability: **Medium**

40. *Answer choices:*
(see index for correct answer)

- a. Rite-Hite
- b. Finished good
- c. Batch production
- d. Lean production

Guidance: level 1

:: International trade ::

_____ involves the transfer of goods or services from one person or entity to another, often in exchange for money. A system or network that allows _____ is called a market.

41. *Answer choices:*

- a. European Union Customs Union
- b. Pauper labor argument
- c. Bureau de change
- d. Trade

Guidance: level 1

:: Finance ::

The _____ of a corporation is the accumulated net income of the corporation that is retained by the corporation at a particular point of time, such as at the end of the reporting period. At the end of that period, the net income at that point is transferred from the Profit and Loss Account to the _____ account. If the balance of the _____ account is negative it may be called accumulated losses, retained losses or accumulated deficit, or similar terminology.

42. *Answer choices:*

- a. Trade idea
- b. Offshore financial centre
- c. Leximetrics
- d. Retained earnings

Guidance: level 1

:: Financial regulatory authorities of the United States ::

The _____ is the revenue service of the United States federal government. The government agency is a bureau of the Department of the Treasury, and is under the immediate direction of the Commissioner of Internal Revenue, who is appointed to a five-year term by the President of the United States. The IRS is responsible for collecting taxes and administering the Internal Revenue Code, the main body of federal statutory tax law of the United States. The duties of the IRS include providing tax assistance to taxpayers and pursuing and resolving instances of erroneous or fraudulent tax filings. The IRS has also overseen various benefits programs, and enforces portions of the Affordable Care Act.

Exam Probability: **Medium**

43. *Answer choices:*
(see index for correct answer)

- a. Operation Choke Point
- b. Securities Investor Protection Corporation
- c. National Credit Union Administration
- d. National Futures Association

Guidance: level 1

:: International taxation ::

_____ is the levying of tax by two or more jurisdictions on the same declared income , asset , or financial transaction . Double liability is mitigated in a number of ways, for example.

Exam Probability: **High**

44. *Answer choices:*
(see index for correct answer)

- a. Double taxation
- b. Withholding
- c. Exchange of information
- d. Foreign Account Tax Compliance Act

Guidance: level 1

:: Management accounting ::

In _____ or managerial accounting, managers use the provisions of accounting information in order to better inform themselves before they decide matters within their organizations, which aids their management and performance of control functions.

45. *Answer choices:*
(see index for correct answer)

- a. Cash and cash equivalents
- b. Corporate travel management
- c. Direct material price variance
- d. Construction accounting

Guidance: level 1

:: ::

_____ is the study and management of exchange relationships. _____ is the business process of creating relationships with and satisfying customers. With its focus on the customer, _____ is one of the premier components of business management.

46. *Answer choices:*
(see index for correct answer)

- a. personal values
- b. hierarchical perspective
- c. corporate values
- d. Marketing

Guidance: level 1

:: Inventory ::

Costs are associated with particular goods using one of the several formulas, including specific identification, first-in first-out , or average cost. Costs include all costs of purchase, costs of conversion and other costs that are incurred in bringing the inventories to their present location and condition. Costs of goods made by the businesses include material, labor, and allocated overhead. The costs of those goods which are not yet sold are deferred as costs of inventory until the inventory is sold or written down in value.

Exam Probability: **High**

47. *Answer choices:*
(see index for correct answer)

- a. Inventory bounce
- b. Average cost method
- c. Cost of goods sold
- d. Stock keeping unit

Guidance: level 1

:: ::

_____ is the collection of techniques, skills, methods, and processes used in the production of goods or services or in the accomplishment of objectives, such as scientific investigation. _____ can be the knowledge of techniques, processes, and the like, or it can be embedded in machines to allow for operation without detailed knowledge of their workings. Systems applying _____ by taking an input, changing it according to the system's use, and then producing an outcome are referred to as _____ systems or technological systems.

Exam Probability: **High**

48. *Answer choices:*
(see index for correct answer)

- a. cultural
- b. Technology
- c. open system
- d. imperative

Guidance: level 1

:: Inventory ::

_____ is the amount of inventory a company has in stock at the end of its fiscal year. It is closely related with _____ cost, which is the amount of money spent to get these goods in stock. It should be calculated at the lower of cost or market.

49. *Answer choices:*
(see index for correct answer)

- a. LIFO
- b. Ending inventory
- c. just-in-time manufacturing
- d. GMROII

Guidance: level 1

:: Financial ratios ::

The _____ or dividend-price ratio of a share is the dividend per share, divided by the price per share. It is also a company's total annual dividend payments divided by its market capitalization, assuming the number of shares is constant. It is often expressed as a percentage.

50. *Answer choices:*
(see index for correct answer)

- a. Sustainable growth rate
- b. Sterling ratio
- c. Dividend yield
- d. Cost accrual ratio

Guidance: level 1

:: ::

A _____ loan or, simply, _____ is used either by purchasers of real property to raise funds to buy real estate, or alternatively by existing property owners to raise funds for any purpose, while putting a lien on the property being _____ d. The loan is "secured" on the borrower's property through a process known as _____ origination. This means that a legal mechanism is put into place which allows the lender to take possession and sell the secured property to pay off the loan in the event the borrower defaults on the loan or otherwise fails to abide by its terms. The word _____ is derived from a Law French term used in Britain in the Middle Ages meaning "death pledge" and refers to the pledge ending when either the obligation is fulfilled or the property is taken through foreclosure. A _____ can also be described as "a borrower giving consideration in the form of a collateral for a benefit ".

Exam Probability: **Low**

51. *Answer choices:*
(see index for correct answer)

- a. Mortgage
- b. empathy
- c. surface-level diversity
- d. cultural

Guidance: level 1

:: Accounting terminology ::

Accounts are typically defined by an identifier and a caption or header and are coded by account type. In computerized accounting systems with computable quantity accounting, the accounts can have a quantity measure definition.

Exam Probability: **High**

52. *Answer choices:*
(see index for correct answer)

- a. managerial accounting
- b. Share premium
- c. Capital expenditure
- d. Chart of accounts

Guidance: level 1

:: Financial ratios ::

_____ is a financial ratio that indicates the percentage of a company's assets that are provided via debt. It is the ratio of total debt and total assets .

Exam Probability: **Medium**

53. *Answer choices:*
(see index for correct answer)

- a. Total revenue share
- b. Earnings yield
- c. Debt ratio
- d. Return on equity

Guidance: level 1

:: Mutualism (movement) ::

A _____ is a professionally managed investment fund that pools money from many investors to purchase securities. These investors may be retail or institutional in nature.

Exam Probability: **High**

54. *Answer choices:*
(see index for correct answer)

- a. Co-buying
- b. ICA Group
- c. Mutual organization
- d. Mutual fund

Guidance: level 1

:: Economics terminology ::

A corporation's share capital or _____ is the portion of a corporation's equity that has been obtained by the issue of shares in the corporation to a shareholder, usually for cash. "Share capital" may also denote the number and types of shares that compose a corporation's share structure.

55. *Answer choices:*

- a. Normal profit
- b. Capital stock
- c. Capital cost
- d. total revenue

Guidance: level 1

:: Commerce ::

A _____ , manufacturing plant or a production plant is an industrial site, usually consisting of buildings and machinery, or more commonly a complex having several buildings, where workers manufacture goods or operate machines processing one product into another.

56. *Answer choices:*

- a. Non-commercial
- b. Hong Kong Mercantile Exchange
- c. Uttarapatha
- d. Factory

Guidance: level 1

:: Insolvency ::

_____ is the process in accounting by which a company is brought to an end in the United Kingdom, Republic of Ireland and United States. The assets and property of the company are redistributed. _____ is also sometimes referred to as winding-up or dissolution, although dissolution technically refers to the last stage of _____ . The process of _____ also arises when customs, an authority or agency in a country responsible for collecting and safeguarding customs duties, determines the final computation or ascertainment of the duties or drawback accruing on an entry.

57. *Answer choices:*

- a. Insolvency law of Russia
- b. Financial distress
- c. Liquidation
- d. United Kingdom insolvency law

Guidance: level 1

:: Currency ::

A _____ , in the most specific sense is money in any form when in use or circulation as a medium of exchange, especially circulating banknotes and coins. A more general definition is that a _____ is a system of money in common use, especially for people in a nation. Under this definition, US dollars , pounds sterling , Australian dollars , European euros , Russian rubles and Indian Rupees are examples of currencies. These various currencies are recognized as stores of value and are traded between nations in foreign exchange markets, which determine the relative values of the different currencies. Currencies in this sense are defined by governments, and each type has limited boundaries of acceptance.

Exam Probability: **High**

58. *Answer choices:*

- a. Nomisma
- b. Pre-decimal currency
- c. Mutilated currency
- d. Monetae cudendae ratio

Guidance: level 1

:: Financial markets ::

In economics and finance, _____ is the practice of taking advantage of a price difference between two or more markets: striking a combination of matching deals that capitalize upon the imbalance, the profit being the difference between the market prices. When used by academics, an _____ is a transaction that involves no negative cash flow at any probabilistic or temporal state and a positive cash flow in at least one state; in simple terms, it is the possibility of a risk-free profit after transaction costs. For example, an _____ opportunity is present when there is the opportunity to instantaneously buy something for a low price and sell it for a higher price.

Exam Probability: **Medium**

59. *Answer choices:*
(see index for correct answer)

- a. Market distortion
- b. Flight-to-quality
- c. Hot equity periods
- d. Round lot

Guidance: level 1

Human resource management

Human resource (HR) management is the strategic approach to the effective management of organization workers so that they help the business gain a competitive advantage. It is designed to maximize employee performance in service of an employer's strategic objectives. HR is primarily concerned with the management of people within organizations, focusing on policies and on systems. HR departments are responsible for overseeing employee-benefits design, employee recruitment, training and development, performance appraisal, and rewarding (e.g., managing pay and benefit systems). HR also concerns itself with organizational change and industrial relations, that is, the balancing of organizational practices with requirements arising from collective bargaining and from governmental laws.

:: Business planning ::

_____ is an organization's process of defining its strategy, or direction, and making decisions on allocating its resources to pursue this strategy. It may also extend to control mechanisms for guiding the implementation of the strategy. _____ became prominent in corporations during the 1960s and remains an important aspect of strategic management. It is executed by strategic planners or strategists, who involve many parties and research sources in their analysis of the organization and its relationship to the environment in which it competes.

Exam Probability: **Low**

1. *Answer choices:*
(see index for correct answer)

- a. operational planning
- b. Business war games
- c. Strategic planning
- d. Open Options Corporation

Guidance: level 1

:: Outsourcing ::

_____ is the relocation of a business process from one country to another—typically an operational process, such as manufacturing, or supporting processes, such as accounting. Typically this refers to a company business, although state governments may also employ _____ . More recently, technical and administrative services have been offshored.

Exam Probability: **Low**

2. *Answer choices:*

- a. Website Management Outsourcing
- b. Media Process Outsourcing
- c. Offshoring
- d. Virtual airline

Guidance: level 1

:: Training ::

_____ is the process of ensuring compliance with laws, regulations, rules, standards, or social norms. By enforcing laws and regulations, governments attempt to effectuate successful implementation of policies.

Exam Probability: **Medium**

3. *Answer choices:*

- a. Practicum
- b. Training
- c. Enforcement
- d. Facila

Guidance: level 1

:: Management ::

A _____ is a method or technique that has been generally accepted as superior to any alternatives because it produces results that are superior to those achieved by other means or because it has become a standard way of doing things, e.g., a standard way of complying with legal or ethical requirements.

4. *Answer choices:*
(see index for correct answer)

- a. Overtime rate
- b. Defensive expenditures
- c. Board of governors
- d. Facilitator

Guidance: level 1

:: Trade union legislation ::

The _____ of 1935 is a foundational statute of United States labor law which guarantees the right of private sector employees to organize into trade unions, engage in collective bargaining, and take collective action such as strikes. The act was written by Senator Robert F. Wagner, passed by the 74th United States Congress, and signed into law by President Franklin D. Roosevelt.

Exam Probability: **Medium**

5. *Answer choices:*
(see index for correct answer)

- a. Employment Act 1982
- b. Labor Management Relations Act
- c. Trade Union Act 1984
- d. Trade Disputes Act 1906

Guidance: level 1

:: Human resource management ::

_____ , also known as organizational socialization, is management jargon first created in 1988 that refers to the mechanism through which new employees acquire the necessary knowledge, skills, and behaviors in order to become effective organizational members and insiders.

Exam Probability: **Low**

6. *Answer choices:*
(see index for correct answer)

- a. Onboarding
- b. Organizational culture

- c. Human resource consulting
- d. Employee retention

Guidance: level 1

:: Employment compensation ::

In government contracting, a _____ is defined as the hourly wage, usual benefits and overtime, paid to the majority of workers, laborers, and mechanics within a particular area. This is usually the union wage.

Exam Probability: **High**

7. *Answer choices:*
(see index for correct answer)

- a. Executive Schedule
- b. Employee stock option
- c. Prevailing wage
- d. Lerman ratio

Guidance: level 1

:: Employment compensation ::

The formula commonly used by compensation professionals to assess the competitiveness of an employee's pay level involves calculating a """ _____ """. _____ is the short form for Comparative ratio.

Exam Probability: **Medium**

8. *Answer choices:*
(see index for correct answer)

- a. Compa-ratio
- b. Duvet day
- c. My Family Care
- d. Law Enforcement Availability Pay

Guidance: level 1

:: ::

Domestic violence is violence or other abuse by one person against another in a domestic setting, such as in marriage or cohabitation. It may be termed intimate partner violence when committed by a spouse or partner in an intimate relationship against the other spouse or partner, and can take place in heterosexual or same-sex relationships, or between former spouses or partners. Domestic violence can also involve violence against children, parents, or the elderly. It takes a number of forms, including physical, verbal, emotional, economic, religious, reproductive, and sexual abuse, which can range from subtle, coercive forms to marital rape and to violent physical abuse such as choking, beating, female genital mutilation, and acid throwing that results in disfigurement or death. Domestic murders include stoning, bride burning, honor killings, and dowry deaths.

Exam Probability: **High**

9. *Answer choices:*
(see index for correct answer)

- a. Family violence
- b. imperative
- c. personal values
- d. deep-level diversity

Guidance: level 1

:: Life skills ::

_____ , emotional leadership , emotional quotient and _____ quotient , is the capability of individuals to recognize their own emotions and those of others, discern between different feelings and label them appropriately, use emotional information to guide thinking and behavior, and manage and/or adjust emotions to adapt to environments or achieve one's goal.

Exam Probability: **Low**

10. *Answer choices:*
(see index for correct answer)

- a. multiple intelligence
- b. Social intelligence
- c. Emotional intelligence
- d. coping mechanism

Guidance: level 1

The _____ is the United States federal agency responsible for conducting research and making recommendations for the prevention of work-related injury and illness. NIOSH is part of the Centers for Disease Control and Prevention within the U.S. Department of Health and Human Services.

Exam Probability: **High**

11. *Answer choices:*
(see index for correct answer)

- a. National Institute for Occupational Safety and Health
- b. WorkSafe Victoria
- c. NEBOSH
- d. Adult Blood Lead Epidemiology and Surveillance

Guidance: level 1

:: ::

_____ are interactive computer-mediated technologies that facilitate the creation and sharing of information, ideas, career interests and other forms of expression via virtual communities and networks. The variety of stand-alone and built-in _____ services currently available introduces challenges of definition; however, there are some common features.

Exam Probability: **Medium**

12. *Answer choices:*
(see index for correct answer)

- a. empathy
- b. cultural
- c. Social media
- d. hierarchical

Guidance: level 1

Centralisation or _____ is the process by which the activities of an organization, particularly those regarding planning and decision-making, framing strategy and policies become concentrated within a particular geographical location group. This moves the important decision-making and planning powers within the center of the organisation.

Exam Probability: **Medium**

13. *Answer choices:*

- a. organic growth
- b. strategic plan
- c. noncommercial
- d. Centralization

Guidance: level 1

:: Sociological terminology ::

In moral and political philosophy, the _____ is a theory or model that originated during the Age of Enlightenment and usually concerns the legitimacy of the authority of the state over the individual. _____ arguments typically posit that individuals have consented, either explicitly or tacitly, to surrender some of their freedoms and submit to the authority in exchange for protection of their remaining rights or maintenance of the social order. The relation between natural and legal rights is often a topic of _____ theory. The term takes its name from The _____ , a 1762 book by Jean-Jacques Rousseau that discussed this concept. Although the antecedents of _____ theory are found in antiquity, in Greek and Stoic philosophy and Roman and Canon Law, the heyday of the _____ was the mid-17th to early 19th centuries, when it emerged as the leading doctrine of political legitimacy.

Exam Probability: **Low**

14. *Answer choices:*

- a. Social contract
- b. Social engagement
- c. Symbolic capital
- d. Anticipatory socialization

:: Human resource management ::

An _____ is a software application that enables the electronic handling of recruitment needs. An ATS can be implemented or accessed online on an enterprise or small business level, depending on the needs of the company and there is also free and open source ATS software available. An ATS is very similar to customer relationship management systems, but are designed for recruitment tracking purposes. In many cases they filter applications automatically based on given criteria such as keywords, skills, former employers, years of experience and schools attended. This has caused many to adapt resume optimization techniques similar to those used in search engine optimization when creating and formatting their résumé.

Exam Probability: **Medium**

15. *Answer choices:*
(see index for correct answer)

- a. Aspiring Minds
- b. Open plan
- c. Applicant tracking system
- d. The war for talent

:: Human resource management ::

_____ is the strategic approach to the effective management of people in an organization so that they help the business to gain a competitive advantage. It is designed to maximize employee performance in service of an employer's strategic objectives. HR is primarily concerned with the management of people within organizations, focusing on policies and on systems. HR departments are responsible for overseeing employee-benefits design, employee recruitment, training and development, performance appraisal, and Reward management . HR also concerns itself with organizational change and industrial relations, that is, the balancing of organizational practices with requirements arising from collective bargaining and from governmental laws.

Exam Probability: **Medium**

16. *Answer choices:*

(see index for correct answer)

- a. CEO succession
- b. Action alert
- c. Adecco Group North America
- d. Human resource management

Guidance: level 1

:: Validity (statistics) ::

In psychometrics, criterion or concrete validity is the extent to which a measure is related to an outcome. _____ is often divided into concurrent and predictive validity. Concurrent validity refers to a comparison between the measure in question and an outcome assessed at the same time. In Standards for Educational & Psychological Tests, it states, "concurrent validity reflects only the status quo at a particular time." Predictive validity, on the other hand, compares the measure in question with an outcome assessed at a later time. Although concurrent and predictive validity are similar, it is cautioned to keep the terms and findings separated. "Concurrent validity should not be used as a substitute for predictive validity without an appropriate supporting rationale."

Exam Probability: **High**

17. *Answer choices:*

(see index for correct answer)

- a. Face validity
- b. Verification and validation
- c. External validity
- d. Incremental validity

Guidance: level 1

:: ::

The _____ of 1938 29 U.S.C. § 203 is a United States labor law that creates the right to a minimum wage, and "time-and-a-half" overtime pay when people work over forty hours a week. It also prohibits most employment of minors in "oppressive child labor". It applies to employees engaged in interstate commerce or employed by an enterprise engaged in commerce or in the production of goods for commerce, unless the employer can claim an exemption from coverage.

Exam Probability: **Medium**

18. *Answer choices:*
(see index for correct answer)

- a. Fair Labor Standards Act
- b. hierarchical perspective
- c. personal values
- d. cultural

Guidance: level 1

:: Design of experiments ::

In the design of experiments, treatments are applied to experimental units in the treatment group. In comparative experiments, members of the complementary group, the _____ , receive either no treatment or a standard treatment.

Exam Probability: **Low**

19. *Answer choices:*
(see index for correct answer)

- a. Vaccine trial
- b. Control group
- c. Case-control study
- d. Self-selection bias

Guidance: level 1

:: Belief ::

_____ is the ability to acquire knowledge without proof, evidence, or conscious reasoning, or without understanding how the knowledge was acquired. Different writers give the word " _____ " a great variety of different meanings, ranging from direct access to unconscious knowledge, unconscious cognition, inner sensing, inner insight to unconscious pattern-recognition and the ability to understand something instinctively, without the need for conscious reasoning.

Exam Probability: **Medium**

20. *Answer choices:*
(see index for correct answer)

- a. Intuition
- b. Ideological assumption
- c. Transubstantiation
- d. Blind men and an elephant

Guidance: level 1

:: Human resource management ::

_____ are the people who make up the workforce of an organization, business sector, or economy. "Human capital" is sometimes used synonymously with " _____ ", although human capital typically refers to a narrower effect . Likewise, other terms sometimes used include manpower, talent, labor, personnel, or simply people.

Exam Probability: **Low**

21. *Answer choices:*
(see index for correct answer)

- a. Labour is not a commodity
- b. Compensation and benefits
- c. Professional employer organization
- d. Human resources

Guidance: level 1

:: Network theory ::

A _____ is a social structure made up of a set of social actors , sets of dyadic ties, and other social interactions between actors. The _____ perspective provides a set of methods for analyzing the structure of whole social entities as well as a variety of theories explaining the patterns observed in these structures. The study of these structures uses _____ analysis to identify local and global patterns, locate influential entities, and examine network dynamics.

Exam Probability: **Low**

22. *Answer choices:*
(see index for correct answer)

- a. Network scheduler
- b. Network Description Language
- c. Social network
- d. Clustering coefficient

Guidance: level 1

:: Survey methodology ::

An _____ is a conversation where questions are asked and answers are given. In common parlance, the word " _____ " refers to a one-on-one conversation between an _____ er and an _____ ee. The _____ er asks questions to which the _____ ee responds, usually so information may be transferred from _____ ee to _____ er . Sometimes, information can be transferred in both directions. It is a communication, unlike a speech, which produces a one-way flow of information.

Exam Probability: **Low**

23. *Answer choices:*
(see index for correct answer)

- a. Self-report
- b. Interview
- c. Census
- d. Survey research

Guidance: level 1

:: ::

According to Torrington, a _____ is usually developed by conducting a job analysis, which includes examining the tasks and sequences of tasks necessary to perform the job. The analysis considers the areas of knowledge and skills needed for the job. A job usually includes several roles. According to Hall, the _____ might be broadened to form a person specification or may be known as "terms of reference". The person/job specification can be presented as a stand-alone document, but in practice it is usually included within the _____ . A _____ is often used by employers in the recruitment process.

Exam Probability: **High**

24. *Answer choices:*
(see index for correct answer)

- • a. cultural
- • b. information systems assessment
- • c. Job description
- • d. Sarbanes-Oxley act of 2002

Guidance: level 1

:: ::

_____ is the extraction of valuable minerals or other geological materials from the earth, usually from an ore body, lode, vein, seam, reef or placer deposit. These deposits form a mineralized package that is of economic interest to the miner.

Exam Probability: **High**

25. *Answer choices:*
(see index for correct answer)

- • a. similarity-attraction theory
- • b. deep-level diversity
- • c. Mining
- • d. process perspective

Guidance: level 1

:: Recruitment ::

A _____ or background investigation is the process of looking up and compiling criminal records, commercial records, and financial records of an individual or an organization. The frequency, purpose, and legitimacy of _____ s varies between countries, industries, and individuals. A variety of methods are used to complete such a check, from comprehensive data base search to personal references.

Exam Probability: **Medium**

26. *Answer choices:*

- a. Jeopardy! audition process
- b. Cravath System
- c. Background check
- d. Purple squirrel

Guidance: level 1

:: Bankruptcy ::

_____ is the concept of a person or group of people taking precedence over another person or group because the former is either older than the latter or has occupied a particular position longer than the latter. _____ is present between parents and children and may be present in other common relationships, such as among siblings of different ages or between workers and their managers.

Exam Probability: **Low**

27. *Answer choices:*

- a. Debt relief order
- b. Seniority
- c. Asset-protection trust
- d. Judgment summons

Guidance: level 1

:: Self ::

_____ is a conscious or subconscious process in which people attempt to influence the perceptions of other people about a person, object or event. They do so by regulating and controlling information in social interaction. It was first conceptualized by Erving Goffman in 1959 in The Presentation of Self in Everyday Life, and then was expanded upon in 1967. An example of _____ theory in play is in sports such as soccer. At an important game, a player would want to showcase themselves in the best light possible, because there are college recruiters watching. This person would have the flashiest pair of cleats and try and perform their best to show off their skills. Their main goal may be to impress the college recruiters in a way that maximizes their chances of being chosen for a college team rather than winning the game.

28. *Answer choices:*
(see index for correct answer)

- a. Self-presentation
- b. Impression management
- c. a person
- d. ecological self

Guidance: level 1

:: Employment discrimination ::

A _____ is a metaphor used to represent an invisible barrier that keeps a given demographic from rising beyond a certain level in a hierarchy.

29. *Answer choices:*
(see index for correct answer)

- a. New South Wales selection bias
- b. Employment discrimination
- c. Glass ceiling
- d. MacBride Principles

Guidance: level 1

:: ::

_____ involves the development of an action plan designed to motivate and guide a person or group toward a goal. _____ can be guided by goal-setting criteria such as SMART criteria. _____ is a major component of personal-development and management literature.

Exam Probability: **Low**

30. *Answer choices:*
(see index for correct answer)

- a. interpersonal communication
- b. Goal setting
- c. Sarbanes-Oxley act of 2002
- d. corporate values

Guidance: level 1

:: Training ::

_____ is action or inaction that is regulated to be in accordance with a particular system of governance. _____ is commonly applied to regulating human and animal behavior, and furthermore, it is applied to each activity-branch in all branches of organized activity, knowledge, and other fields of study and observation. _____ can be a set of expectations that are required by any governing entity including the self, groups, classes, fields, industries, or societies.

Exam Probability: **Medium**

31. *Answer choices:*
(see index for correct answer)

- a. Endurance training
- b. Facila
- c. Simulation game
- d. Discipline

Guidance: level 1

:: Employment ::

_____ is the probability that an individual will keep his/her job; a job with a high level of _____ is such that a person with the job would have a small chance of losing it.

Exam Probability: **Low**

32. *Answer choices:*
(see index for correct answer)

- a. Work-in
- b. Job security
- c. Psychological contract
- d. Career assessment

Guidance: level 1

:: Problem solving ::

A _____ is a unit or formation established to work on a single defined task or activity. Originally introduced by the United States Navy, the term has now caught on for general usage and is a standard part of NATO terminology. Many non-military organizations now create " _____ s" or task groups for temporary activities that might have once been performed by ad hoc committees.

Exam Probability: **High**

33. *Answer choices:*
(see index for correct answer)

- a. Einstellung effect
- b. Lateral computing
- c. Curiosity
- d. 5 Whys

Guidance: level 1

:: ::

A _____ is the ability to carry out a task with determined results often within a given amount of time, energy, or both. _____ s can often be divided into domain-general and domain-specific _____ s. For example, in the domain of work, some general _____ s would include time management, teamwork and leadership, self-motivation and others, whereas domain-specific _____ s would be used only for a certain job. _____ usually requires certain environmental stimuli and situations to assess the level of _____ being shown and used.

Exam Probability: **Medium**

34. *Answer choices:*
(see index for correct answer)

- a. imperative
- b. Skill
- c. personal values
- d. levels of analysis

Guidance: level 1

:: ::

Educational technology is "the study and ethical practice of facilitating learning and improving performance by creating, using, and managing appropriate technological processes and resources".

Exam Probability: **Medium**

35. *Answer choices:*
(see index for correct answer)

- a. co-culture
- b. levels of analysis
- c. E-learning
- d. personal values

Guidance: level 1

:: ::

An _____ is a process where candidates are examined to determine their suitability for specific types of employment, especially management or military command. The candidates' personality and aptitudes are determined by techniques including interviews, group exercises, presentations, examinations and psychometric testing.

Exam Probability: **Medium**

36. *Answer choices:*
(see index for correct answer)

- a. open system
- b. co-culture
- c. corporate values
- d. Assessment center

Guidance: level 1

:: Business law ::

A pre-entry _____ is a form of union security agreement under which the employer agrees to hire union members only, and employees must remain members of the union at all times in order to remain employed. This is different from a post-entry _____ , which is an agreement requiring all employees to join the union if they are not already members. In a union shop, the union must accept as a member any person hired by the employer.

Exam Probability: **Medium**

37. *Answer choices:*
(see index for correct answer)

- a. Administration
- b. Closed shop
- c. Stick licensing
- d. Turnkey

Guidance: level 1

:: ::

The U.S. _____ is a federal agency that administers and enforces civil rights laws against workplace discrimination. The EEOC investigates discrimination complaints based on an individual's race, children, national origin, religion, sex, age, disability, sexual orientation, gender identity, genetic information, and retaliation for reporting, participating in, and/or opposing a discriminatory practice.

Exam Probability: **Medium**

38. *Answer choices:*
(see index for correct answer)

- a. cultural
- b. Sarbanes-Oxley act of 2002
- c. imperative
- d. Equal Employment Opportunity Commission

Guidance: level 1

:: Human resource management ::

_____ refers to the anticipation of required human capital for an organization and the planning to meet those needs. The field increased in popularity after McKinsey's 1997 research and the 2001 book on The War for Talent. _____ in this context does not refer to the management of entertainers.

Exam Probability: **Low**

39. *Answer choices:*
(see index for correct answer)

- a. Organizational orientations
- b. Potential analysis
- c. Talent management
- d. Applicant tracking system

Guidance: level 1

:: United States employment discrimination case law ::

_____ , 524 U.S. 775 , is a US labor law case of the United States Supreme Court in which the Court identified the circumstances under which an employer may be held liable under Title VII of the Civil Rights Act of 1964 for the acts of a supervisory employee whose sexual harassment of subordinates has created a hostile work environment amounting to employment discrimination. The court held that "an employer is vicariously liable for actionable discrimination caused by a supervisor, but subject to an affirmative defense looking to the reasonableness of the employer's conduct as well as that of a plaintiff victim."

Exam Probability: **High**

40. *Answer choices:*
(see index for correct answer)

- a. Faragher v. City of Boca Raton
- b. Price Waterhouse v. Hopkins
- c. Hosanna-Tabor Evangelical Lutheran Church and School v. Equal Employment Opportunity Commission
- d. Vance v. Ball State University

Guidance: level 1

:: Sociological theories ::

A _____ is a systematic process for determining and addressing needs, or "gaps" between current conditions and desired conditions or "wants". The discrepancy between the current condition and wanted condition must be measured to appropriately identify the need. The need can be a desire to improve current performance or to correct a deficiency.

Exam Probability: **Medium**

41. *Answer choices:*
(see index for correct answer)

- a. comfort zone
- b. social constructionism
- c. resource mobilization
- d. Needs assessment

Guidance: level 1

:: Survey methodology ::

_____ is often used to assess thoughts, opinions, and feelings. Surveys can be specific and limited, or they can have more global, widespread goals. Psychologists and sociologists often use surveys to analyze behavior, while it is also used to meet the more pragmatic needs of the media, such as, in evaluating political candidates, public health officials, professional organizations, and advertising and marketing directors. A survey consists of a predetermined set of questions that is given to a sample. With a representative sample, that is, one that is representative of the larger population of interest, one can describe the attitudes of the population from which the sample was drawn. Further, one can compare the attitudes of different populations as well as look for changes in attitudes over time. A good sample selection is key as it allows one to generalize the findings from the sample to the population, which is the whole purpose of _____ .

Exam Probability: **High**

42. *Answer choices:*
(see index for correct answer)

- a. Administrative error
- b. Self-report
- c. Inverse probability weighting
- d. Coverage error

Guidance: level 1

:: Employment ::

A _____ , a concept developed in contemporary research by organizational scholar Denise Rousseau, represents the mutual beliefs, perceptions and informal obligations between an employer and an employee. It sets the dynamics for the relationship and defines the detailed practicality of the work to be done. It is distinguishable from the formal written contract of employment which, for the most part, only identifies mutual duties and responsibilities in a generalized form.

Exam Probability: **High**

43. *Answer choices:*
(see index for correct answer)

- a. Psychological contract
- b. Academic job market

- c. Work-in
- d. Ethical job

Guidance: level 1

:: Management ::

_____ is a technique used by some employers to rotate their employees' assigned jobs throughout their employment. Employers practice this technique for a number of reasons. It was designed to promote flexibility of employees and to keep employees interested into staying with the company/organization which employs them. There is also research that shows how _____ s help relieve the stress of employees who work in a job that requires manual labor.

Exam Probability: **Medium**

44. *Answer choices:*
(see index for correct answer)

- a. Outrage constraint
- b. Management entrenchment
- c. Statistical process control
- d. Job rotation

Guidance: level 1

:: Training ::

_____ is a phase of training needs analysis directed at identifying which individuals within an organization should receive training.

Exam Probability: **High**

45. *Answer choices:*
(see index for correct answer)

- a. Confidence-based learning
- b. Compliance training
- c. Person Analysis
- d. Biography Work

Guidance: level 1

:: Organizational behavior ::

_____ is the act of matching attitudes, beliefs, and behaviors to group norms or politics. Norms are implicit, specific rules, shared by a group of individuals, that guide their interactions with others. People often choose to conform to society rather than to pursue personal desires because it is often easier to follow the path others have made already, rather than creating a new one. This tendency to conform occurs in small groups and/or society as a whole, and may result from subtle unconscious influences , or direct and overt social pressure. _____ can occur in the presence of others, or when an individual is alone. For example, people tend to follow social norms when eating or watching television, even when alone.

Exam Probability: **Low**

46. *Answer choices:*
(see index for correct answer)

- a. Self-policing
- b. Conformity
- c. Behavioral systems analysis
- d. Micro-initiative

Guidance: level 1

:: ::

_____ , also known as alcohol use disorder , is a broad term for any drinking of alcohol that results in mental or physical health problems. The disorder was previously divided into two types: alcohol abuse and alcohol dependence. In a medical context, _____ is said to exist when two or more of the following conditions are present: a person drinks large amounts of alcohol over a long time period, has difficulty cutting down, acquiring and drinking alcohol takes up a great deal of time, alcohol is strongly desired, usage results in not fulfilling responsibilities, usage results in social problems, usage results in health problems, usage results in risky situations, withdrawal occurs when stopping, and alcohol tolerance has occurred with use. Risky situations include drinking and driving or having unsafe sex, among other things. Alcohol use can affect all parts of the body, but it particularly affects the brain, heart, liver, pancreas and immune system. This can result in mental illness, Wernicke–Korsakoff syndrome, irregular heartbeat, an impaired immune response, liver cirrhosis and increased cancer risk, among other diseases Drinking during pregnancy can cause damage to the baby resulting in fetal alcohol spectrum disorders. Women are generally more sensitive than men to the harmful physical and mental effects of alcohol.

Exam Probability: **Low**

47. *Answer choices:*
(see index for correct answer)

- a. open system
- b. co-culture
- c. Character
- d. Alcoholism

Guidance: level 1

:: Financial accounting ::

_____ is the intangible value of a business, covering its people, the value relating to its relationships, and everything that is left when the employees go home, of which intellectual property is but one component. It is the sum of everything everybody in a company knows that gives it a competitive edge. The term is used in academia in an attempt to account for the value of intangible assets not listed explicitly on a company's balance sheets. On a national level _____ refers to national intangible capital, NIC. A second meaning that is used in academia and was adopted in large corporations is focused on the recycling of knowledge via knowledge management and _____ management. Creating, shaping and updating the stock of _____ requires the formulation of a strategic vision, which blends together all three dimensions of _____ within the organisational context through exploration, exploitation, measurement, and disclosure. _____ is used in the context of assessing the wealth of organizations. A metric for the value of _____ is the amount by which the enterprise value of a firm exceeds the value of its tangible assets. Directly visible on corporate books is capital embodied in its physical assets and financial capital; however all three make up the value of an enterprise. Measuring the real value and the total performance of _____'s components is a critical part of running a company in the knowledge economy and Information Age. Understanding the _____ in an enterprise allows leveraging of its intellectual assets. For a corporation, the result will optimize its stock price.

Exam Probability: **Medium**

48. *Answer choices:*
(see index for correct answer)

- a. Convenience translation
- b. Controlling interest
- c. Intellectual capital
- d. Floating capital

Guidance: level 1

:: Human resource management ::

_____ is the application of information technology for both networking and supporting at least two individual or collective actors in their shared performing of HR activities.

49. *Answer choices:*

(see index for correct answer)

- a. E-HRM
- b. Voluntary redundancy
- c. Bradford Factor
- d. Labour is not a commodity

Guidance: level 1

:: Stress ::

_____ means beneficial stress—either psychological, physical , or biochemical/radiological .

50. *Answer choices:*

(see index for correct answer)

- a. CernySmith Assessment
- b. Military sexual trauma
- c. Eustress
- d. Critical incident stress management

Guidance: level 1

:: ::

_____ medicine is an approach to medical practice intended to optimize decision-making by emphasizing the use of evidence from well-designed and well-conducted research. Although all medicine based on science has some degree of empirical support, EBM goes further, classifying evidence by its epistemologic strength and requiring that only the strongest types can yield strong recommendations; weaker types can yield only weak recommendations. The term was originally used to describe an approach to teaching the practice of medicine and improving decisions by individual physicians about individual patients. Use of the term rapidly expanded to include a previously described approach that emphasized the use of evidence in the design of guidelines and policies that apply to groups of patients and populations . It has subsequently spread to describe an approach to decision-making that is used at virtually every level of health care as well as other fields .

51. *Answer choices:*
(see index for correct answer)

- a. deep-level diversity
- b. similarity-attraction theory
- c. Evidence-based
- d. surface-level diversity

Guidance: level 1

:: Corporate governance ::

An _____ is generally a person responsible for running an organization, although the exact nature of the role varies depending on the organization. In many militaries, an _____ , or "XO," is the second-in-command, reporting to the commanding officer. The XO is typically responsible for the management of day-to-day activities, freeing the commander to concentrate on strategy and planning the unit's next move.

52. *Answer choices:*
(see index for correct answer)

- a. Board-only
- b. Chief operating officer
- c. Executive officer
- d. Chief audit executive

Guidance: level 1

:: ::

_____ is the process of collecting, analyzing and/or reporting information regarding the performance of an individual, group, organization, system or component. _____ is not a new concept, some of the earliest records of human activity relate to the counting or recording of activities.

53. *Answer choices:*
(see index for correct answer)

- a. Performance measurement
- b. empathy
- c. process perspective
- d. Character

Guidance: level 1

:: ::

A _____ , medical practitioner, medical doctor, or simply doctor, is a professional who practises medicine, which is concerned with promoting, maintaining, or restoring health through the study, diagnosis, prognosis and treatment of disease, injury, and other physical and mental impairments. _____ s may focus their practice on certain disease categories, types of patients, and methods of treatment—known as specialities—or they may assume responsibility for the provision of continuing and comprehensive medical care to individuals, families, and communities—known as general practice. Medical practice properly requires both a detailed knowledge of the academic disciplines, such as anatomy and physiology, underlying diseases and their treatment—the science of medicine—and also a decent competence in its applied practice—the art or craft of medicine.

Exam Probability: **Low**

54. *Answer choices:*
(see index for correct answer)

- a. co-culture
- b. deep-level diversity
- c. Physician
- d. levels of analysis

Guidance: level 1

:: Recruitment ::

_____ is a specialized recruitment service which organizations pay to seek out and recruit highly qualified candidates for senior-level and executive jobs . Headhunters may also seek out and recruit other highly specialized and/or skilled positions in organizations for which there is strong competition in the job market for the top talent, such as senior data analysts or computer programmers. The method usually involves commissioning a third-party organization, typically an _____ firm, but possibly a standalone consultant or consulting firm, to research the availability of suitable qualified candidates working for competitors or related businesses or organizations. Having identified a shortlist of qualified candidates who match the client's requirements, the _____ firm may act as an intermediary to contact the individual and see if they might be interested in moving to a new employer. The _____ firm may also carry out initial screening of the candidate, negotiations on remuneration and benefits, and preparing the employment contract. In some markets there has been a move towards using _____ for lower positions driven by the fact that there are less candidates for some positions even on lower levels than executive.

Exam Probability: **Low**

55. *Answer choices:*
(see index for correct answer)

- a. Employee referral
- b. Jeopardy! audition process
- c. Campus placement
- d. Executive search

Guidance: level 1

:: Employment compensation ::

A _____ is pay and benefits employees receive when they leave employment at a company unwillfully. In addition to their remaining regular pay, it may include some of the following.

Exam Probability: **Low**

56. *Answer choices:*
(see index for correct answer)

- a. The Theory of Wages
- b. salary sacrifice

- c. Scanlon plan
- d. Severance package

Guidance: level 1

:: Labour relations ::

An _____ is a place of employment at which one is not required to join or financially support a union as a condition of hiring or continued employment. _____ is also known as a merit shop.

Exam Probability: **Low**

57. *Answer choices:*
(see index for correct answer)

- a. Picketing
- b. Merit shop
- c. Open shop
- d. Comprehensive campaign

Guidance: level 1

:: ::

_____ is a belief that hard work and diligence have a moral benefit and an inherent ability, virtue or value to strengthen character and individual abilities. It is a set of values centered on importance of work and manifested by determination or desire to work hard. Social ingrainment of this value is considered to enhance character through hard work that is respective to an individual's field of work.

Exam Probability: **High**

58. *Answer choices:*
(see index for correct answer)

- a. empathy
- b. Work ethic
- c. interpersonal communication
- d. information systems assessment

Guidance: level 1

:: Human resource management ::

_____ refers to the ability of an organization to retain its employees. _____ can be represented by a simple statistic . However, many consider _____ as relating to the efforts by which employers attempt to retain the employees in their workforce. In this sense, retention becomes the strategies rather than the outcome.

Exam Probability: **High**

59. *Answer choices:*

- a. Internal communications
- b. Continuing professional development
- c. Employment testing
- d. Action alert

Guidance: level 1

Information systems

Information systems (IS) are formal, sociotechnical, organizational systems designed to collect, process, store, and distribute information. In a sociotechnical perspective Information Systems are composed by four components: technology, process, people and organizational structure.

:: ::

A _____ is a structure / access pattern specific to data warehouse environments, used to retrieve client-facing data. The _____ is a subset of the data warehouse and is usually oriented to a specific business line or team. Whereas data warehouses have an enterprise-wide depth, the information in _____ s pertains to a single department. In some deployments, each department or business unit is considered the owner of its _____ including all the hardware, software and data. This enables each department to isolate the use, manipulation and development of their data. In other deployments where conformed dimensions are used, this business unit ownership will not hold true for shared dimensions like customer, product, etc.

Exam Probability: **Low**

1. *Answer choices:*
(see index for correct answer)

- a. Sarbanes-Oxley act of 2002
- b. functional perspective
- c. hierarchical
- d. open system

Guidance: level 1

:: Computing input devices ::

In computing, an _____ is a piece of computer hardware equipment used to provide data and control signals to an information processing system such as a computer or information appliance. Examples of _____ s include keyboards, mouse, scanners, digital cameras and joysticks. Audio _____ s may be used for purposes including speech recognition. Many companies are utilizing speech recognition to help assist users to use their device.

Exam Probability: **Medium**

2. *Answer choices:*
(see index for correct answer)

- a. Graffiti 2
- b. IntelliMouse
- c. Input device
- d. Project Digits

Guidance: level 1

:: Internet governance ::

A _____ is one of the domains at the highest level in the hierarchical Domain Name System of the Internet. The _____ names are installed in the root zone of the name space. For all domains in lower levels, it is the last part of the domain name, that is, the last label of a fully qualified domain name. For example, in the domain name www.example.com, the _____ is com. Responsibility for management of most _____ s is delegated to specific organizations by the Internet Corporation for Assigned Names and Numbers , which operates the Internet Assigned Numbers Authority , and is in charge of maintaining the DNS root zone.

Exam Probability: **Medium**

3. *Answer choices:*
(see index for correct answer)

- a. Foretec Seminars
- b. Uniform Domain-Name Dispute-Resolution Policy
- c. Top-level domain
- d. Internet governance

Guidance: level 1

:: Computer memory ::

_____ is a type of non-volatile memory used in computers and other electronic devices. Data stored in ROM can only be modified slowly, with difficulty, or not at all, so it is mainly used to store firmware or application software in plug-in cartridges.

Exam Probability: **Medium**

4. *Answer choices:*
(see index for correct answer)

- a. Flash memory controller
- b. Read-only memory
- c. Memory ProteXion
- d. Flat memory model

Guidance: level 1

:: Geographic information systems ::

_____ is the computational process of transforming a physical address description to a location on the Earth`s surface . Reverse _____ , on the other hand, converts geographic coordinates to a description of a location, usually the name of a place or an addressable location. _____ relies on a computer representation of address points, the street / road network, together with postal and administrative boundaries.

Exam Probability: **Medium**

5. *Answer choices:*
(see index for correct answer)

- a. GeoWeb Conference
- b. Route
- c. Geography Markup Language
- d. Geocoding

Guidance: level 1

:: Internet privacy ::

An _____ is a private network accessible only to an organization's staff. Often, a wide range of information and services are available on an organization's internal _____ that are unavailable to the public, unlike the Internet. A company-wide _____ can constitute an important focal point of internal communication and collaboration, and provide a single starting point to access internal and external resources. In its simplest form, an _____ is established with the technologies for local area networks and wide area networks . Many modern _____ s have search engines, user profiles, blogs, mobile apps with notifications, and events planning within their infrastructure.

Exam Probability: **High**

6. *Answer choices:*
(see index for correct answer)

- a. Phoenix Labs
- b. Intranet
- c. Local shared object
- d. Secure communication

Guidance: level 1

:: Automatic identification and data capture ::

_____ is the trademark for a type of matrix barcode first designed in 1994 for the automotive industry in Japan. A barcode is a machine-readable optical label that contains information about the item to which it is attached. In practice, _____ s often contain data for a locator, identifier, or tracker that points to a website or application. A _____ uses four standardized encoding modes to store data efficiently; extensions may also be used.

Exam Probability: **High**

7. *Answer choices:*
(see index for correct answer)

- a. IBeacon
- b. RCD Technology
- c. Track and trace
- d. QR code

Guidance: level 1

_____ , Inc. is an American online social media and social networking service company based in Menlo Park, California. It was founded by Mark Zuckerberg, along with fellow Harvard College students and roommates Eduardo Saverin, Andrew McCollum, Dustin Moskovitz and Chris Hughes. It is considered one of the Big Four technology companies along with Amazon, Apple, and Google.

Exam Probability: **High**

8. *Answer choices:*
(see index for correct answer)

- a. Facebook
- b. similarity-attraction theory
- c. functional perspective
- d. information systems assessment

Guidance: level 1

:: Marketing ::

_____ is a business model in which consumers create value and businesses consume that value. For example, when a consumer writes reviews or when a consumer gives a useful idea for new product development then that consumer is creating value for the business if the business adopts the input. In the C2B model, a reverse auction or demand collection model, enables buyers to name or demand their own price, which is often binding, for a specific good or service. Inside of a consumer to business market the roles involved in the transaction must be established and the consumer must offer something of value to the business.

Exam Probability: **High**

9. *Answer choices:*
(see index for correct answer)

- a. Klondike Big Inch Land Promotion
- b. Need
- c. Marketing communications
- d. Performance-based advertising

Guidance: level 1

:: Data management ::

_____ is "data [information] that provides information about other data". Many distinct types of _____ exist, among these descriptive _____ , structural _____ , administrative _____ , reference _____ and statistical _____ .

Exam Probability: **Medium**

10. *Answer choices:*
(see index for correct answer)

- a. Vocabulary-based transformation
- b. Data set
- c. Log trigger
- d. Data archive

Guidance: level 1

:: Reputation management ::

A _____ is an astronomical object consisting of a luminous spheroid of plasma held together by its own gravity. The nearest _____ to Earth is the Sun. Many other _____ s are visible to the naked eye from Earth during the night, appearing as a multitude of fixed luminous points in the sky due to their immense distance from Earth. Historically, the most prominent _____ s were grouped into constellations and asterisms, the brightest of which gained proper names. Astronomers have assembled _____ catalogues that identify the known _____ s and provide standardized stellar designations. However, most of the estimated 300 sextillion _____ s in the Universe are invisible to the naked eye from Earth, including all _____ s outside our galaxy, the Milky Way.

Exam Probability: **High**

11. *Answer choices:*
(see index for correct answer)

- a. EigenTrust
- b. Star
- c. 123people
- d. Moderation system

Guidance: level 1

_____ comprises the strategies and technologies used by enterprises for the data analysis of business information. BI technologies provide historical, current and predictive views of business operations. Common functions of _____ technologies include reporting, online analytical processing, analytics, data mining, process mining, complex event processing, business performance management, benchmarking, text mining, predictive analytics and prescriptive analytics. BI technologies can handle large amounts of structured and sometimes unstructured data to help identify, develop and otherwise create new strategic business opportunities. They aim to allow for the easy interpretation of these big data. Identifying new opportunities and implementing an effective strategy based on insights can provide businesses with a competitive market advantage and long-term stability.

Exam Probability: **High**

12. *Answer choices:*
(see index for correct answer)

- a. Fabricator
- b. Business intelligence
- c. Electro-optical MASINT
- d. Geophysical MASINT

Guidance: level 1

In information technology, a _____ , or data _____ , or the process of backing up, refers to the copying into an archive file of computer data that is already in secondary storage—so that it may be used to restore the original after a data loss event. The verb form is "back up" , whereas the noun and adjective form is " _____ ".

Exam Probability: **High**

13. *Answer choices:*
(see index for correct answer)

- a. Separation of duties
- b. Federation Against Software Theft
- c. Alternative compensation system

- d. Backup

Guidance: level 1

:: Virtual reality ::

_____ is an experience taking place within simulated and immersive environments that can be similar to or completely different from the real world. Applications of _____ can include entertainment and educational purposes . Other, distinct types of VR style technology include augmented reality and mixed reality.

Exam Probability: **High**

14. *Answer choices:*
(see index for correct answer)

- a. GT Racing Cockpit
- b. Normal mapping
- c. Virtual reality
- d. Digital Molecular Matter

Guidance: level 1

:: Online companies ::

_____ is a business directory service and crowd-sourced review forum, and a public company of the same name that is headquartered in San Francisco, California. The company develops, hosts and markets the _____ .com website and the _____ mobile app, which publish crowd-sourced reviews about businesses. It also operates an online reservation service called _____ Reservations.

Exam Probability: **Low**

15. *Answer choices:*
(see index for correct answer)

- a. Yelp
- b. Justdial
- c. Geekologie
- d. Pinstorm

Guidance: level 1

A _____ is a group of interacting or interrelated entities that form a unified whole. A _____ is delineated by its spatial and temporal boundaries, surrounded and influenced by its environment, described by its structure and purpose and expressed in its functioning.

Exam Probability: **Medium**

16. *Answer choices:*
(see index for correct answer)

- a. co-design
- b. Black box
- c. System
- d. equifinality

Guidance: level 1

_____ s are many different distantly related animals that typically have a long cylindrical tube-like body and no limbs. _____ s vary in size from microscopic to over 1 metre in length for marine polychaete _____ s , 6.7 metres for the African giant earth _____ , Microchaetus rappi, and 58 metres for the marine nemertean _____ , Lineus longissimus. Various types of _____ occupy a small variety of parasitic niches, living inside the bodies of other animals. Free-living _____ species do not live on land, but instead, live in marine or freshwater environments, or underground by burrowing.In biology, " _____ " refers to an obsolete taxon, vermes, used by Carolus Linnaeus and Jean-Baptiste Lamarck for all non-arthropod invertebrate animals, now seen to be paraphyletic. The name stems from the Old English word wyrm. Most animals called " _____ s" are invertebrates, but the term is also used for the amphibian caecilians and the slow _____ Anguis, a legless burrowing lizard. Invertebrate animals commonly called " _____ s" include annelids , nematodes , platyhelminthes , marine nemertean _____ s , marine Chaetognatha , priapulid _____ s, and insect larvae such as grubs and maggots.

Exam Probability: **High**

17. *Answer choices:*

- a. High Mark Credit Information Services
- b. Worm
- c. Zyfin
- d. Media Technology Monitor

Guidance: level 1

:: Stochastic processes ::

_____ in its modern meaning is a "new idea, creative thoughts, new imaginations in form of device or method". _____ is often also viewed as the application of better solutions that meet new requirements, unarticulated needs, or existing market needs. Such _____ takes place through the provision of more-effective products, processes, services, technologies, or business models that are made available to markets, governments and society. An _____ is something original and more effective and, as a consequence, new, that "breaks into" the market or society. _____ is related to, but not the same as, invention, as _____ is more apt to involve the practical implementation of an invention to make a meaningful impact in the market or society, and not all _____ s require an invention. _____ often manifests itself via the engineering process, when the problem being solved is of a technical or scientific nature. The opposite of _____ is exnovation.

Exam Probability: **High**

18. *Answer choices:*

- a. Local time
- b. Stochastic quantization
- c. Fluid queue
- d. Innovation

Guidance: level 1

:: Payment systems ::

_____ s are part of a payment system issued by financial institutions, such as a bank, to a customer that enables its owner to access the funds in the customer's designated bank accounts, or through a credit account and make payments by electronic funds transfer and access automated teller machines . Such cards are known by a variety of names including bank cards, ATM cards, MAC , client cards, key cards or cash cards.

19. *Answer choices:*
(see index for correct answer)

- a. Payment card
- b. Direct corporate access
- c. Money order
- d. BACHO record format

Guidance: level 1

:: Management ::

Porter's Five Forces Framework is a tool for analyzing competition of a business. It draws from industrial organization economics to derive five forces that determine the competitive intensity and, therefore, the attractiveness of an industry in terms of its profitability. An "unattractive" industry is one in which the effect of these five forces reduces overall profitability. The most unattractive industry would be one approaching "pure competition", in which available profits for all firms are driven to normal profit levels. The five-forces perspective is associated with its originator, Michael E. Porter of Harvard University. This framework was first published in Harvard Business Review in 1979.

20. *Answer choices:*
(see index for correct answer)

- a. Porter five forces analysis
- b. Technology scouting
- c. Management buyout
- d. Concept of operations

Guidance: level 1

_____ is an electronic non-volatile computer storage medium that can be electrically erased and reprogrammed.

Exam Probability: **Medium**

21. *Answer choices:*
(see index for correct answer)

- a. Flash memory
- b. Offset
- c. 6264
- d. Shift register lookup table

Guidance: level 1

:: World Wide Web ::

A _____ is a document that is suitable to act as a web resource on the World Wide Web. In order to graphically display a _____ , a web browser is needed. This is a type of software that can retrieve _____ s from the Internet. When accessed by a web browser it may be displayed as a _____ on a monitor or mobile device. Typical _____ s are hypertext documents which contain hyperlinks, often referred to as links, for browsing to other _____ s.

Exam Probability: **Medium**

22. *Answer choices:*
(see index for correct answer)

- a. Simple Common Gateway Interface
- b. Hypertargeting
- c. Web page
- d. Isabel Maxwell

Guidance: level 1

:: Supply chain management ::

_____ is the removal of intermediaries in economics from a supply chain, or cutting out the middlemen in connection with a transaction or a series of transactions. Instead of going through traditional distribution channels, which had some type of intermediary , companies may now deal with customers directly, for example via the Internet. Hence, the use of factory direct and direct from the factory to mean the same thing.

Exam Probability: **High**

23. *Answer choices:*

- a. Procurement
- b. Universal Product Code ,
- c. Supply chain diversification
- d. Avercast

Guidance: level 1

:: ::

_____ LLC is an American multinational technology company that specializes in Internet-related services and products, which include online advertising technologies, search engine, cloud computing, software, and hardware. It is considered one of the Big Four technology companies, alongside Amazon, Apple and Facebook.

Exam Probability: **Low**

24. *Answer choices:*

- a. similarity-attraction theory
- b. interpersonal communication
- c. information systems assessment
- d. levels of analysis

Guidance: level 1

:: Survey methodology ::

A _____ is the procedure of systematically acquiring and recording information about the members of a given population. The term is used mostly in connection with national population and housing _____ es; other common _____ es include agriculture, business, and traffic _____ es. The United Nations defines the essential features of population and housing _____ es as "individual enumeration, universality within a defined territory, simultaneity and defined periodicity", and recommends that population _____ es be taken at least every 10 years. United Nations recommendations also cover _____ topics to be collected, official definitions, classifications and other useful information to co-ordinate international practice.

Exam Probability: **Medium**

25. *Answer choices:*

- a. Census
- b. Swiss Centre of Expertise in the Social Sciences
- c. Self-report
- d. National Health Interview Survey

Guidance: level 1

:: Data transmission ::

In telecommunication a _____ is the means of connecting one location to another for the purpose of transmitting and receiving digital information. It can also refer to a set of electronics assemblies, consisting of a transmitter and a receiver and the interconnecting data telecommunication circuit. These are governed by a link protocol enabling digital data to be transferred from a data source to a data sink.

Exam Probability: **Low**

26. *Answer choices:*

- a. Data link
- b. Scancode
- c. User information bit
- d. Flag sequence

Guidance: level 1

:: Virtual economies ::

_____ is an online virtual world, developed and owned by the San Francisco-based firm Linden Lab and launched on June 23, 2003. By 2013, _____ had approximately one million regular users; at the end of 2017 active user count totals "between 800,000 and 900,000". In many ways, _____ is similar to massively multiplayer online role-playing games; however, Linden Lab is emphatic that their creation is not a game: "There is no manufactured conflict, no set objective".

Exam Probability: **Low**

27. *Answer choices:*
(see index for correct answer)

- a. Monopoly money
- b. Second Life
- c. Empire Avenue
- d. There

Guidance: level 1

:: ::

_____ is a kind of action that occur as two or more objects have an effect upon one another. The idea of a two-way effect is essential in the concept of _____ , as opposed to a one-way causal effect. A closely related term is interconnectivity, which deals with the _____ s of _____ s within systems: combinations of many simple _____ s can lead to surprising emergent phenomena. _____ has different tailored meanings in various sciences. Changes can also involve _____ .

Exam Probability: **Low**

28. *Answer choices:*
(see index for correct answer)

- a. hierarchical
- b. levels of analysis
- c. Interaction
- d. corporate values

Guidance: level 1

_____ is a free email service developed by Google. Users can access _____ on the web and using third-party programs that synchronize email content through POP or IMAP protocols. _____ started as a limited beta release on April 1, 2004 and ended its testing phase on July 7, 2009.

Exam Probability: **High**

29. *Answer choices:*
(see index for correct answer)

- a. cultural
- b. Gmail
- c. surface-level diversity
- d. similarity-attraction theory

Guidance: level 1

:: Information science ::

_____ has been defined as "the branch of ethics that focuses on the relationship between the creation, organization, dissemination, and use of information, and the ethical standards and moral codes governing human conduct in society". It examines the morality that comes from information as a resource, a product, or as a target. It provides a critical framework for considering moral issues concerning informational privacy, moral agency , new environmental issues , problems arising from the life-cycle of information .
It is very vital to understand that librarians, archivists, information professionals among others, really understand the importance of knowing how to disseminate proper information as well as being responsible with their actions when addressing information.

Exam Probability: **Low**

30. *Answer choices:*
(see index for correct answer)

- a. Information ethics
- b. Informatics
- c. User-subjective approach
- d. Humanities Advanced Technology and Information Institute

Guidance: level 1

In business, a _____ is the attribute that allows an organization to outperform its competitors. A _____ may include access to natural resources, such as high-grade ores or a low-cost power source, highly skilled labor, geographic location, high entry barriers, and access to new technology.

Exam Probability: **Low**

31. *Answer choices:*
(see index for correct answer)

- a. Cross ownership
- b. Competitive advantage
- c. Community of practice
- d. Meeting system

Guidance: level 1

_____ is a type of fraud that occurs on the Internet in pay-per-click online advertising. In this type of advertising, the owners of websites that post the ads are paid an amount of money determined by how many visitors to the sites click on the ads. Fraud occurs when a person, automated script or computer program imitates a legitimate user of a web browser, clicking on such an ad without having an actual interest in the target of the ad's link. _____ is the subject of some controversy and increasing litigation due to the advertising networks being a key beneficiary of the fraud.

Exam Probability: **High**

32. *Answer choices:*
(see index for correct answer)

- a. ProStores
- b. Click fraud
- c. RapidBuyr
- d. Notice and take down

Guidance: level 1

The _____ is an extension of the World Wide Web through standards by the World Wide Web Consortium . The standards promote common data formats and exchange protocols on the Web, most fundamentally the Resource Description Framework . According to the W3C, "The _____ provides a common framework that allows data to be shared and reused across application, enterprise, and community boundaries". The _____ is therefore regarded as an integrator across different content, information applications and systems.

Exam Probability: **Medium**

33. *Answer choices:*
(see index for correct answer)

- a. Knowledge engineering
- b. Semantic Web
- c. Collaborative innovation network
- d. Knowledge modeling

Guidance: level 1

:: ::

A database is an organized collection of data, generally stored and accessed electronically from a computer system. Where databases are more complex they are often developed using formal design and modeling techniques.

Exam Probability: **Medium**

34. *Answer choices:*
(see index for correct answer)

- a. hierarchical perspective
- b. open system
- c. Database management system
- d. process perspective

Guidance: level 1

:: Business ::

_____ is a sourcing model in which individuals or organizations obtain goods and services, including ideas and finances, from a large, relatively open and often rapidly-evolving group of internet users; it divides work between participants to achieve a cumulative result. The word _____ itself is a portmanteau of crowd and outsourcing, and was coined in 2005. As a mode of sourcing, _____ existed prior to the digital age .

Exam Probability: **Medium**

35. *Answer choices:*
(see index for correct answer)

- a. Post-transaction marketing
- b. Intangible asset finance
- c. Crowdsourcing
- d. Sales

Guidance: level 1

:: Data management ::

_____ , or OLAP , is an approach to answer multi-dimensional analytical queries swiftly in computing. OLAP is part of the broader category of business intelligence, which also encompasses relational databases, report writing and data mining. Typical applications of OLAP include business reporting for sales, marketing, management reporting, business process management , budgeting and forecasting, financial reporting and similar areas, with new applications emerging, such as agriculture. The term OLAP was created as a slight modification of the traditional database term online transaction processing .

Exam Probability: **High**

36. *Answer choices:*
(see index for correct answer)

- a. Content re-appropriation
- b. Data virtualization
- c. Chunked transfer encoding
- d. Bitmap index

Guidance: level 1

:: ::

A _____ is the event in which two or more bodies exert forces on each other in about a relatively short time. Although the most common use of the word _____ refers to incidents in which two or more objects collide with great force, the scientific use of the term implies nothing about the magnitude of the force.

Exam Probability: **Medium**

37. *Answer choices:*
(see index for correct answer)

- a. empathy
- b. similarity-attraction theory
- c. process perspective
- d. Collision

Guidance: level 1

:: Data ::

In computer main memory, auxiliary storage and computer buses, _____ is the existence of data that is additional to the actual data and permits correction of errors in stored or transmitted data. The additional data can simply be a complete copy of the actual data, or only select pieces of data that allow detection of errors and reconstruction of lost or damaged data up to a certain level.

Exam Probability: **High**

38. *Answer choices:*
(see index for correct answer)

- a. Synthetic data
- b. GS1 DataBar Coupon
- c. Biological data
- d. Data acquisition

Guidance: level 1

:: Data management ::

In business, _____ is a method used to define and manage the critical data of an organization to provide, with data integration, a single point of reference. The data that is mastered may include reference data- the set of permissible values, and the analytical data that supports decision making.

Exam Probability: **High**

39. *Answer choices:*
(see index for correct answer)

- a. Novell Storage Manager
- b. Modular concurrency control
- c. Data proliferation
- d. Linear medium

Guidance: level 1

:: ::

A _____ is a control panel usually located directly ahead of a vehicle's driver, displaying instrumentation and controls for the vehicle's operation.

Exam Probability: **High**

40. *Answer choices:*
(see index for correct answer)

- a. personal values
- b. Sarbanes-Oxley act of 2002
- c. levels of analysis
- d. corporate values

Guidance: level 1

:: Business planning ::

_____ is an organization's process of defining its strategy, or direction, and making decisions on allocating its resources to pursue this strategy. It may also extend to control mechanisms for guiding the implementation of the strategy. _____ became prominent in corporations during the 1960s and remains an important aspect of strategic management. It is executed by strategic planners or strategists, who involve many parties and research sources in their analysis of the organization and its relationship to the environment in which it competes.

Exam Probability: **Medium**

41. *Answer choices:*
(see index for correct answer)

- a. Business war games
- b. Community Futures
- c. operational planning
- d. Strategic planning

Guidance: level 1

:: Google services ::

A blog is a discussion or informational website published on the World Wide Web consisting of discrete, often informal diary-style text entries . Posts are typically displayed in reverse chronological order, so that the most recent post appears first, at the top of the web page. Until 2009, blogs were usually the work of a single individual, occasionally of a small group, and often covered a single subject or topic. In the 2010s, "multi-author blogs" emerged, featuring the writing of multiple authors and sometimes professionally edited. MABs from newspapers, other media outlets, universities, think tanks, advocacy groups, and similar institutions account for an increasing quantity of blog traffic. The rise of Twitter and other "microblogging" systems helps integrate MABs and single-author blogs into the news media. Blog can also be used as a verb, meaning to maintain or add content to a blog.

Exam Probability: **Low**

42. *Answer choices:*
(see index for correct answer)

- a. Google Traffic
- b. Google App Engine

- c. Blogger
- d. Google Translator Toolkit

:: Fraud ::

In law, _____ is intentional deception to secure unfair or unlawful gain, or to deprive a victim of a legal right. _____ can violate civil law , a criminal law , or it may cause no loss of money, property or legal right but still be an element of another civil or criminal wrong. The purpose of _____ may be monetary gain or other benefits, for example by obtaining a passport, travel document, or driver's license, or mortgage _____ , where the perpetrator may attempt to qualify for a mortgage by way of false statements.

Exam Probability: **High**

43. *Answer choices:*
(see index for correct answer)

- a. Intrinsic fraud
- b. Hijacked journal
- c. Regummed stamp
- d. Fraud

:: Data analysis ::

_____ is a process of inspecting, cleansing, transforming, and modeling data with the goal of discovering useful information, informing conclusions, and supporting decision-making. _____ has multiple facets and approaches, encompassing diverse techniques under a variety of names, and is used in different business, science, and social science domains. In today's business world, _____ plays a role in making decisions more scientific and helping businesses operate more effectively.

Exam Probability: **Medium**

44. *Answer choices:*
(see index for correct answer)

- a. Data fusion

- b. Proxy
- c. Rasdaman
- d. Data analysis

:: ::

_____ Holdings, Inc. is an American company operating a worldwide online payments system that supports online money transfers and serves as an electronic alternative to traditional paper methods like checks and money orders. The company operates as a payment processor for online vendors, auction sites, and many other commercial users, for which it charges a fee in exchange for benefits such as one-click transactions and password memory. _____ 's payment system, also called _____ , is considered a type of payment rail.

Exam Probability: **High**

45. *Answer choices:*
(see index for correct answer)

- a. hierarchical
- b. open system
- c. functional perspective
- d. PayPal

:: Management ::

In organizational studies, _____ is the efficient and effective development of an organization's resources when they are needed. Such resources may include financial resources, inventory, human skills, production resources, or information technology and natural resources.

Exam Probability: **Medium**

46. *Answer choices:*
(see index for correct answer)

- a. Focused improvement
- b. Information excellence
- c. DMSMS
- d. Security management

:: Management ::

A _____ defines or constrains some aspect of business and always resolves to either true or false. _____ s are intended to assert business structure or to control or influence the behavior of the business. _____ s describe the operations, definitions and constraints that apply to an organization. _____ s can apply to people, processes, corporate behavior and computing systems in an organization, and are put in place to help the organization achieve its goals.

Exam Probability: **Low**

47. *Answer choices:*
(see index for correct answer)

- a. Pareto analysis
- b. Staff management
- c. Business rule
- d. Public sector consulting

:: Information systems ::

A _____ is an information system that supports business or organizational decision-making activities. DSSs serve the management, operations and planning levels of an organization and help people make decisions about problems that may be rapidly changing and not easily specified in advance—i.e. unstructured and semi-structured decision problems. _____ s can be either fully computerized or human-powered, or a combination of both.

Exam Probability: **Medium**

48. *Answer choices:*
(see index for correct answer)

- a. Validis
- b. Information silo
- c. Enterprise information access
- d. Decision support system

In information technology to _____ means to move from one place to another, information to detailed data by focusing in on something. In a GUI-environment, "drilling-down" may involve clicking on some representation in order to reveal more detail.

Exam Probability: **High**

49. *Answer choices:*
(see index for correct answer)

- a. Enterprise output management
- b. Drill down
- c. Professional Petroleum Data Management Association
- d. XML/EDIFACT

Guidance: level 1

:: Marketing by medium ::

_____ , also called online marketing or Internet advertising or web advertising, is a form of marketing and advertising which uses the Internet to deliver promotional marketing messages to consumers. Many consumers find _____ disruptive and have increasingly turned to ad blocking for a variety of reasons. When software is used to do the purchasing, it is known as programmatic advertising.

Exam Probability: **High**

50. *Answer choices:*
(see index for correct answer)

- a. Brand infiltration
- b. Digital marketing
- c. Social video marketing
- d. Online advertising

Guidance: level 1

:: Information science ::

In discourse-based grammatical theory, _____ is any tracking of referential information by speakers. Information may be new, just introduced into the conversation; given, already active in the speakers' consciousness; or old, no longer active. The various types of activation, and how these are defined, are model-dependent.

Exam Probability: **Low**

51. *Answer choices:*

- a. Retrievability
- b. Ontology for Biomedical Investigations
- c. Intergovernmental Bureau for Informatics
- d. The Royal School of Library and Information Science

Guidance: level 1

:: Web security exploits ::

A _____ is a baked or cooked food that is small, flat and sweet. It usually contains flour, sugar and some type of oil or fat. It may include other ingredients such as raisins, oats, chocolate chips, nuts, etc.

Exam Probability: **Low**

52. *Answer choices:*

- a. Cookie
- b. Cross-site cooking
- c. Cookiemonster attack
- d. HTTP header injection

Guidance: level 1

:: Information systems ::

_____ are formal, sociotechnical, organizational systems designed to collect, process, store, and distribute information. In a sociotechnical perspective, _____ are composed by four components: task, people, structure , and technology.

53. *Answer choices:*

- a. Information engineering
- b. Information systems
- c. Spatial decision support system
- d. Labvantage

Guidance: level 1

:: Tag editors ::

_____ is a media player, media library, Internet radio broadcaster, and mobile device management application developed by Apple Inc. It was announced on January 9, 2001. It is used to play, download, and organize digital multimedia files, including music and video, on personal computers running the macOS and Windows operating systems. Content must be purchased through the _____ Store, whereas _____ is the software letting users manage their purchases.

Exam Probability: **Medium**

54. *Answer choices:*

- a. CD Player
- b. Puddletag
- c. Nightingale
- d. ITunes

Guidance: level 1

:: Mereology ::

_____ , in the abstract, is what belongs to or with something, whether as an attribute or as a component of said thing. In the context of this article, it is one or more components , whether physical or incorporeal, of a person's estate; or so belonging to, as in being owned by, a person or jointly a group of people or a legal entity like a corporation or even a society. Depending on the nature of the _____ , an owner of _____ has the right to consume, alter, share, redefine, rent, mortgage, pawn, sell, exchange, transfer, give away or destroy it, or to exclude others from doing these things, as well as to perhaps abandon it; whereas regardless of the nature of the _____ , the owner thereof has the right to properly use it , or at the very least exclusively keep it.

Exam Probability: **Low**

55. *Answer choices:*
(see index for correct answer)

- a. Non-wellfounded mereology
- b. Mereological nihilism
- c. Property
- d. Mereological essentialism

Guidance: level 1

:: Production and manufacturing ::

_____ is the manufacturing approach of using computers to control entire production process. This integration allows individual processes to exchange information with each other and initiate actions. Although manufacturing can be faster and less error-prone by the integration of computers, the main advantage is the ability to create automated manufacturing processes. Typically CIM relies of closed-loop control processes, based on real-time input from sensors. It is also known as flexible design and manufacturing.

Exam Probability: **Medium**

56. *Answer choices:*
(see index for correct answer)

- a. Production equipment control
- b. Program evaluation and review technique
- c. SERCOS III

- d. Computer-integrated manufacturing

Guidance: level 1

:: Fraud ::

_____ is the deliberate use of someone else's identity, usually as a method to gain a financial advantage or obtain credit and other benefits in the other person's name, and perhaps to the other person's disadvantage or loss. The person whose identity has been assumed may suffer adverse consequences, especially if they are held responsible for the perpetrator's actions.

_____ occurs when someone uses another's personally identifying information, like their name, identifying number, or credit card number, without their permission, to commit fraud or other crimes. The term _____ was coined in 1964. Since that time, the definition of _____ has been statutorily prescribed throughout both the U.K. and the United States as the theft of personally identifying information, generally including a person's name, date of birth, social security number, driver's license number, bank account or credit card numbers, PIN numbers, electronic signatures, fingerprints, passwords, or any other information that can be used to access a person's financial resources.

Exam Probability: **High**

57. *Answer choices:*
(see index for correct answer)

- a. Address fraud
- b. Customer not present
- c. Identity theft
- d. Corporate scandal

Guidance: level 1

:: Management ::

_____ is the discipline of strategically planning for, and managing, all interactions with third party organizations that supply goods and/or services to an organization in order to maximize the value of those interactions. In practice, SRM entails creating closer, more collaborative relationships with key suppliers in order to uncover and realize new value and reduce risk of failure.

Exam Probability: **Medium**

58. *Answer choices:*
(see index for correct answer)

- a. Total security management
- b. Supplier relationship management
- c. Task-oriented and relationship-oriented leadership
- d. Information excellence

Guidance: level 1

:: ::

_____ is a brand name associated with the development of the _____ web browser. It is now owned by Verizon Media, a subsidiary of Verizon. The brand belonged to the _____ Communications Corporation , an independent American computer services company, whose headquarters were in Mountain View, California, and later Dulles, Virginia. The browser was once dominant but lost to Internet Explorer and other competitors after the so-called first browser war, its market share falling from more than 90 percent in the mid-1990s to less than 1 percent in 2006.

Exam Probability: **Low**

59. *Answer choices:*
(see index for correct answer)

- a. Netscape
- b. co-culture
- c. process perspective
- d. levels of analysis

Guidance: level 1

Marketing

Marketing is the study and management of exchange relationships. Marketing is the business process of creating relationships with and satisfying customers. With its focus on the customer, marketing is one of the premier components of business management.

Marketing is defined by the American Marketing Association as "the activity, set of institutions, and processes for creating, communicating, delivering, and exchanging offerings that have value for customers, clients, partners, and society at large."

:: Survey methodology ::

An _____ is a conversation where questions are asked and answers are given. In common parlance, the word "_____" refers to a one-on-one conversation between an _____ er and an _____ ee. The _____ er asks questions to which the _____ ee responds, usually so information may be transferred from _____ ee to _____ er . Sometimes, information can be transferred in both directions. It is a communication, unlike a speech, which produces a one-way flow of information.

Exam Probability: **Medium**

1. *Answer choices:*
(see index for correct answer)

- a. Census
- b. Sampling
- c. Group concept mapping
- d. Survey research

Guidance: level 1

:: ::

Retail is the process of selling consumer goods or services to customers through multiple channels of distribution to earn a profit. Retailers satisfy demand identified through a supply chain. The term "retailer" is typically applied where a service provider fills the small orders of a large number of individuals, who are end-users, rather than large orders of a small number of wholesale, corporate or government clientele. Shopping generally refers to the act of buying products. Sometimes this is done to obtain final goods, including necessities such as food and clothing; sometimes it takes place as a recreational activity. Recreational shopping often involves window shopping and browsing; it does not always result in a purchase.

2. *Answer choices:*
(see index for correct answer)

- a. levels of analysis
- b. deep-level diversity
- c. co-culture
- d. empathy

Guidance: level 1

:: Monopoly (economics) ::

A _____ is a form of intellectual property that gives its owner the legal right to exclude others from making, using, selling, and importing an invention for a limited period of years, in exchange for publishing an enabling public disclosure of the invention. In most countries _____ rights fall under civil law and the _____ holder needs to sue someone infringing the _____ in order to enforce his or her rights. In some industries _____ s are an essential form of competitive advantage; in others they are irrelevant.

3. *Answer choices:*
(see index for correct answer)

- a. Patent
- b. Cost per procedure
- c. Natural monopoly
- d. Supracompetitive pricing

:: Marketing ::

_____ is the marketing of products that are presumed to be environmentally safe. It incorporates a broad range of activities, including product modification, changes to the production process, sustainable packaging, as well as modifying advertising. Yet defining _____ is not a simple task where several meanings intersect and contradict each other; an example of this will be the existence of varying social, environmental and retail definitions attached to this term. Other similar terms used are environmental marketing and ecological marketing.

Exam Probability: **High**

4. *Answer choices:*
(see index for correct answer)

- a. Green marketing
- b. Customer franchise
- c. Demand signal repository
- d. Hakan Okay

:: ::

In marketing, a _____ is a ticket or document that can be redeemed for a financial discount or rebate when purchasing a product.

Exam Probability: **High**

5. *Answer choices:*
(see index for correct answer)

- a. information systems assessment
- b. co-culture
- c. Coupon
- d. cultural

:: ::

An _____ is an area of the production, distribution, or trade, and consumption of goods and services by different agents. Understood in its broadest sense, 'The _____ is defined as a social domain that emphasize the practices, discourses, and material expressions associated with the production, use, and management of resources'. Economic agents can be individuals, businesses, organizations, or governments. Economic transactions occur when two parties agree to the value or price of the transacted good or service, commonly expressed in a certain currency. However, monetary transactions only account for a small part of the economic domain.

Exam Probability: **Low**

6. *Answer choices:*
(see index for correct answer)

- a. cultural
- b. Economy
- c. process perspective
- d. information systems assessment

Guidance: level 1

:: Advertising techniques ::

In promotion and of advertising, a _____ or show consists of a person's written or spoken statement extolling the virtue of a product. The term " _____ " most commonly applies to the sales-pitches attributed to ordinary citizens, whereas the word "endorsement" usually applies to pitches by celebrities. _____ s can be part of communal marketing. Sometimes, the cartoon character can be a _____ in a commercial.

Exam Probability: **Low**

7. *Answer choices:*
(see index for correct answer)

- a. Unipole sign
- b. Testimonial
- c. Inconsistent comparison
- d. Soft sell

Guidance: level 1

A _____ service is an online platform which people use to build social networks or social relationship with other people who share similar personal or career interests, activities, backgrounds or real-life connections.

Exam Probability: **Medium**

8. *Answer choices:*

(see index for correct answer)

- a. hierarchical perspective
- b. Social networking
- c. similarity-attraction theory
- d. process perspective

Guidance: level 1

:: Data analysis ::

_____ is a process of inspecting, cleansing, transforming, and modeling data with the goal of discovering useful information, informing conclusions, and supporting decision-making. _____ has multiple facets and approaches, encompassing diverse techniques under a variety of names, and is used in different business, science, and social science domains. In today's business world, _____ plays a role in making decisions more scientific and helping businesses operate more effectively.

Exam Probability: **High**

9. *Answer choices:*

(see index for correct answer)

- a. Stationary subspace analysis
- b. Collocation
- c. Smoothing
- d. Data analysis

Guidance: level 1

:: Retailing ::

_____ is the process of selling consumer goods or services to customers through multiple channels of distribution to earn a profit. _____ ers satisfy demand identified through a supply chain. The term " _____ er" is typically applied where a service provider fills the small orders of a large number of individuals, who are end-users, rather than large orders of a small number of wholesale, corporate or government clientele. Shopping generally refers to the act of buying products. Sometimes this is done to obtain final goods, including necessities such as food and clothing; sometimes it takes place as a recreational activity. Recreational shopping often involves window shopping and browsing; it does not always result in a purchase.

Exam Probability: **Medium**

10. *Answer choices:*

- a. Dry goods
- b. Bulk bins
- c. Second-hand shop
- d. Retail

Guidance: level 1

:: ::

An _____ is a contingent motivator. Traditional _____ s are extrinsic motivators which reward actions to yield a desired outcome. The effectiveness of traditional _____ s has changed as the needs of Western society have evolved. While the traditional _____ model is effective when there is a defined procedure and goal for a task, Western society started to require a higher volume of critical thinkers, so the traditional model became less effective. Institutions are now following a trend in implementing strategies that rely on intrinsic motivations rather than the extrinsic motivations that the traditional _____ s foster.

Exam Probability: **Low**

11. *Answer choices:*

- a. imperative
- b. Sarbanes-Oxley act of 2002
- c. Incentive

- d. cultural

Guidance: level 1

:: Legal terms ::

A _____ is a person who is called upon to issue a response to a communication made by another. The term is used in legal contexts, in survey methodology, and in psychological conditioning.

Exam Probability: **High**

12. *Answer choices:*
(see index for correct answer)

- a. Call of duty
- b. Divesting abandonment
- c. Respondent
- d. Person of interest

Guidance: level 1

:: ::

The _____ is an agreement signed by Canada, Mexico, and the United States, creating a trilateral trade bloc in North America. The agreement came into force on January 1, 1994, and superseded the 1988 Canada–United States Free Trade Agreement between the United States and Canada. The NAFTA trade bloc is one of the largest trade blocs in the world by gross domestic product.

Exam Probability: **Medium**

13. *Answer choices:*
(see index for correct answer)

- a. hierarchical perspective
- b. Sarbanes-Oxley act of 2002
- c. process perspective
- d. North American Free Trade Agreement

Guidance: level 1

:: Services management and marketing ::

_____ is a specialised branch of marketing. _____ emerged as a separate field of study in the early 1980s, following the recognition that the unique characteristics of services required different strategies compared with the marketing of physical goods.

14. *Answer choices:*
(see index for correct answer)

- a. Internet hosting service
- b. Night service
- c. Reverse bounty
- d. Services marketing

Guidance: level 1

:: Evaluation methods ::

In natural and social sciences, and sometimes in other fields, _____ is the systematic empirical investigation of observable phenomena via statistical, mathematical, or computational techniques. The objective of _____ is to develop and employ mathematical models, theories, and hypotheses pertaining to phenomena. The process of measurement is central to _____ because it provides the fundamental connection between empirical observation and mathematical expression of quantitative relationships.

15. *Answer choices:*
(see index for correct answer)

- a. Rubric
- b. Qualitative research
- c. Ethnography
- d. Quantitative research

Guidance: level 1

:: Consumer behaviour ::

Convenient procedures, products and services are those intended to increase ease in accessibility, save resources and decrease frustration. A modern _____ is a labor-saving device, service or substance which make a task easier or more efficient than a traditional method. _____ is a relative concept, and depends on context. For example, automobiles were once considered a _____ , yet today are regarded as a normal part of life.

Exam Probability: **Medium**

16. *Answer choices:*
(see index for correct answer)

- a. Canadian Index of Consumer Confidence
- b. Post-consumerism
- c. Convenience
- d. Center for a New American Dream

Guidance: level 1

:: Competition regulators ::

The _____ is an independent agency of the United States government, established in 1914 by the _____ Act. Its principal mission is the promotion of consumer protection and the elimination and prevention of anticompetitive business practices, such as coercive monopoly. It is headquartered in the _____ Building in Washington, D.C.

Exam Probability: **High**

17. *Answer choices:*
(see index for correct answer)

- a. Competition Bureau
- b. Federal Trade Commission
- c. Competition Authority
- d. Directorate-General for Competition

Guidance: level 1

:: Survey methodology ::

A _____ is the procedure of systematically acquiring and recording information about the members of a given population. The term is used mostly in connection with national population and housing _____ es; other common _____ es include agriculture, business, and traffic _____ es. The United Nations defines the essential features of population and housing _____ es as "individual enumeration, universality within a defined territory, simultaneity and defined periodicity", and recommends that population _____ es be taken at least every 10 years. United Nations recommendations also cover _____ topics to be collected, official definitions, classifications and other useful information to co-ordinate international practice.

Exam Probability: **High**

18. *Answer choices:*
(see index for correct answer)

- a. Group concept mapping
- b. Sampling
- c. Inverse probability weighting
- d. World Association for Public Opinion Research

Guidance: level 1

:: Monopoly (economics) ::

The _____ of 1890 was a United States antitrust law that regulates competition among enterprises, which was passed by Congress under the presidency of Benjamin Harrison.

Exam Probability: **Low**

19. *Answer choices:*
(see index for correct answer)

- a. Economies of scope
- b. Network effect
- c. Sherman Antitrust Act
- d. Bilateral monopoly

Guidance: level 1

:: Direct marketing ::

_____ is a form of advertising where organizations communicate directly to customers through a variety of media including cell phone text messaging, email, websites, online adverts, database marketing, fliers, catalog distribution, promotional letters, targeted television, newspapers, magazine advertisements, and outdoor advertising. Among practitioners, it is also known as direct response marketing.

Exam Probability: **Low**

20. *Answer choices:*

(see index for correct answer)

- a. Cold calling
- b. Ginsu
- c. Solo Ads
- d. Publishers Clearing House

Guidance: level 1

:: ::

Market segmentation is the activity of dividing a broad consumer or business market, normally consisting of existing and potential customers, into sub-groups of consumers based on some type of shared characteristics. In dividing or segmenting markets, researchers typically look for common characteristics such as shared needs, common interests, similar lifestyles or even similar demographic profiles. The overall aim of segmentation is to identify high yield segments – that is, those segments that are likely to be the most profitable or that have growth potential – so that these can be selected for special attention .

Exam Probability: **Medium**

21. *Answer choices:*

(see index for correct answer)

- a. interpersonal communication
- b. Market segments
- c. similarity-attraction theory
- d. levels of analysis

Guidance: level 1

_____ is a means of protection from financial loss. It is a form of risk management, primarily used to hedge against the risk of a contingent or uncertain loss

Exam Probability: **High**

22. *Answer choices:*
(see index for correct answer)

- a. deep-level diversity
- b. Insurance
- c. open system
- d. levels of analysis

Guidance: level 1

In law, a _____ is a coming together of parties to a dispute, to present information in a tribunal, a formal setting with the authority to adjudicate claims or disputes. One form of tribunal is a court. The tribunal, which may occur before a judge, jury, or other designated trier of fact, aims to achieve a resolution to their dispute.

Exam Probability: **High**

23. *Answer choices:*
(see index for correct answer)

- a. hierarchical
- b. Sarbanes-Oxley act of 2002
- c. surface-level diversity
- d. co-culture

Guidance: level 1

:: Television commercials ::

_____ is a characteristic that distinguishes physical entities that have biological processes, such as signaling and self-sustaining processes, from those that do not, either because such functions have ceased , or because they never had such functions and are classified as inanimate. Various forms of _____ exist, such as plants, animals, fungi, protists, archaea, and bacteria. The criteria can at times be ambiguous and may or may not define viruses, viroids, or potential synthetic _____ as "living". Biology is the science concerned with the study of _____ .

Exam Probability: **Medium**

24. *Answer choices:*
(see index for correct answer)

- a. Orange Man
- b. Write the Future
- c. Little Mikey
- d. Gay Mountain

Guidance: level 1

:: ::

_____ is both a research area and a practical skill encompassing the ability of an individual or organization to "lead" or guide other individuals, teams, or entire organizations. Specialist literature debates various viewpoints, contrasting Eastern and Western approaches to _____ , and also United States versus European approaches. U.S. academic environments define _____ as "a process of social influence in which a person can enlist the aid and support of others in the accomplishment of a common task".

Exam Probability: **Medium**

25. *Answer choices:*
(see index for correct answer)

- a. functional perspective
- b. imperative
- c. Leadership
- d. co-culture

Guidance: level 1

:: Business models ::

_____ es are privately owned corporations, partnerships, or sole proprietorships that have fewer employees and/or less annual revenue than a regular-sized business or corporation. Businesses are defined as "small" in terms of being able to apply for government support and qualify for preferential tax policy varies depending on the country and industry.

_____ es range from fifteen employees under the Australian Fair Work Act 2009, fifty employees according to the definition used by the European Union, and fewer than five hundred employees to qualify for many U.S. _____ Administration programs. While _____ es can also be classified according to other methods, such as annual revenues, shipments, sales, assets, or by annual gross or net revenue or net profits, the number of employees is one of the most widely used measures.

26. *Answer choices:*

- a. Technology push
- b. Legacy carrier
- c. Subscription business model
- d. Premium business model

Guidance: level 1

:: Marketing ::

_____ s are structured marketing strategies designed by merchants to encourage customers to continue to shop at or use the services of businesses associated with each program. These programs exist covering most types of commerce, each one having varying features and rewards-schemes.

27. *Answer choices:*

- a. Generic brand
- b. Adobe Social
- c. Franchise fee
- d. Loyalty program

Guidance: level 1

A _____ or sample _____ is a single measure of some attribute of a sample . It is calculated by applying a function to the values of the items of the sample, which are known together as a set of data.

Exam Probability: **Medium**

28. *Answer choices:*
(see index for correct answer)

- a. functional perspective
- b. similarity-attraction theory
- c. Statistic
- d. hierarchical perspective

Guidance: level 1

Distribution is one of the four elements of the marketing mix. Distribution is the process of making a product or service available for the consumer or business user who needs it. This can be done directly by the producer or service provider, or using indirect channels with distributors or intermediaries. The other three elements of the marketing mix are product, pricing, and promotion.

Exam Probability: **Low**

29. *Answer choices:*
(see index for correct answer)

- a. information systems assessment
- b. personal values
- c. similarity-attraction theory
- d. open system

Guidance: level 1

:: Decision theory ::

Within economics the concept of _____ is used to model worth or value, but its usage has evolved significantly over time. The term was introduced initially as a measure of pleasure or satisfaction within the theory of utilitarianism by moral philosophers such as Jeremy Bentham and John Stuart Mill. But the term has been adapted and reapplied within neoclassical economics, which dominates modern economic theory, as a _____ function that represents a consumer's preference ordering over a choice set. As such, it is devoid of its original interpretation as a measurement of the pleasure or satisfaction obtained by the consumer from that choice.

Exam Probability: **Medium**

30. *Answer choices:*
(see index for correct answer)

- a. Nash equilibrium
- h. Outcome primacy
- c. Trade-off talking rational economic person
- d. VIKOR method

Guidance: level 1

:: Information technology management ::

B2B is often contrasted with business-to-consumer . In B2B commerce, it is often the case that the parties to the relationship have comparable negotiating power, and even when they do not, each party typically involves professional staff and legal counsel in the negotiation of terms, whereas B2C is shaped to a far greater degree by economic implications of information asymmetry. However, within a B2B context, large companies may have many commercial, resource and information advantages over smaller businesses. The United Kingdom government, for example, created the post of Small Business Commissioner under the Enterprise Act 2016 to "enable small businesses to resolve disputes" and "consider complaints by small business suppliers about payment issues with larger businesses that they supply."

Exam Probability: **High**

31. *Answer choices:*
(see index for correct answer)

- a. Contract management
- b. Cable management

- c. Business-to-business
- d. ISO/IEC 20000

:: Management ::

_____ is the organizational discipline which focuses on the practical application of marketing orientation, techniques and methods inside enterprises and organizations and on the management of a firm's marketing resources and activities.

Exam Probability: **High**

32. *Answer choices:*
(see index for correct answer)

- a. Concept of operations
- b. Meeting system
- c. Shamrock Organization
- d. Industrial democracy

:: Market research ::

_____ is the action of defining, gathering, analyzing, and distributing intelligence about products, customers, competitors, and any aspect of the environment needed to support executives and managers in strategic decision making for an organization.

Exam Probability: **High**

33. *Answer choices:*
(see index for correct answer)

- a. Voter News Service
- b. Market surveillance
- c. Nonprobability sampling
- d. Competitive intelligence

:: Contract law ::

In contract law, a _____ is a promise which is not a condition of the contract or an innominate term: it is a term "not going to the root of the contract", and which only entitles the innocent party to damages if it is breached: i.e. the _____ is not true or the defaulting party does not perform the contract in accordance with the terms of the _____ . A _____ is not guarantee. It is a mere promise. It may be enforced if it is breached by an award for the legal remedy of damages.

Exam Probability: **High**

34. *Answer choices:*
(see index for correct answer)

- a. Pirate code
- b. Warranty
- c. Marriage privatization
- d. Baseball business rules

Guidance: level 1

:: Consumer theory ::

_____ is the quantity of a good that consumers are willing and able to purchase at various prices during a given period of time.

Exam Probability: **High**

35. *Answer choices:*
(see index for correct answer)

- a. Compensated demand
- b. Marshallian demand function
- c. Demand
- d. Joint demand

Guidance: level 1

:: Marketing ::

A _____ is a group of customers within a business's serviceable available market at which a business aims its marketing efforts and resources. A _____ is a subset of the total market for a product or service. The _____ typically consists of consumers who exhibit similar characteristics and are considered most likely to buy a business's market offerings or are likely to be the most profitable segments for the business to service.

Exam Probability: **Low**

36. *Answer choices:*
(see index for correct answer)

- a. Art Infusion
- b. Configurator
- c. Mandatory labelling
- d. Target market

Guidance: level 1

:: Evaluation methods ::

_____ is a scientific method of observation to gather non-numerical data. This type of research "refers to the meanings, concepts definitions, characteristics, metaphors, symbols, and description of things" and not to their "counts or measures." This research answers why and how a certain phenomenon may occur rather than how often. _____ approaches are employed across many academic disciplines, focusing particularly on the human elements of the social and natural sciences; in less academic contexts, areas of application include qualitative market research, business, service demonstrations by non-profits, and journalism.

Exam Probability: **Low**

37. *Answer choices:*
(see index for correct answer)

- a. Self-assessment
- b. Embedded case study
- c. Program process monitoring
- d. Qualitative research

Guidance: level 1

:: Income ::

_____ is a ratio between the net profit and cost of investment resulting from an investment of some resources. A high ROI means the investment's gains favorably to its cost. As a performance measure, ROI is used to evaluate the efficiency of an investment or to compare the efficiencies of several different investments. In purely economic terms, it is one way of relating profits to capital invested. _____ is a performance measure used by businesses to identify the efficiency of an investment or number of different investments.

Exam Probability: **High**

38. *Answer choices:*

- a. Property Investment calculator
- b. Return on investment
- c. Mandatory tipping
- d. Giganomics

Guidance: level 1

:: Market research ::

_____ is "the process or set of processes that links the producers, customers, and end users to the marketer through information used to identify and define marketing opportunities and problems; generate, refine, and evaluate marketing actions; monitor marketing performance; and improve understanding of marketing as a process. _____ specifies the information required to address these issues, designs the method for collecting information, manages and implements the data collection process, analyzes the results, and communicates the findings and their implications."

Exam Probability: **Low**

39. *Answer choices:*

- a. Travel survey
- b. Marketing research
- c. Monroe Mendelsohn Research
- d. Ecological model of competition

:: Brand management ::

_____ refers to the extent to which customers are able to recall or recognise a brand. _____ is a key consideration in consumer behavior, advertising management, brand management and strategy development. The consumer's ability to recognise or recall a brand is central to purchasing decision-making. Purchasing cannot proceed unless a consumer is first aware of a product category and a brand within that category. Awareness does not necessarily mean that the consumer must be able to recall a specific brand name, but he or she must be able to recall sufficient distinguishing features for purchasing to proceed. For instance, if a consumer asks her friend to buy her some gum in a "blue pack", the friend would be expected to know which gum to buy, even though neither friend can recall the precise brand name at the time.

Exam Probability: **Medium**

40. *Answer choices:*
(see index for correct answer)

- a. Brand awareness
- b. VCU Brandcenter
- c. Napa Declaration on Place
- d. Principle Group

:: Market research ::

An _____ or lighthouse customer is an early customer of a given company, product, or technology. The term originates from Everett M. Rogers' Diffusion of Innovations .

Exam Probability: **Medium**

41. *Answer choices:*
(see index for correct answer)

- a. Indian Readership Survey
- b. Mode effect
- c. Simple random sample
- d. Early adopter

:: ::

In communications and information processing, _____ is a system of rules to convert information—such as a letter, word, sound, image, or gesture—into another form or representation, sometimes shortened or secret, for communication through a communication channel or storage in a storage medium. An early example is the invention of language, which enabled a person, through speech, to communicate what they saw, heard, felt, or thought to others. But speech limits the range of communication to the distance a voice can carry, and limits the audience to those present when the speech is uttered. The invention of writing, which converted spoken language into visual symbols, extended the range of communication across space and time.

Exam Probability: **Low**

42. *Answer choices:*
(see index for correct answer)

- a. similarity-attraction theory
- b. Code
- c. co-culture
- d. hierarchical

:: Investment ::

In finance, the benefit from an _____ is called a return. The return may consist of a gain realised from the sale of property or an _____, unrealised capital appreciation , or _____ income such as dividends, interest, rental income etc., or a combination of capital gain and income. The return may also include currency gains or losses due to changes in foreign currency exchange rates.

Exam Probability: **High**

43. *Answer choices:*
(see index for correct answer)

- a. Security characteristic line

- b. Investment
- c. Market sentiment
- d. Investor profile

:: Marketing ::

_____ uses different marketing channels and tools in combination: Marketing communication channels focus on any way a business communicates a message to its desired market, or the market in general. A marketing communication tool can be anything from: advertising, personal selling, direct marketing, sponsorship, communication, and promotion to public relations.

Exam Probability: **High**

44. *Answer choices:*
(see index for correct answer)

- a. Predatory pricing
- b. Marketing communications
- c. Mass customization
- d. Cultural consumer

:: Commercial item transport and distribution ::

In commerce, supply-chain management , the management of the flow of goods and services, involves the movement and storage of raw materials, of work-in-process inventory, and of finished goods from point of origin to point of consumption. Interconnected or interlinked networks, channels and node businesses combine in the provision of products and services required by end customers in a supply chain. Supply-chain management has been defined as the "design, planning, execution, control, and monitoring of supply-chain activities with the objective of creating net value, building a competitive infrastructure, leveraging worldwide logistics, synchronizing supply with demand and measuring performance globally."SCM practice draws heavily from the areas of industrial engineering, systems engineering, operations management, logistics, procurement, information technology, and marketing and strives for an integrated approach. Marketing channels play an important role in supply-chain management. Current research in supply-chain management is concerned with topics related to sustainability and risk management, among others. Some suggest that the "people dimension" of SCM, ethical issues, internal integration, transparency/visibility, and human capital/talent management are topics that have, so far, been underrepresented on the research agenda.

Exam Probability: **Low**

45. *Answer choices:*
(see index for correct answer)

- a. Dautel
- b. Supply chain management
- c. Chain conveyor
- d. Standard Carrier Alpha Code

Guidance: level 1

:: ::

A _____ is an organized collection of data, generally stored and accessed electronically from a computer system. Where _____ s are more complex they are often developed using formal design and modeling techniques.

Exam Probability: **Low**

46. *Answer choices:*
(see index for correct answer)

- a. Database
- b. Sarbanes-Oxley act of 2002
- c. levels of analysis
- d. deep-level diversity

Guidance: level 1

:: ::

Business is the activity of making one's living or making money by producing or buying and selling products . Simply put, it is "any activity or enterprise entered into for profit. It does not mean it is a company, a corporation, partnership, or have any such formal organization, but it can range from a street peddler to General Motors."

Exam Probability: **High**

47. *Answer choices:*
(see index for correct answer)

- a. corporate values
- b. cultural
- c. Firm
- d. surface-level diversity

Guidance: level 1

:: ::

_____ or commercialisation is the process of introducing a new product or production method into commerce—making it available on the market. The term often connotes especially entry into the mass market , but it also includes a move from the laboratory into commerce. Many technologies begin in a research and development laboratory or in an inventor's workshop and may not be practical for commercial use in their infancy . The "development" segment of the "research and development" spectrum requires time and money as systems are engineered with a view to making the product or method a paying commercial proposition. The product launch of a new product is the final stage of new product development - at this point advertising, sales promotion, and other marketing efforts encourage commercial adoption of the product or method. Beyond _____ can lie consumerization .

Exam Probability: **High**

48. *Answer choices:*

- a. Commercialization
- b. surface-level diversity
- c. levels of analysis
- d. imperative

Guidance: level 1

:: ::

_____ , or auditory perception, is the ability to perceive sounds by detecting vibrations, changes in the pressure of the surrounding medium through time, through an organ such as the ear. The academic field concerned with _____ is auditory science.

Exam Probability: **High**

49. *Answer choices:*

- a. open system
- b. hierarchical perspective
- c. Hearing
- d. Sarbanes-Oxley act of 2002

Guidance: level 1

:: Promotion and marketing communications ::

_____ is one of the elements of the promotional mix. . _____ uses both media and non-media marketing communications for a pre-determined, limited time to increase consumer demand, stimulate market demand or improve product availability. Examples include contests, coupons, freebies, loss leaders, point of purchase displays, premiums, prizes, product samples, and rebates.

Exam Probability: **High**

50. *Answer choices:*

- a. Custom media
- b. Underwriting spot
- c. Sales promotion
- d. Communication planning

:: Communication design ::

An _____ is a series of advertisement messages that share a single idea and theme which make up an integrated marketing communication . An IMC is a platform in which a group of people can group their ideas, beliefs, and concepts into one large media base. _____ s utilize diverse media channels over a particular time frame and target identified audiences.

Exam Probability: **High**

51. *Answer choices:*
(see index for correct answer)

- a. Celestino Piatti
- b. Peter Saville
- c. Advertising campaign
- d. Colin Forbes

:: ::

_____ refers to a business or organization attempting to acquire goods or services to accomplish its goals. Although there are several organizations that attempt to set standards in the _____ process, processes can vary greatly between organizations. Typically the word " _____ " is not used interchangeably with the word "procurement", since procurement typically includes expediting, supplier quality, and transportation and logistics in addition to _____ .

Exam Probability: **High**

52. *Answer choices:*
(see index for correct answer)

- a. personal values
- b. interpersonal communication
- c. process perspective
- d. hierarchical

:: Commerce ::

A _____ is a company or individual that purchases goods or services with the intention of selling them rather than consuming or using them. This is usually done for profit . One example can be found in the industry of telecommunications, where companies buy excess amounts of transmission capacity or call time from other carriers and resell it to smaller carriers.

Exam Probability: **Medium**

53. *Answer choices:*
(see index for correct answer)

- a. TradeCard
- b. Trade credit
- c. Reseller
- d. Non-commercial

Guidance: level 1

:: Planning ::

_____ is a high level plan to achieve one or more goals under conditions of uncertainty. In the sense of the "art of the general," which included several subsets of skills including tactics, siegecraft, logistics etc., the term came into use in the 6th century C.E. in East Roman terminology, and was translated into Western vernacular languages only in the 18th century. From then until the 20th century, the word " _____ " came to denote "a comprehensive way to try to pursue political ends, including the threat or actual use of force, in a dialectic of wills" in a military conflict, in which both adversaries interact.

Exam Probability: **Medium**

54. *Answer choices:*
(see index for correct answer)

- a. Event scheduling
- b. Enterprise architecture planning
- c. Parish plan
- d. Strategy

Guidance: level 1

:: Packaging ::

In work place, _____ or job _____ means good ranking with the hypothesized conception of requirements of a role. There are two types of job _____ s: contextual and task. Task _____ is related to cognitive ability while contextual _____ is dependent upon personality. Task _____ are behavioral roles that are recognized in job descriptions and by remuneration systems, they are directly related to organizational _____, whereas, contextual _____ are value based and additional behavioral roles that are not recognized in job descriptions and covered by compensation; they are extra roles that are indirectly related to organizational _____. Citizenship _____ like contextual _____ means a set of individual activity/contribution that supports the organizational culture.

Exam Probability: **Low**

55. *Answer choices:*
(see index for correct answer)

- a. Performance
- b. Tamper resistance
- c. Shake well
- d. Permeation

Guidance: level 1

:: Pricing ::

_____ is a pricing strategy in which the selling price is determined by adding a specific amount markup to a product's unit cost. An alternative pricing method is value-based pricing.

Exam Probability: **High**

56. *Answer choices:*
(see index for correct answer)

- a. Net metering
- b. Average usage billing
- c. Cost-plus pricing
- d. Asymmetric price transmission

Guidance: level 1

In legal terminology, a _____ is any formal legal document that sets out the facts and legal reasons that the filing party or parties believes are sufficient to support a claim against the party or parties against whom the claim is brought that entitles the plaintiff to a remedy . For example, the Federal Rules of Civil Procedure that govern civil litigation in United States courts provide that a civil action is commenced with the filing or service of a pleading called a _____ . Civil court rules in states that have incorporated the Federal Rules of Civil Procedure use the same term for the same pleading.

Exam Probability: **Medium**

57. *Answer choices:*
(see index for correct answer)

- a. surface-level diversity
- b. personal values
- c. process perspective
- d. Complaint

Guidance: level 1

_____ or globalisation is the process of interaction and integration among people, companies, and governments worldwide. As a complex and multifaceted phenomenon, _____ is considered by some as a form of capitalist expansion which entails the integration of local and national economies into a global, unregulated market economy. _____ has grown due to advances in transportation and communication technology. With the increased global interactions comes the growth of international trade, ideas, and culture. _____ is primarily an economic process of interaction and integration that's associated with social and cultural aspects. However, conflicts and diplomacy are also large parts of the history of _____ , and modern _____ .

Exam Probability: **Low**

58. *Answer choices:*
(see index for correct answer)

- a. Reciprocity
- b. Monopolistic advantage theory
- c. Absolute advantage
- d. Globalization

Guidance: level 1

:: Auctioneering ::

An _____ is a process of buying and selling goods or services by offering them up for bid, taking bids, and then selling the item to the highest bidder. The open ascending price _____ is arguably the most common form of _____ in use today. Participants bid openly against one another, with each subsequent bid required to be higher than the previous bid. An _____ eer may announce prices, bidders may call out their bids themselves , or bids may be submitted electronically with the highest current bid publicly displayed. In a Dutch _____ , the _____ eer begins with a high asking price for some quantity of like items; the price is lowered until a participant is willing to accept the _____ eer's price for some quantity of the goods in the lot or until the seller's reserve price is met. While _____ s are most associated in the public imagination with the sale of antiques, paintings, rare collectibles and expensive wines, _____ s are also used for commodities, livestock, radio spectrum and used cars. In economic theory, an _____ may refer to any mechanism or set of trading rules for exchange.

Exam Probability: **Low**

59. *Answer choices:*
(see index for correct answer)

- a. Walton School of Auctioneering
- b. Auction
- c. Virginity auction
- d. Auctionata

Guidance: level 1

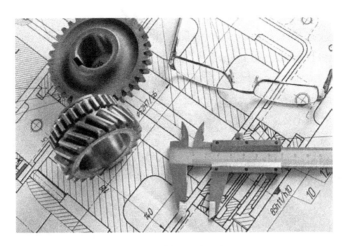

Manufacturing

Manufacturing is the production of merchandise for use or sale using labor and machines, tools, chemical and biological processing, or formulation. The term may refer to a range of human activity, from handicraft to high tech, but is most commonly applied to industrial design , in which raw materials are transformed into finished goods on a large scale. Such finished goods may be sold to other manufacturers for the production of other, more complex products, such as aircraft, household appliances, furniture, sports equipment or automobiles, or sold to wholesalers, who in turn sell them to retailers, who then sell them to end users and consumers.

:: Project management ::

_____ is the right to exercise power, which can be formalized by a state and exercised by way of judges, appointed executives of government, or the ecclesiastical or priestly appointed representatives of a God or other deities.

Exam Probability: **Low**

1. *Answer choices:*
(see index for correct answer)

- a. Project Management Professional
- b. Project blog
- c. Opportunity management
- d. Project network

Guidance: level 1

:: Management ::

_____ is the process of thinking about the activities required to achieve a desired goal. It is the first and foremost activity to achieve desired results. It involves the creation and maintenance of a plan, such as psychological aspects that require conceptual skills. There are even a couple of tests to measure someone's capability of _____ well. As such, _____ is a fundamental property of intelligent behavior. An important further meaning, often just called " _____ " is the legal context of permitted building developments.

Exam Probability: **High**

2. *Answer choices:*
(see index for correct answer)

- a. Remedial action
- b. Planning
- c. Vasa syndrome
- d. Knowledge Based Decision Making

Guidance: level 1

:: Auditing ::

_____ is the process of systematic examination of a quality system carried out by an internal or external _____ or or an audit team. It is an important part of an organization's quality management system and is a key element in the ISO quality system standard, ISO 9001.

Exam Probability: **High**

3. *Answer choices:*
(see index for correct answer)

- a. Quality audit
- b. Assurance services
- c. Certified Internal Control Auditors
- d. Circulation Verification Council

Guidance: level 1

:: Alchemical processes ::

In chemistry, a _____ is a special type of homogeneous mixture composed of two or more substances. In such a mixture, a solute is a substance dissolved in another substance, known as a solvent. The mixing process of a _____ happens at a scale where the effects of chemical polarity are involved, resulting in interactions that are specific to solvation. The _____ assumes the phase of the solvent when the solvent is the larger fraction of the mixture, as is commonly the case. The concentration of a solute in a _____ is the mass of that solute expressed as a percentage of the mass of the whole _____ . The term aqueous _____ is when one of the solvents is water.

Exam Probability: **High**

4. *Answer choices:*
(see index for correct answer)

- a. Solution
- b. Corporification
- c. Congelation
- d. Projection

Guidance: level 1

:: Knowledge representation ::

_____ s are causal diagrams created by Kaoru Ishikawa that show the causes of a specific event.

Exam Probability: **Medium**

5. *Answer choices:*
(see index for correct answer)

- a. Procedural reasoning system
- b. Knowledge integration
- c. Ishikawa diagram
- d. Personal knowledge base

Guidance: level 1

:: ::

An _____ is, most an organized examination or formal evaluation exercise. In engineering activities _____ involves the measurements, tests, and gauges applied to certain characteristics in regard to an object or activity. The results are usually compared to specified requirements and standards for determining whether the item or activity is in line with these targets, often with a Standard _____ Procedure in place to ensure consistent checking. _____ s are usually non-destructive.

Exam Probability: **Medium**

6. *Answer choices:*

(see index for correct answer)

- a. personal values
- b. Inspection
- c. information systems assessment
- d. similarity-attraction theory

Guidance: level 1

:: Planning ::

_____ is a high level plan to achieve one or more goals under conditions of uncertainty. In the sense of the "art of the general," which included several subsets of skills including tactics, siegecraft, logistics etc., the term came into use in the 6th century C.E. in East Roman terminology, and was translated into Western vernacular languages only in the 18th century. From then until the 20th century, the word " _____ " came to denote "a comprehensive way to try to pursue political ends, including the threat or actual use of force, in a dialectic of wills" in a military conflict, in which both adversaries interact.

Exam Probability: **Low**

7. *Answer choices:*

(see index for correct answer)

- a. School timetable
- b. Strategy
- c. Implementation intention
- d. Plano Trienal

Guidance: level 1

:: Data management ::

_____ refers to a data-driven improvement cycle used for improving, optimizing and stabilizing business processes and designs. The _____ improvement cycle is the core tool used to drive Six Sigma projects. However, _____ is not exclusive to Six Sigma and can be used as the framework for other improvement applications.

Exam Probability: **Medium**

8. *Answer choices:*
(see index for correct answer)

- a. Data management
- b. Match report
- c. Concurrency control
- d. Hierarchical classifier

Guidance: level 1

:: Costs ::

In process improvement efforts, _____ or cost of quality is a means to quantify the total cost of quality-related efforts and deficiencies. It was first described by Armand V. Feigenbaum in a 1956 Harvard Business Review article.

Exam Probability: **Low**

9. *Answer choices:*
(see index for correct answer)

- a. Further processing cost
- b. Psychic cost
- c. Quality costs
- d. Cost per paper

Guidance: level 1

:: Consortia ::

A _____ is an association of two or more individuals, companies, organizations or governments with the objective of participating in a common activity or pooling their resources for achieving a common goal.

10. *Answer choices:*
(see index for correct answer)

- a. Open Handset Alliance
- b. Y Chromosome Consortium
- c. Consortium
- d. Service Availability Forum

Guidance: level 1

:: Information technology management ::

_____ within quality management systems and information technology systems is a process—either formal or informal—used to ensure that changes to a product or system are introduced in a controlled and coordinated manner. It reduces the possibility that unnecessary changes will be introduced to a system without forethought, introducing faults into the system or undoing changes made by other users of software. The goals of a _____ procedure usually include minimal disruption to services, reduction in back-out activities, and cost-effective utilization of resources involved in implementing change.

11. *Answer choices:*
(see index for correct answer)

- a. Change control
- b. EFx Factory
- c. Runbook
- d. ESCM-CL

Guidance: level 1

:: Costs ::

In economics, _____ is the total economic cost of production and is made up of variable cost, which varies according to the quantity of a good produced and includes inputs such as labour and raw materials, plus fixed cost, which is independent of the quantity of a good produced and includes inputs that cannot be varied in the short term: fixed costs such as buildings and machinery, including sunk costs if any. Since cost is measured per unit of time, it is a flow variable.

Exam Probability: **Low**

12. *Answer choices:*
(see index for correct answer)

- a. Prospective costs
- b. Cost of poor quality
- c. Total cost
- d. Further processing cost

Guidance: level 1

:: Materials ::

A _____ , also known as a feedstock, unprocessed material, or primary commodity, is a basic material that is used to produce goods, finished products, energy, or intermediate materials which are feedstock for future finished products. As feedstock, the term connotes these materials are bottleneck assets and are highly important with regard to producing other products. An example of this is crude oil, which is a _____ and a feedstock used in the production of industrial chemicals, fuels, plastics, and pharmaceutical goods; lumber is a _____ used to produce a variety of products including all types of furniture. The term " _____ " denotes materials in minimally processed or unprocessed in states; e.g., raw latex, crude oil, cotton, coal, raw biomass, iron ore, air, logs, or water i.e. "...any product of agriculture, forestry, fishing and any other mineral that is in its natural form or which has undergone the transformation required to prepare it for internationally marketing in substantial volumes."

Exam Probability: **Medium**

13. *Answer choices:*
(see index for correct answer)

- a. Refractory
- b. Tensometer
- c. Slurry
- d. Saturated-surface-dry

Guidance: level 1

:: Monopoly (economics) ::

_____ are "efficiencies formed by variety, not volume" . For example, a gas station that sells gasoline can sell soda, milk, baked goods, etc through their customer service representatives and thus achieve gasoline companies _____ .

Exam Probability: **Medium**

14. *Answer choices:*
(see index for correct answer)

- a. Patent
- b. Quasi-rent
- c. Electricity liberalization
- d. Building block model

Guidance: level 1

:: ::

_____ refers to the confirmation of certain characteristics of an object, person, or organization. This confirmation is often, but not always, provided by some form of external review, education, assessment, or audit. Accreditation is a specific organization's process of _____ . According to the National Council on Measurement in Education, a _____ test is a credentialing test used to determine whether individuals are knowledgeable enough in a given occupational area to be labeled "competent to practice" in that area.

Exam Probability: **Medium**

15. *Answer choices:*
(see index for correct answer)

- a. similarity-attraction theory
- b. open system
- c. Sarbanes-Oxley act of 2002

- d. Certification

Guidance: level 1

:: Project management ::

A _____ is the approximation of the cost of a program, project, or operation. The _____ is the product of the cost estimating process. The _____ has a single total value and may have identifiable component values. A problem with a cost overrun can be avoided with a credible, reliable, and accurate _____ . A cost estimator is the professional who prepares _____ s. There are different types of cost estimators, whose title may be preceded by a modifier, such as building estimator, or electrical estimator, or chief estimator. Other professionals such as quantity surveyors and cost engineers may also prepare _____ s or contribute to _____ s. In the US, according to the Bureau of Labor Statistics, there were 185,400 cost estimators in 2010. There are around 75,000 professional quantity surveyors working in the UK.

Exam Probability: **Medium**

16. *Answer choices:*

(see index for correct answer)

- a. Cost estimate
- b. Akihabara syndrome
- c. The International Association of Project and Program Management
- d. Effective Development Group

Guidance: level 1

:: Help desk ::

A high-explosive anti-tank warhead is a type of shaped charge explosive that uses the Munroe effect to penetrate thick tank armor. The warhead functions by having the explosive charge collapse a metal liner inside the warhead into a high-velocity superplastic jet. This superplastic jet is capable of penetrating armor steel to a depth of seven or more times the diameter of the charge but is usually used to immobilize or destroy tanks. Due to the way they work, they do not have to be fired as fast as an armor piercing shell, allowing less recoil. Contrary to a widespread misconception , the jet does not melt its way through armor, as its effect is purely kinetic in nature. The _____ warhead has become less effective against tanks and other armored vehicles due to the use of composite armor, explosive-reactive armor, and active protection systems which destroy the _____ warhead before it hits the tank. Even though _____ rounds are less effective against the heavy armor found on 2010s main battle tanks, _____ warheads remain a threat against less-armored parts of a main battle tank and against lighter armored vehicles or unarmored vehicles and helicopters.

Exam Probability: **High**

17. *Answer choices:*
(see index for correct answer)

- a. OTRS
- b. Liberum Help Desk
- c. HEAT
- d. Virtual help desk

Guidance: level 1

:: ::

_____ is the production of products for use or sale using labour and machines, tools, chemical and biological processing, or formulation. The term may refer to a range of human activity, from handicraft to high tech, but is most commonly applied to industrial design, in which raw materials are transformed into finished goods on a large scale. Such finished goods may be sold to other manufacturers for the production of other, more complex products, such as aircraft, household appliances, furniture, sports equipment or automobiles, or sold to wholesalers, who in turn sell them to retailers, who then sell them to end users and consumers.

18. *Answer choices:*
(see index for correct answer)

- a. co-culture
- b. surface-level diversity
- c. corporate values
- d. functional perspective

Guidance: level 1

:: Management ::

_____ is a process by which entities review the quality of all factors involved in production. ISO 9000 defines _____ as "A part of quality management focused on fulfilling quality requirements".

Exam Probability: **Low**

19. *Answer choices:*
(see index for correct answer)

- a. Adhocracy
- b. Completed Staff Work
- c. Product breakdown structure
- d. Knowledge Based Decision Making

Guidance: level 1

:: Finance ::

_____ is a financial estimate intended to help buyers and owners determine the direct and indirect costs of a product or system. It is a management accounting concept that can be used in full cost accounting or even ecological economics where it includes social costs.

Exam Probability: **Medium**

20. *Answer choices:*
(see index for correct answer)

- a. Convention of conservatism
- b. Dynamic financial analysis
- c. Revaluation of fixed assets
- d. Total cost of ownership

:: Commerce ::

A _____ is an employee within a company, business or other organization who is responsible at some level for buying or approving the acquisition of goods and services needed by the company. Responsible for buying the best quality products, goods and services for their company at the most competitive prices, _____ s work in a wide range of sectors for many different organizations. The position responsibilities may be the same as that of a buyer or purchasing agent, or may include wider supervisory or managerial responsibilities. A _____ may oversee the acquisition of materials needed for production, general supplies for offices and facilities, equipment, or construction contracts. A _____ often supervises purchasing agents and buyers, but in small companies the _____ may also be the purchasing agent or buyer. The _____ position may also carry the title "Procurement Manager" or in the public sector, "Procurement Officer". He or she can come from both an Engineering or Economics background.

Exam Probability: **Medium**

21. *Answer choices:*
(see index for correct answer)

- a. Factory
- b. Perfect tender rule
- c. Non-commercial
- d. Purchasing manager

:: Management ::

An _____ is a loosely coupled, self-organizing network of firms that combine their economic output to provide products and services offerings to the market. Firms in the _____ may operate independently, for example, through market mechanisms, or cooperatively through agreements and contracts. They provide value added service or product to the OEM .

Exam Probability: **High**

22. *Answer choices:*

- a. Fall guy
- b. Earned schedule
- c. Office management
- d. Project cost management

Guidance: level 1

:: Project management ::

_____ is a process of setting goals, planning and/or controlling the organizing and leading the execution of any type of activity, such as.

Exam Probability: **Medium**

23. *Answer choices:*

- a. Management process
- b. Multidisciplinary approach
- c. Direct changeover
- d. Time horizon

Guidance: level 1

:: Costs ::

The _____ is computed by dividing the total cost of goods available for sale by the total units available for sale. This gives a weighted-average unit cost that is applied to the units in the ending inventory.

Exam Probability: **Medium**

24. *Answer choices:*

- a. Incremental cost-effectiveness ratio
- b. Explicit cost
- c. Average cost
- d. Quality costs

Guidance: level 1

:: Outsourcing ::

_____ is an institutional procurement process that continuously improves and re-evaluates the purchasing activities of a company. In the services industry, _____ refers to a service solution, sometimes called a strategic partnership, which is specifically customized to meet the client's individual needs. In a production environment, it is often considered one component of supply chain management. Modern supply chain management professionals have placed emphasis on defining the distinct differences between _____ and procurement. Procurement operations support tactical day-to-day transactions such as issuing Purchase Orders to suppliers, whereas _____ represents to strategic planning, supplier development, contract negotiation, supply chain infrastructure, and outsourcing models.

Exam Probability: **Medium**

25. *Answer choices:*
(see index for correct answer)

- a. Virtual CFO
- b. Pillsbury Winthrop Shaw Pittman
- c. Strategic sourcing
- d. Oregon Bridge Delivery Partners

Guidance: level 1

:: Production economics ::

_____ is the creation of a whole that is greater than the simple sum of its parts. The term _____ comes from the Attic Greek word sea synergia from synergos, , meaning "working together".

Exam Probability: **High**

26. *Answer choices:*
(see index for correct answer)

- a. Synergy
- b. The labor problem
- c. Value and Capital
- d. Specialization

Guidance: level 1

:: Industrial design ::

In physics and mathematics, the _____ of a mathematical space is informally defined as the minimum number of coordinates needed to specify any point within it. Thus a line has a _____ of one because only one coordinate is needed to specify a point on it for example, the point at 5 on a number line. A surface such as a plane or the surface of a cylinder or sphere has a _____ of two because two coordinates are needed to specify a point on it for example, both a latitude and longitude are required to locate a point on the surface of a sphere. The inside of a cube, a cylinder or a sphere is three- _____ al because three coordinates are needed to locate a point within these spaces.

Exam Probability: **Low**

27. *Answer choices:*
(see index for correct answer)

- a. Design and Technology
- b. Dimension
- c. Aeolipile
- d. Danish design

Guidance: level 1

:: Quality ::

The _____ , formerly the _____ Control , is a knowledge-based global community of quality professionals, with nearly 80,000 members dedicated to promoting and advancing quality tools, principles, and practices in their workplaces and communities.

Exam Probability: **Low**

28. *Answer choices:*
(see index for correct answer)

- a. American Society for Quality
- b. Robustification
- c. Cleaning validation
- d. Independent test organization

Guidance: level 1

:: ::

A _____ or till is a mechanical or electronic device for registering and calculating transactions at a point of sale. It is usually attached to a drawer for storing cash and other valuables. A modern _____ is usually attached to a printer that can print out receipts for record-keeping purposes.

Exam Probability: **Medium**

29. *Answer choices:*
(see index for correct answer)

- a. co-culture
- b. hierarchical perspective
- c. levels of analysis
- d. Cash register

Guidance: level 1

:: Project management ::

In political science, an _____ is a means by which a petition signed by a certain minimum number of registered voters can force a government to choose to either enact a law or hold a public vote in parliament in what is called indirect _____ , or under direct _____ , the proposition is immediately put to a plebiscite or referendum, in what is called a Popular initiated Referendum or citizen-initiated referendum).

Exam Probability: **Medium**

30. *Answer choices:*
(see index for correct answer)

- a. 10,000ft
- b. Australian Institute of Project Management
- c. Fast-track construction
- d. Initiative

Guidance: level 1

:: Production and manufacturing ::

_____ is a production planning, scheduling, and inventory control system used to manage manufacturing processes. Most MRP systems are software-based, but it is possible to conduct MRP by hand as well.

Exam Probability: **Medium**

31. *Answer choices:*
(see index for correct answer)

- a. ISO/TS 16949
- b. Enterprise control
- c. Material requirements planning
- d. Food processing

Guidance: level 1

:: Casting (manufacturing) ::

A _____ is a regularity in the world, man-made design, or abstract ideas. As such, the elements of a _____ repeat in a predictable manner. A geometric _____ is a kind of _____ formed of geometric shapes and typically repeated like a wallpaper design.

Exam Probability: **High**

32. *Answer choices:*
(see index for correct answer)

- a. Castability
- b. AutoCAST
- c. Ceramic mold casting
- d. Institute of Cast Metals Engineers

Guidance: level 1

:: Fault-tolerant computer systems ::

_____ decision-making is a group decision-making process in which group members develop, and agree to support a decision in the best interest of the whole group or common goal. _____ may be defined professionally as an acceptable resolution, one that can be supported, even if not the "favourite" of each individual. It has its origin in the Latin word consensus , which is from consentio meaning literally feel together. It is used to describe both the decision and the process of reaching a decision. _____ decision-making is thus concerned with the process of deliberating and finalizing a decision, and the social, economic, legal, environmental and political effects of applying this process.

Exam Probability: **Low**

33. *Answer choices:*
(see index for correct answer)

- a. Virtual synchrony
- b. Consensus
- c. Gbcast
- d. N-version programming

Guidance: level 1

:: Production economics ::

_____ is the joint use of a resource or space. It is also the process of dividing and distributing. In its narrow sense, it refers to joint or alternating use of inherently finite goods, such as a common pasture or a shared residence. Still more loosely, " _____ " can actually mean giving something as an outright gift: for example, to "share" one's food really means to give some of it as a gift. _____ is a basic component of human interaction, and is responsible for strengthening social ties and ensuring a person's well-being.

Exam Probability: **High**

34. *Answer choices:*
(see index for correct answer)

- a. Sharing
- b. Capacity utilization
- c. Factor price
- d. Division of work

:: Metalworking ::

A _____ is a round object with various uses. It is used in _____ games, where the play of the game follows the state of the _____ as it is hit, kicked or thrown by players. _____ s can also be used for simpler activities, such as catch or juggling. _____ s made from hard-wearing materials are used in engineering applications to provide very low friction bearings, known as _____ bearings. Black-powder weapons use stone and metal _____ s as projectiles.

Exam Probability: **High**

35. *Answer choices:*
(see index for correct answer)

- a. Filing
- b. Ball
- c. Chemical milling
- d. Ironwork

:: Packaging ::

In work place, _____ or job _____ means good ranking with the hypothesized conception of requirements of a role. There are two types of job _____ s: contextual and task. Task _____ is related to cognitive ability while contextual _____ is dependent upon personality. Task _____ are behavioral roles that are recognized in job descriptions and by remuneration systems, they are directly related to organizational _____ , whereas, contextual _____ are value based and additional behavioral roles that are not recognized in job descriptions and covered by compensation; they are extra roles that are indirectly related to organizational _____ .
Citizenship _____ like contextual _____ means a set of individual activity/contribution that supports the organizational culture.

Exam Probability: **High**

36. *Answer choices:*
(see index for correct answer)

- a. Intermediate bulk container
- b. Tetra Brik
- c. Reel
- d. Wrap rage

Guidance: level 1

:: Industrial engineering ::

_____ , in its contemporary conceptualisation, is a comparison of perceived expectations of a service with perceived performance , giving rise to the equation SQ=P-E. This conceptualistion of _____ has its origins in the expectancy-disconfirmation paradigm.

Exam Probability: **Low**

37. *Answer choices:*
(see index for correct answer)

- a. Optimal design
- b. Continuous emissions monitoring system
- c. Service quality
- d. Time and motion study

Guidance: level 1

:: ::

A _____ consists of an orchestrated and repeatable pattern of business activity enabled by the systematic organization of resources into processes that transform materials, provide services, or process information. It can be depicted as a sequence of operations, the work of a person or group, the work of an organization of staff, or one or more simple or complex mechanisms.

Exam Probability: **Low**

38. *Answer choices:*
(see index for correct answer)

- a. Workflow
- b. deep-level diversity
- c. hierarchical perspective
- d. interpersonal communication

Guidance: level 1

:: Accounting source documents ::

A _____ is a commercial document and first official offer issued by a buyer to a seller indicating types, quantities, and agreed prices for products or services. It is used to control the purchasing of products and services from external suppliers. _____ s can be an essential part of enterprise resource planning system orders.

Exam Probability: **Low**

39. *Answer choices:*

(see index for correct answer)

- a. Purchase order
- b. Bank statement
- c. Parcel audit
- d. Superbill

Guidance: level 1

:: Debt ::

_____ is the trust which allows one party to provide money or resources to another party wherein the second party does not reimburse the first party immediately , but promises either to repay or return those resources at a later date. In other words, _____ is a method of making reciprocity formal, legally enforceable, and extensible to a large group of unrelated people.

Exam Probability: **High**

40. *Answer choices:*

(see index for correct answer)

- a. External debt
- b. Cessio bonorum
- c. Credit
- d. Household debt

Guidance: level 1

:: Costs ::

_____ is the process used by companies to reduce their costs and increase their profits. Depending on a company's services or product, the strategies can vary. Every decision in the product development process affects cost.

Exam Probability: **Low**

41. *Answer choices:*
(see index for correct answer)

- a. Cost reduction
- b. Implicit cost
- c. Total cost of acquisition
- d. labor cost

Guidance: level 1

:: Management ::

In economics and marketing, _____ is the process of distinguishing a product or service from others, to make it more attractive to a particular target market. This involves differentiating it from competitors' products as well as a firm's own products. The concept was proposed by Edward Chamberlin in his 1933 The Theory of Monopolistic Competition.

Exam Probability: **Low**

42. *Answer choices:*
(see index for correct answer)

- a. Crisis plan
- b. Dynamic enterprise modeling
- c. Product differentiation
- d. Focused improvement

Guidance: level 1

:: Management ::

Business _____ is a discipline in operations management in which people use various methods to discover, model, analyze, measure, improve, optimize, and automate business processes. BPM focuses on improving corporate performance by managing business processes. Any combination of methods used to manage a company's business processes is BPM. Processes can be structured and repeatable or unstructured and variable. Though not required, enabling technologies are often used with BPM.

Exam Probability: **High**

43. *Answer choices:*
(see index for correct answer)

- a. Project team builder
- b. Process management
- c. Energy management software
- d. Business rule

Guidance: level 1

:: Production and manufacturing ::

_____ is a set of techniques and tools for process improvement. Though as a shortened form it may be found written as 6S, it should not be confused with the methodology known as 6S .

Exam Probability: **Low**

44. *Answer choices:*
(see index for correct answer)

- a. Six Sigma
- b. Miniaturization
- c. Product layout
- d. Zero Defects

Guidance: level 1

:: ::

_____ refers to a business or organization attempting to acquire goods or services to accomplish its goals. Although there are several organizations that attempt to set standards in the _____ process, processes can vary greatly between organizations. Typically the word " _____ " is not used interchangeably with the word "procurement", since procurement typically includes expediting, supplier quality, and transportation and logistics in addition to _____ .

Exam Probability: **High**

45. *Answer choices:*
(see index for correct answer)

- a. deep-level diversity
- b. information systems assessment
- c. Sarbanes-Oxley act of 2002
- d. Purchasing

Guidance: level 1

:: Management accounting ::

_____ are costs that are not directly accountable to a cost object . _____ may be either fixed or variable. _____ include administration, personnel and security costs. These are those costs which are not directly related to production. Some _____ may be overhead. But some overhead costs can be directly attributed to a project and are direct costs.

Exam Probability: **High**

46. *Answer choices:*
(see index for correct answer)

- a. Chartered Cost Accountant
- b. Throughput accounting
- c. Variance
- d. Indirect costs

Guidance: level 1

:: Metals ::

A _____ is a material that, when freshly prepared, polished, or fractured, shows a lustrous appearance, and conducts electricity and heat relatively well. _____ s are typically malleable or ductile . A _____ may be a chemical element such as iron, or an alloy such as stainless steel.

Exam Probability: **High**

47. *Answer choices:*
(see index for correct answer)

- a. Metal
- b. Light metal
- c. Metal toxicity
- d. Metallurgy

Guidance: level 1

:: Management ::

_____ is a term used in business and Information Technology to describe the in-depth process of capturing customer's expectations, preferences and aversions. Specifically, the _____ is a market research technique that produces a detailed set of customer wants and needs, organized into a hierarchical structure, and then prioritized in terms of relative importance and satisfaction with current alternatives. _____ studies typically consist of both qualitative and quantitative research steps. They are generally conducted at the start of any new product, process, or service design initiative in order to better understand the customer's wants and needs, and as the key input for new product definition, Quality Function Deployment , and the setting of detailed design specifications.

Exam Probability: **Medium**

48. *Answer choices:*
(see index for correct answer)

- a. Stakeholder
- b. Hierarchical organization
- c. Voice of the customer
- d. Power to the edge

Guidance: level 1

:: Time management ::

_____ is the process of planning and exercising conscious control of time spent on specific activities, especially to increase effectiveness, efficiency, and productivity. It involves a juggling act of various demands upon a person relating to work, social life, family, hobbies, personal interests and commitments with the finiteness of time. Using time effectively gives the person "choice" on spending/managing activities at their own time and expediency.

Exam Probability: **Medium**

49. *Answer choices:*
(see index for correct answer)

- a. Time management
- b. Maestro concept
- c. Time allocation
- d. Getting Things Done

Guidance: level 1

:: Semiconductor companies ::

_____ Corporation is a Japanese multinational conglomerate corporation headquartered in Konan, Minato, Tokyo. Its diversified business includes consumer and professional electronics, gaming, entertainment and financial services. The company owns the largest music entertainment business in the world, the largest video game console business and one of the largest video game publishing businesses, and is one of the leading manufacturers of electronic products for the consumer and professional markets, and a leading player in the film and television entertainment industry. _____ was ranked 97th on the 2018 Fortune Global 500 list.

Exam Probability: **Low**

50. *Answer choices:*
(see index for correct answer)

- a. NXP Semiconductors
- b. Sitronics
- c. Qulsar
- d. Sony

:: Non-parametric statistics ::

A _____ is an accurate representation of the distribution of numerical data. It is an estimate of the probability distribution of a continuous variable and was first introduced by Karl Pearson. It differs from a bar graph, in the sense that a bar graph relates two variables, but a _____ relates only one. To construct a _____ , the first step is to "bin" the range of values—that is, divide the entire range of values into a series of intervals—and then count how many values fall into each interval. The bins are usually specified as consecutive, non-overlapping intervals of a variable. The bins must be adjacent, and are often of equal size.

Exam Probability: **Medium**

51. *Answer choices:*
(see index for correct answer)

- a. Chi-squared test
- b. Kernel regression
- c. Durbin test
- d. Binomial test

:: Procurement ::

Purchasing is the formal process of buying goods and services. The _____ can vary from one organization to another, but there are some common key elements.

Exam Probability: **Low**

52. *Answer choices:*
(see index for correct answer)

- a. Request for information
- b. Government contract proposal
- c. Bulk purchasing
- d. Proposal theme statement

:: Asset ::

In financial accounting, an _____ is any resource owned by the business. Anything tangible or intangible that can be owned or controlled to produce value and that is held by a company to produce positive economic value is an _____ . Simply stated, _____ s represent value of ownership that can be converted into cash . The balance sheet of a firm records the monetary value of the _____ s owned by that firm. It covers money and other valuables belonging to an individual or to a business.

Exam Probability: **Medium**

53. *Answer choices:*
(see index for correct answer)

- a. Fixed asset
- b. Asset

Guidance: level 1

:: Quality ::

A _____ is an initiating cause of either a condition or a causal chain that leads to an outcome or effect of interest. The term denotes the earliest, most basic, 'deepest', cause for a given behavior; most often a fault. The idea is that you can only see an error by its manifest signs. Those signs can be widespread, multitudinous, and convoluted, whereas the _____ leading to them often is a lot simpler.

Exam Probability: **High**

54. *Answer choices:*
(see index for correct answer)

- a. Market Driven Quality
- b. Root cause
- c. Dualistic Petri nets
- d. Shigeo Shingo

Guidance: level 1

:: Project management ::

In economics and business decision-making, a sunk cost is a cost that has already been incurred and cannot be recovered.

55. *Answer choices:*
(see index for correct answer)

- a. Project team
- b. Collaborative planning software
- c. American Society of Professional Estimators
- d. Sunk costs

Guidance: level 1

:: Data management ::

_____ is the ability of a physical product to remain functional, without requiring excessive maintenance or repair, when faced with the challenges of normal operation over its design lifetime. There are several measures of _____ in use, including years of life, hours of use, and number of operational cycles. In economics, goods with a long usable life are referred to as durable goods.

56. *Answer choices:*
(see index for correct answer)

- a. Edge data integration
- b. Single customer view
- c. Master data
- d. Storage model

Guidance: level 1

:: Decision theory ::

_____ is a method developed in Japan beginning in 1966 to help transform the voice of the customer into engineering characteristics for a product. Yoji Akao, the original developer, described QFD as a "method to transform qualitative user demands into quantitative parameters, to deploy the functions forming quality, and to deploy methods for achieving the design quality into subsystems and component parts, and ultimately to specific elements of the manufacturing process." The author combined his work in quality assurance and quality control points with function deployment used in value engineering.

Exam Probability: **Medium**

57. *Answer choices:*
(see index for correct answer)

- a. Quality function deployment
- b. Influence diagram
- c. Normative model of decision-making
- d. Secretary problem

Guidance: level 1

:: Packaging materials ::

_____ is a thin material produced by pressing together moist fibres of cellulose pulp derived from wood, rags or grasses, and drying them into flexible sheets.It is a versatile material with many uses, including writing, printing, packaging, cleaning, decorating, and a number of industrial and construction processes. _____ s are essential in legal or non-legal documentation.

Exam Probability: **Low**

58. *Answer choices:*
(see index for correct answer)

- a. Molded pulp
- b. Filament tape
- c. Label
- d. Soilon

Guidance: level 1

The _____ recognizes U.S. organizations in the business, health care, education, and nonprofit sectors for performance excellence. The Baldrige Award is the only formal recognition of the performance excellence of both public and private U.S. organizations given by the President of the United States. It is administered by the Baldrige Performance Excellence Program, which is based at and managed by the National Institute of Standards and Technology , an agency of the U.S. Department of Commerce.

Exam Probability: **High**

59. *Answer choices:*

(see index for correct answer)

- a. Philippine Quality Award
- b. Canada Awards for Excellence
- c. Malcolm Baldrige National Quality Award
- d. Deming Prize

Guidance: level 1

Commerce

Commerce relates to "the exchange of goods and services, especially on a large scale." It includes legal, economic, political, social, cultural and technological systems that operate in any country or internationally.

:: Marketing ::

The _____ is a foundation model for businesses. The _____ has been defined as the "set of marketing tools that the firm uses to pursue its marketing objectives in the target market". Thus the _____ refers to four broad levels of marketing decision, namely: product, price, place, and promotion. Marketing practice has been occurring for millennia, but marketing theory emerged in the early twentieth century. The contemporary _____, or the 4 Ps, which has become the dominant framework for marketing management decisions, was first published in 1960. In services marketing, an extended _____ is used, typically comprising 7 Ps, made up of the original 4 Ps extended by process, people, and physical evidence. Occasionally service marketers will refer to 8 Ps, comprising these 7 Ps plus performance.

Exam Probability: **Medium**

1. *Answer choices:*

(see index for correct answer)

- a. Free Comic Book Day
- b. Marketing mix
- c. Pharmaceutical marketing
- d. Adobe Media Optimizer

Guidance: level 1

:: Insolvency ::

_____ is a legal process through which people or other entities who cannot repay debts to creditors may seek relief from some or all of their debts. In most jurisdictions, _____ is imposed by a court order, often initiated by the debtor.

Exam Probability: **High**

2. *Answer choices:*
(see index for correct answer)

- a. Insolvency
- b. Bankruptcy
- c. Official Committee of Equity Security Holders
- d. Insolvency law of Russia

Guidance: level 1

:: Cryptography ::

In cryptography, _____ is the process of encoding a message or information in such a way that only authorized parties can access it and those who are not authorized cannot. _____ does not itself prevent interference, but denies the intelligible content to a would-be interceptor. In an _____ scheme, the intended information or message, referred to as plaintext, is encrypted using an _____ algorithm – a cipher – generating ciphertext that can be read only if decrypted. For technical reasons, an _____ scheme usually uses a pseudo-random _____ key generated by an algorithm. It is in principle possible to decrypt the message without possessing the key, but, for a well-designed _____ scheme, considerable computational resources and skills are required. An authorized recipient can easily decrypt the message with the key provided by the originator to recipients but not to unauthorized users.

Exam Probability: **Medium**

3. *Answer choices:*
(see index for correct answer)

- a. plaintext
- b. Encryption
- c. cryptosystem
- d. Electronic Signature

Guidance: level 1

" _____ " means the Government Service which is responsible for the administration of _____ law and the collection of duties and taxes and which also has the responsibility for the application of other laws and regulations relating to the importation, exportation, movement or storage of goods.

Exam Probability: **High**

4. *Answer choices:*
(see index for correct answer)

- a. Animal and Plant Health Inspection Service
- b. Export of cryptography from the United States
- c. Customs valuation
- d. Customs

Guidance: level 1

An _____ , or automated clearinghouse, is an electronic network for financial transactions, generally domestic low value payments. An ACH is a computer-based clearing house and settlement facility established to process the exchange of electronic transactions between participating financial institutions. It is a form of clearing house that is specifically for payments and may support both credit transfers and direct debits.

Exam Probability: **Low**

5. *Answer choices:*
(see index for correct answer)

- a. Online shopping
- b. ESewa
- c. Automated Clearing House
- d. Mobile commerce

Guidance: level 1

The _____ , now also known as the First _____ , was the transition to new manufacturing processes in Europe and the US, in the period from about 1760 to sometime between 1820 and 1840. This transition included going from hand production methods to machines, new chemical manufacturing and iron production processes, the increasing use of steam power and water power, the development of machine tools and the rise of the mechanized factory system. The _____ also led to an unprecedented rise in the rate of population growth.

Exam Probability: **Medium**

6. *Answer choices:*
(see index for correct answer)

- a. Coke
- b. Great Migration of Canada
- c. Industrial Revolution
- d. Luddite

Guidance: level 1

:: ::

Senior management, executive management, upper management, or a _____ is generally a team of individuals at the highest level of management of an organization who have the day-to-day tasks of managing that organization — sometimes a company or a corporation.

Exam Probability: **Medium**

7. *Answer choices:*
(see index for correct answer)

- a. Management team
- b. process perspective
- c. information systems assessment
- d. Character

Guidance: level 1

:: ::

_____ is a type of government support for the citizens of that society. _____ may be provided to people of any income level, as with social security , but it is usually intended to ensure that the poor can meet their basic human needs such as food and shelter. _____ attempts to provide poor people with a minimal level of well-being, usually either a free- or a subsidized-supply of certain goods and social services, such as healthcare, education, and vocational training.

Exam Probability: **Low**

8. *Answer choices:*
(see index for correct answer)

- a. Welfare
- b. open system
- c. functional perspective
- d. process perspective

Guidance: level 1

:: ::

Competition arises whenever at least two parties strive for a goal which cannot be shared: where one's gain is the other's loss .

Exam Probability: **Medium**

9. *Answer choices:*
(see index for correct answer)

- a. hierarchical perspective
- b. co-culture
- c. Competitor
- d. similarity-attraction theory

Guidance: level 1

:: Management ::

_____ is the identification, evaluation, and prioritization of risks followed by coordinated and economical application of resources to minimize, monitor, and control the probability or impact of unfortunate events or to maximize the realization of opportunities.

Exam Probability: **Medium**

10. *Answer choices:*
(see index for correct answer)

- a. Technology scouting
- b. Risk management
- c. Topple rate
- d. Oriental management

Guidance: level 1

:: ::

A _____ is a structured form of play, usually undertaken for enjoyment and sometimes used as an educational tool. _____ s are distinct from work, which is usually carried out for remuneration, and from art, which is more often an expression of aesthetic or ideological elements. However, the distinction is not clear-cut, and many _____ s are also considered to be work or art .

Exam Probability: **High**

11. *Answer choices:*
(see index for correct answer)

- a. Game
- b. co-culture
- c. process perspective
- d. open system

Guidance: level 1

:: Scientific method ::

In the social sciences and life sciences, a _____ is a research method involving an up-close, in-depth, and detailed examination of a subject of study , as well as its related contextual conditions.

12. *Answer choices:*
(see index for correct answer)

- a. Case study
- b. pilot project
- c. Preference test
- d. Causal research

Guidance: level 1

:: Supply chain management :::

_____ is the removal of intermediaries in economics from a supply chain, or cutting out the middlemen in connection with a transaction or a series of transactions. Instead of going through traditional distribution channels, which had some type of intermediary , companies may now deal with customers directly, for example via the Internet. Hence, the use of factory direct and direct from the factory to mean the same thing.

13. *Answer choices:*
(see index for correct answer)

- a. Manugistics
- b. Application service provider
- c. Helveta
- d. Disintermediation

Guidance: level 1

:: Budgets ::

A _____ is a financial plan for a defined period, often one year. It may also include planned sales volumes and revenues, resource quantities, costs and expenses, assets, liabilities and cash flows. Companies, governments, families and other organizations use it to express strategic plans of activities or events in measurable terms.

Exam Probability: **High**

14. *Answer choices:*
(see index for correct answer)

- a. Budget
- b. Budgeted cost of work scheduled
- c. Performance-based budgeting
- d. Zero-based budgeting

Guidance: level 1

:: Information retrieval ::

_____ is a technique used by recommender systems. _____ has two senses, a narrow one and a more general one.

Exam Probability: **Low**

15. *Answer choices:*
(see index for correct answer)

- a. Federated search
- b. Datanet
- c. Dynatext
- d. Collaborative filtering

Guidance: level 1

:: Logistics ::

_____ is generally the detailed organization and implementation of a complex operation. In a general business sense, _____ is the management of the flow of things between the point of origin and the point of consumption in order to meet requirements of customers or corporations. The resources managed in _____ may include tangible goods such as materials, equipment, and supplies, as well as food and other consumable items. The _____ of physical items usually involves the integration of information flow, materials handling, production, packaging, inventory, transportation, warehousing, and often security.

Exam Probability: **High**

16. *Answer choices:*
(see index for correct answer)

- a. Logistics
- b. Navy lighterage pontoons
- c. Tracking number
- d. International Society of Logistics

Guidance: level 1

:: Marketing ::

_____ or stock is the goods and materials that a business holds for the ultimate goal of resale .

Exam Probability: **High**

17. *Answer choices:*
(see index for correct answer)

- a. Lingerie party
- b. The Cellar
- c. Mystery shopping
- d. Marketing myopia

Guidance: level 1

:: Generally Accepted Accounting Principles ::

Expenditure is an outflow of money to another person or group to pay for an item or service, or for a category of costs. For a tenant, rent is an _____ . For students or parents, tuition is an _____ . Buying food, clothing, furniture or an automobile is often referred to as an _____ . An _____ is a cost that is "paid" or "remitted", usually in exchange for something of value. Something that seems to cost a great deal is "expensive". Something that seems to cost little is "inexpensive". " _____ s of the table" are _____ s of dining, refreshments, a feast, etc.

Exam Probability: **Medium**

18. *Answer choices:*

- a. Financial position of the United States
- b. Expense
- c. Operating profit
- d. Shares outstanding

Guidance: level 1

:: Securities (finance) ::

A _____ is a container that is traditionally constructed from stiff fibers, and can be made from a range of materials, including wood splints, runners, and cane. While most _____ s are made from plant materials, other materials such as horsehair, baleen, or metal wire can be used. _____ s are generally woven by hand. Some _____ s are fitted with a lid, while others are left open on top.

Exam Probability: **Low**

19. *Answer choices:*

- a. Tracking stock
- b. Trust-preferred
- c. Interest in securities
- d. Basket

Guidance: level 1

:: ::

_____ is a term frequently used in marketing. It is a measure of how products and services supplied by a company meet or surpass customer expectation. _____ is defined as "the number of customers, or percentage of total customers, whose reported experience with a firm, its products, or its services exceeds specified satisfaction goals."

Exam Probability: **Medium**

20. *Answer choices:*
(see index for correct answer)

- a. open system
- b. Customer satisfaction
- c. cultural
- d. similarity-attraction theory

Guidance: level 1

:: Commodities ::

In economics, a _____ is an economic good or service that has full or substantial fungibility: that is, the market treats instances of the good as equivalent or nearly so with no regard to who produced them. Most commodities are raw materials, basic resources, agricultural, or mining products, such as iron ore, sugar, or grains like rice and wheat. Commodities can also be mass-produced unspecialized products such as chemicals and computer memory.

Exam Probability: **High**

21. *Answer choices:*
(see index for correct answer)

- a. Commodity money
- b. Sample grade
- c. Commoditization
- d. Commodity

Guidance: level 1

:: Statutory law ::

_____ or statute law is written law set down by a body of legislature or by a singular legislator . This is as opposed to oral or customary law; or regulatory law promulgated by the executive or common law of the judiciary. Statutes may originate with national, state legislatures or local municipalities.

22. *Answer choices:*
(see index for correct answer)

- a. ratification
- b. incorporation by reference
- c. Statute of repose
- d. statute law

Guidance: level 1

:: Commercial item transport and distribution ::

In commerce, supply-chain management , the management of the flow of goods and services, involves the movement and storage of raw materials, of work-in-process inventory, and of finished goods from point of origin to point of consumption. Interconnected or interlinked networks, channels and node businesses combine in the provision of products and services required by end customers in a supply chain. Supply-chain management has been defined as the "design, planning, execution, control, and monitoring of supply-chain activities with the objective of creating net value, building a competitive infrastructure, leveraging worldwide logistics, synchronizing supply with demand and measuring performance globally."SCM practice draws heavily from the areas of industrial engineering, systems engineering, operations management, logistics, procurement, information technology, and marketing and strives for an integrated approach. Marketing channels play an important role in supply-chain management. Current research in supply-chain management is concerned with topics related to sustainability and risk management, among others. Some suggest that the "people dimension" of SCM, ethical issues, internal integration, transparency/visibility, and human capital/talent management are topics that have, so far, been underrepresented on the research agenda.

- a. Supply chain management
- b. Unit load
- c. Delivery order
- d. Toll Global Resources

Guidance: level 1

:: ::

_____ s and acquisitions are transactions in which the ownership of companies, other business organizations, or their operating units are transferred or consolidated with other entities. As an aspect of strategic management, M&A can allow enterprises to grow or downsize, and change the nature of their business or competitive position.

Exam Probability: **Low**

- a. Merger
- b. imperative
- c. empathy
- d. cultural

Guidance: level 1

:: ::

_____ is the collaborative effort of a team to achieve a common goal or to complete a task in the most effective and efficient way. This concept is seen within the greater framework of a team, which is a group of interdependent individuals who work together towards a common goal. Basic requirements for effective _____ are an adequate team size , available resources for the team to make use of , and clearly defined roles within the team in order for everyone to have a clear purpose. _____ is present in any context where a group of people are working together to achieve a common goal. These contexts include an industrial organization , athletics , a school , and the healthcare system . In each of these settings, the level of _____ and interdependence can vary from low , to intermediate , to high , depending on the amount of communication, interaction, and collaboration present between team members.

Exam Probability: **Low**

25. *Answer choices:*

- a. Character
- b. Teamwork
- c. co-culture
- d. process perspective

Guidance: level 1

:: Project management ::

_____ is the right to exercise power, which can be formalized by a state and exercised by way of judges, appointed executives of government, or the ecclesiastical or priestly appointed representatives of a God or other deities.

Exam Probability: **Medium**

26. *Answer choices:*

- a. International Project Management Association
- b. Akihabara syndrome
- c. Scope statement
- d. Student syndrome

Guidance: level 1

A _____ is a deliberate system of principles to guide decisions and achieve rational outcomes. A _____ is a statement of intent, and is implemented as a procedure or protocol. Policies are generally adopted by a governance body within an organization. Policies can assist in both subjective and objective decision making. Policies to assist in subjective decision making usually assist senior management with decisions that must be based on the relative merits of a number of factors, and as a result are often hard to test objectively, e.g. work-life balance _____ . In contrast policies to assist in objective decision making are usually operational in nature and can be objectively tested, e.g. password _____ .

Exam Probability: **High**

27. *Answer choices:*

(see index for correct answer)

- a. Decision aids
- b. Policy
- c. Belief decision matrix
- d. Applied information economics

Guidance: level 1

An _____ is a contingent motivator. Traditional _____ s are extrinsic motivators which reward actions to yield a desired outcome. The effectiveness of traditional _____ s has changed as the needs of Western society have evolved. While the traditional _____ model is effective when there is a defined procedure and goal for a task, Western society started to require a higher volume of critical thinkers, so the traditional model became less effective. Institutions are now following a trend in implementing strategies that rely on intrinsic motivations rather than the extrinsic motivations that the traditional _____ s foster.

Exam Probability: **Medium**

28. *Answer choices:*

(see index for correct answer)

- a. cultural
- b. Incentive
- c. hierarchical
- d. functional perspective

Guidance: level 1

:: ::

_____ is an abstract concept of management of complex systems according to a set of rules and trends. In systems theory, these types of rules exist in various fields of biology and society, but the term has slightly different meanings according to context. For example.

Exam Probability: **High**

29. *Answer choices:*
(see index for correct answer)

- a. process perspective
- b. Regulation
- c. interpersonal communication
- d. levels of analysis

Guidance: level 1

:: ::

_____ is both a research area and a practical skill encompassing the ability of an individual or organization to "lead" or guide other individuals, teams, or entire organizations. Specialist literature debates various viewpoints, contrasting Eastern and Western approaches to _____ , and also United States versus European approaches. U.S. academic environments define _____ as "a process of social influence in which a person can enlist the aid and support of others in the accomplishment of a common task".

Exam Probability: **High**

30. *Answer choices:*
(see index for correct answer)

- a. functional perspective
- b. Leadership
- c. hierarchical perspective
- d. imperative

:: Production economics ::

In economics long run is a theoretical concept where all markets are in equilibrium, and all prices and quantities have fully adjusted and are in equilibrium. The long run contrasts with the _____ where there are some constraints and markets are not fully in equilibrium.

Exam Probability: **Low**

31. *Answer choices:*

(see index for correct answer)

- a. Economic batch quantity
- b. Producer's risk
- c. Marginal product
- d. Cost-of-production theory of value

:: Consortia ::

A _____ is an association of two or more individuals, companies, organizations or governments with the objective of participating in a common activity or pooling their resources for achieving a common goal.

Exam Probability: **High**

32. *Answer choices:*

(see index for correct answer)

- a. RNAi Global Initiative
- b. Euronews SA
- c. Linguistic Data Consortium
- d. QIVICON

:: E-commerce ::

_____ is the activity of buying or selling of products on online services or over the Internet. Electronic commerce draws on technologies such as mobile commerce, electronic funds transfer, supply chain management, Internet marketing, online transaction processing, electronic data interchange , inventory management systems, and automated data collection systems.

Exam Probability: **High**

33. *Answer choices:*
(see index for correct answer)

- a. Storefront
- b. Virtual workplace
- c. Quisk
- d. E-commerce

Guidance: level 1

:: Data interchange standards ::

_____ is the concept of businesses electronically communicating information that was traditionally communicated on paper, such as purchase orders and invoices. Technical standards for EDI exist to facilitate parties transacting such instruments without having to make special arrangements.

Exam Probability: **Medium**

34. *Answer choices:*
(see index for correct answer)

- a. ASC X12
- b. Domain Application Protocol
- c. Uniform Communication Standard
- d. Electronic data interchange

Guidance: level 1

:: Management ::

_____ is a process by which entities review the quality of all factors involved in production. ISO 9000 defines _____ as "A part of quality management focused on fulfilling quality requirements".

35. *Answer choices:*

(see index for correct answer)

- a. Radical transparency
- b. Quality control
- c. Corporate recovery
- d. Allegiance

Guidance: level 1

:: Marketing techniques ::

_____ is the activity of dividing a broad consumer or business market, normally consisting of existing and potential customers, into sub-groups of consumers based on some type of shared characteristics. In dividing or segmenting markets, researchers typically look for common characteristics such as shared needs, common interests, similar lifestyles or even similar demographic profiles. The overall aim of segmentation is to identify high yield segments – that is, those segments that are likely to be the most profitable or that have growth potential – so that these can be selected for special attention .

Exam Probability: **Low**

36. *Answer choices:*

(see index for correct answer)

- a. As seen on TV
- b. Loss leader
- c. Unique selling language
- d. Market segmentation

Guidance: level 1

:: ::

_____ is an emotion involving pleasure, , or anxiety in considering or awaiting an expected event.

Exam Probability: **Low**

37. *Answer choices:*

(see index for correct answer)

- a. levels of analysis
- b. similarity-attraction theory
- c. Anticipation
- d. empathy

Guidance: level 1

:: ::

Employment is a relationship between two parties, usually based on a contract where work is paid for, where one party, which may be a corporation, for profit, not-for-profit organization, co-operative or other entity is the employer and the other is the employee. Employees work in return for payment, which may be in the form of an hourly wage, by piecework or an annual salary, depending on the type of work an employee does or which sector she or he is working in. Employees in some fields or sectors may receive gratuities, bonus payment or stock options. In some types of employment, employees may receive benefits in addition to payment. Benefits can include health insurance, housing, disability insurance or use of a gym. Employment is typically governed by employment laws, regulations or legal contracts.

Exam Probability: **Low**

38. *Answer choices:*

(see index for correct answer)

- a. Personnel
- b. similarity-attraction theory
- c. hierarchical
- d. hierarchical perspective

Guidance: level 1

:: ::

_____ is the amount of time someone works beyond normal working hours. The term is also used for the pay received for this time. Normal hours may be determined in several ways.

Exam Probability: **High**

39. *Answer choices:*

(see index for correct answer)

- a. deep-level diversity
- b. empathy
- c. cultural
- d. Overtime

Guidance: level 1

:: Auctioneering ::

_____ are electronic auctions, which can be used by sellers to sell their items to many potential buyers. Sellers and buyers can be individuals, organizations etc.

Exam Probability: **Low**

40. *Answer choices:*
(see index for correct answer)

- a. Auto auction
- b. Forward auction
- c. Public auction
- d. Bidding fee auction

Guidance: level 1

:: Decision theory ::

Within economics the concept of _____ is used to model worth or value, but its usage has evolved significantly over time. The term was introduced initially as a measure of pleasure or satisfaction within the theory of utilitarianism by moral philosophers such as Jeremy Bentham and John Stuart Mill. But the term has been adapted and reapplied within neoclassical economics, which dominates modern economic theory, as a _____ function that represents a consumer's preference ordering over a choice set. As such, it is devoid of its original interpretation as a measurement of the pleasure or satisfaction obtained by the consumer from that choice.

Exam Probability: **Medium**

41. *Answer choices:*
(see index for correct answer)

- a. Menu dependence
- b. Utility
- c. Rational Focal Point

- d. Applied information economics

Guidance: level 1

:: Commercial item transport and distribution ::

In a contract of carriage, the _____ is the entity who is financially responsible for the receipt of a shipment. Generally, but not always, the _____ is the same as the receiver.

Exam Probability: **Low**

42. *Answer choices:*
(see index for correct answer)

- a. Consignee
- b. Container crane
- c. Mid-stream operation
- d. Air cargo

Guidance: level 1

:: ::

A _____ is monetary compensation paid by an employer to an employee in exchange for work done. Payment may be calculated as a fixed amount for each task completed , or at an hourly or daily rate , or based on an easily measured quantity of work done.

Exam Probability: **Low**

43. *Answer choices:*
(see index for correct answer)

- a. process perspective
- b. cultural
- c. functional perspective
- d. corporate values

Guidance: level 1

:: ::

_____ or accountancy is the measurement, processing, and communication of financial information about economic entities such as businesses and corporations. The modern field was established by the Italian mathematician Luca Pacioli in 1494. _____ , which has been called the "language of business", measures the results of an organization's economic activities and conveys this information to a variety of users, including investors, creditors, management, and regulators. Practitioners of _____ are known as accountants. The terms "_____" and "financial reporting" are often used as synonyms.

Exam Probability: **High**

44. *Answer choices:*
(see index for correct answer)

- a. cultural
- b. imperative
- c. Accounting
- d. corporate values

Guidance: level 1

:: Industrial automation ::

_____ is the technology by which a process or procedure is performed with minimal human assistance. _____ or automatic control is the use of various control systems for operating equipment such as machinery, processes in factories, boilers and heat treating ovens, switching on telephone networks, steering and stabilization of ships, aircraft and other applications and vehicles with minimal or reduced human intervention.

Exam Probability: **High**

45. *Answer choices:*
(see index for correct answer)

- a. PLCopen
- b. Advanced Plant Management System
- c. Automation
- d. Stack light

Guidance: level 1

:: Payment systems ::

_____ s are part of a payment system issued by financial institutions, such as a bank, to a customer that enables its owner to access the funds in the customer's designated bank accounts, or through a credit account and make payments by electronic funds transfer and access automated teller machines . Such cards are known by a variety of names including bank cards, ATM cards, MAC , client cards, key cards or cash cards.

Exam Probability: **Medium**

46. *Answer choices:*
(see index for correct answer)

- a. Telegraphic transfer
- b. GreenZap
- c. Certified check
- d. Payment card

Guidance: level 1

:: Quality management ::

_____ ensures that an organization, product or service is consistent. It has four main components: quality planning, quality assurance, quality control and quality improvement. _____ is focused not only on product and service quality, but also on the means to achieve it. _____ , therefore, uses quality assurance and control of processes as well as products to achieve more consistent quality. What a customer wants and is willing to pay for it determines quality. It is written or unwritten commitment to a known or unknown consumer in the market . Thus, quality can be defined as fitness for intended use or, in other words, how well the product performs its intended function

Exam Probability: **Low**

47. *Answer choices:*
(see index for correct answer)

- a. Germanischer Lloyd
- b. Quality management
- c. Quality policy
- d. Quality Management Maturity Grid

Guidance: level 1

A _____ is a technical term in psychology, economics and philosophy usually used in relation to choosing between alternatives. For example, someone prefers A over B if they would rather choose A than B.

Exam Probability: **Medium**

48. *Answer choices:*
(see index for correct answer)

- a. Engel curve
- b. Compensated demand
- c. Slutsky equation
- d. Preference

Guidance: level 1

:: E-commerce ::

_____ is the business-to-business or business-to-consumer or business-to-government purchase and sale of supplies, work, and services through the Internet as well as other information and networking systems, such as electronic data interchange and enterprise resource planning.

Exam Probability: **High**

49. *Answer choices:*
(see index for correct answer)

- a. Mobimoneybox
- b. Live banner
- c. E-commerce in Southeast Asia
- d. E-procurement

Guidance: level 1

:: Packaging ::

In work place, _____ or job _____ means good ranking with the hypothesized conception of requirements of a role. There are two types of job _____ s: contextual and task. Task _____ is related to cognitive ability while contextual _____ is dependent upon personality. Task _____ are behavioral roles that are recognized in job descriptions and by remuneration systems, they are directly related to organizational _____ , whereas, contextual _____ are value based and additional behavioral roles that are not recognized in job descriptions and covered by compensation; they are extra roles that are indirectly related to organizational _____ . Citizenship _____ like contextual _____ means a set of individual activity/contribution that supports the organizational culture.

Exam Probability: **Low**

50. *Answer choices:*
(see index for correct answer)

- a. Video game packaging
- b. Food labeling regulations
- c. Cyperus tegetiformis
- d. Performance

Guidance: level 1

:: ::

A _____ is a professional who provides expert advice in a particular area such as security , management, education, accountancy, law, human resources, marketing , finance, engineering, science or any of many other specialized fields.

Exam Probability: **High**

51. *Answer choices:*
(see index for correct answer)

- a. levels of analysis
- b. Consultant
- c. interpersonal communication
- d. co-culture

Guidance: level 1

_____ or stock control can be broadly defined as "the activity of checking a shop's stock." However, a more focused definition takes into account the more science-based, methodical practice of not only verifying a business` inventory but also focusing on the many related facets of inventory management "within an organisation to meet the demand placed upon that business economically." Other facets of _____ include supply chain management, production control, financial flexibility, and customer satisfaction. At the root of _____ , however, is the _____ problem, which involves determining when to order, how much to order, and the logistics of those decisions.

Exam Probability: **Medium**

52. *Answer choices:*
(see index for correct answer)

- a. Inventory control
- b. Audience segmentation
- c. Demand generation
- d. Emailing

Guidance: level 1

Unlike sealed-bid auctions , an _____ is "open" or fully transparent, as the identity of all bidders is disclosed to each other during the auction. More generally, an auction mechanism is considered "English" if it involves an iterative process of adjusting the price in a direction that is unfavorable to the bidders . In contrast, a Dutch auction would adjust the price in a direction that favored the bidders .

Exam Probability: **High**

53. *Answer choices:*
(see index for correct answer)

- a. English auction
- b. Calor licitantis
- c. Auction catalog
- d. Bidding fee auction

:: Regulators ::

A _____ is a public authority or government agency responsible for exercising autonomous authority over some area of human activity in a regulatory or supervisory capacity. An independent _____ is a _____ that is independent from other branches or arms of the government.

Exam Probability: **Medium**

54. *Answer choices:*

(see index for correct answer)

- a. Regulatory agency
- b. Independent regulatory agencies in Turkey
- c. Crofters Commission
- d. Croatian Regulatory Authority for Network Industries

:: ::

Business is the activity of making one's living or making money by producing or buying and selling products . Simply put, it is "any activity or enterprise entered into for profit. It does not mean it is a company, a corporation, partnership, or have any such formal organization, but it can range from a street peddler to General Motors."

Exam Probability: **Low**

55. *Answer choices:*

(see index for correct answer)

- a. Character
- b. empathy
- c. Firm
- d. information systems assessment

:: Real property law ::

A _____ is the grant of authority or rights, stating that the granter formally recognizes the prerogative of the recipient to exercise the rights specified. It is implicit that the granter retains superiority , and that the recipient admits a limited status within the relationship, and it is within that sense that _____ s were historically granted, and that sense is retained in modern usage of the term.

Exam Probability: **High**

56. *Answer choices:*
(see index for correct answer)

- a. Land contract
- b. Disseisor
- c. Retaliatory eviction
- d. Charter

Guidance: level 1

:: Supply chain management ::

_____ is a variable pricing strategy, based on understanding, anticipating and influencing consumer behavior in order to maximize revenue or profits from a fixed, time-limited resource . As a specific, inventory-focused branch of revenue management, _____ involves strategic control of inventory to sell the right product to the right customer at the right time for the right price. This process can result in price discrimination, in which customers consuming identical goods or services are charged different prices. _____ is a large revenue generator for several major industries; Robert Crandall, former Chairman and CEO of American Airlines, gave _____ its name and has called it "the single most important technical development in transportation management since we entered deregulation."

Exam Probability: **Low**

57. *Answer choices:*
(see index for correct answer)

- a. National Centre for Cold-chain Development
- b. Chain of responsibility
- c. Yield management
- d. ERP system

Guidance: level 1

IBM _____ also known as WCS is a software platform framework for e-commerce, including marketing, sales, customer and order processing functionality in a tailorable, integrated package. It is a single, unified platform which offers the ability to do business directly with consumers, with businesses, indirectly through channel partners, or all of these simultaneously. _____ is a customizable, scalable and high availability solution built on the Java - Java EE platform using open standards, such as XML, and Web services.

Exam Probability: **Low**

58. *Answer choices:*
(see index for correct answer)

- a. Private electronic market
- b. AS 2805
- c. SIE
- d. WebSphere Commerce

Guidance: level 1

_____ refers to a business or organization attempting to acquire goods or services to accomplish its goals. Although there are several organizations that attempt to set standards in the _____ process, processes can vary greatly between organizations. Typically the word " _____ " is not used interchangeably with the word "procurement", since procurement typically includes expediting, supplier quality, and transportation and logistics in addition to _____ .

Exam Probability: **Low**

59. *Answer choices:*
(see index for correct answer)

- a. Purchasing
- b. interpersonal communication
- c. corporate values
- d. functional perspective

Guidance: level 1

Business ethics

Business ethics (also known as corporate ethics) is a form of applied ethics or professional ethics, that examines ethical principles and moral or ethical problems that can arise in a business environment. It applies to all aspects of business conduct and is relevant to the conduct of individuals and entire organizations. These ethics originate from individuals, organizational statements or from the legal system. These norms, values, ethical, and unethical practices are what is used to guide business. They help those businesses maintain a better connection with their stakeholders.

:: United States federal labor legislation ::

The _____ of 1988 is a United States federal law that generally prevents employers from using polygraph tests, either for pre-employment screening or during the course of employment, with certain exemptions.

Exam Probability: **High**

1. *Answer choices:*
(see index for correct answer)

- a. Federal Employers Liability Act
- b. Employee Polygraph Protection Act
- c. Water Resources Development Act of 2007
- d. Age Discrimination in Employment Act

Guidance: level 1

:: ::

_____ is an eight-block-long street running roughly northwest to southeast from Broadway to South Street, at the East River, in the Financial District of Lower Manhattan in New York City. Over time, the term has become a metonym for the financial markets of the United States as a whole, the American financial services industry , or New York–based financial interests.

Exam Probability: **Medium**

2. *Answer choices:*

(see index for correct answer)

- a. Sarbanes-Oxley act of 2002
- b. co-culture
- c. Wall Street
- d. surface-level diversity

Guidance: level 1

:: Environmental economics ::

_____ is the process of people maintaining change in a balanced environment, in which the exploitation of resources, the direction of investments, the orientation of technological development and institutional change are all in harmony and enhance both current and future potential to meet human needs and aspirations. For many in the field, _____ is defined through the following interconnected domains or pillars: environment, economic and social, which according to Fritjof Capra is based on the principles of Systems Thinking. Sub-domains of sustainable development have been considered also: cultural, technological and political. While sustainable development may be the organizing principle for _____ for some, for others, the two terms are paradoxical . Sustainable development is the development that meets the needs of the present without compromising the ability of future generations to meet their own needs. Brundtland Report for the World Commission on Environment and Development introduced the term of sustainable development.

Exam Probability: **Low**

3. *Answer choices:*

(see index for correct answer)

- a. Predicting the timing of peak oil
- b. Commodification of nature
- c. Sustainability

- d. Peak oil

Guidance: level 1

:: Minimum wage ::

The _____ are working people whose incomes fall below a given poverty line due to lack of work hours and/or low wages.Largely because they are earning such low wages, the _____ face numerous obstacles that make it difficult for many of them to find and keep a job, save up money, and maintain a sense of self-worth.

Exam Probability: **Medium**

4. *Answer choices:*
(see index for correct answer)

- a. Working poor
- b. Minimum wage in the United States
- c. National Anti-Sweating League
- d. Minimum wage in Taiwan

Guidance: level 1

:: Corporations law ::

A normal _____ consists of various departments that contribute to the company's overall mission and goals. Common departments include Marketing, [Finance, [[Operations managementOperations, Human Resource, and IT. These five divisions represent the major departments within a publicly traded company, though there are often smaller departments within autonomous firms. There is typically a CEO, and Board of Directors composed of the directors of each department. There are also company presidents, vice presidents, and CFOs.There is a great diversity in corporate forms as enterprises may range from single company to multi-corporate conglomerate. The four main _____ s are Functional, Divisional, Geographic, and the Matrix.Realistically, most corporations tend to have a "hybrid" structure, which is a combination of different models with one dominant strategy.

Exam Probability: **High**

5. *Answer choices:*
(see index for correct answer)

- a. Duty of loyalty
- b. General incorporation law
- c. Articles of Incorporation
- d. Corporate structure

:: Coal ::

_____ is a combustible black or brownish-black sedimentary rock, formed as rock strata called _____ seams. _____ is mostly carbon with variable amounts of other elements; chiefly hydrogen, sulfur, oxygen, and nitrogen. _____ is formed if dead plant matter decays into peat and over millions of years the heat and pressure of deep burial converts the peat into _____ . Vast deposits of _____ originates in former wetlands—called _____ forests—that covered much of the Earth's tropical land areas during the late Carboniferous and Permian times.

Exam Probability: **High**

6. *Answer choices:*
(see index for correct answer)

- a. Coalite
- b. World Coal Association
- c. Pulverized coal-fired boiler
- d. Azienda Nazionale Idrogenazione Combustibili

:: Ethical banking ::

A _____ or community development finance institution - abbreviated in both cases to CDFI - is a financial institution that provides credit and financial services to underserved markets and populations, primarily in the USA but also in the UK. A CDFI may be a community development bank, a community development credit union , a community development loan fund , a community development venture capital fund , a microenterprise development loan fund, or a community development corporation.

Exam Probability: **Low**

7. *Answer choices:*
(see index for correct answer)

- a. Community development financial institution
- b. Cultura Sparebank
- c. JAK Members Bank
- d. The Co-operative Bank

Guidance: level 1

:: Social enterprise ::

Corporate social responsibility   is a type of international private business self-regulation. While once it was possible to describe CSR as an internal organisational policy or a corporate ethic strategy, that time has passed as various international laws have been developed and various organisations have used their authority to push it beyond individual or even industry-wide initiatives. While it has been considered a form of corporate self-regulation for some time, over the last decade or so it has moved considerably from voluntary decisions at the level of individual organisations, to mandatory schemes at regional, national and even transnational levels.

Exam Probability: **Medium**

8. *Answer choices:*
(see index for correct answer)

- a. Social venture
- b. Social enterprise

Guidance: level 1

:: ::

_____ is "property consisting of land and the buildings on it, along with its natural resources such as crops, minerals or water; immovable property of this nature; an interest vested in this an item of real property, buildings or housing in general. Also: the business of _____ ; the profession of buying, selling, or renting land, buildings, or housing." It is a legal term used in jurisdictions whose legal system is derived from English common law, such as India, England, Wales, Northern Ireland, United States, Canada, Pakistan, Australia, and New Zealand.

Exam Probability: **Low**

9. *Answer choices:*
(see index for correct answer)

- a. imperative
- b. levels of analysis
- c. Real estate
- d. Sarbanes-Oxley act of 2002

Guidance: level 1

:: Financial markets ::

The _____ is a United States federal government organization, established by Title I of the Dodd–Frank Wall Street Reform and Consumer Protection Act, which was signed into law by President Barack Obama on July 21, 2010. The Office of Financial Research is intended to provide support to the council.

Exam Probability: **Low**

10. *Answer choices:*
(see index for correct answer)

- a. Financial Stability Oversight Council
- b. QuickFIX
- c. Latino Community Foundation
- d. Ugly Americans: The True Story of the Ivy League Cowboys Who Raided the Asian Markets for Millions

Guidance: level 1

:: ::

_____ is a non-governmental environmental organization with offices in over 39 countries and an international coordinating body in Amsterdam, the Netherlands. _____ was founded in 1971 by Irving Stowe, and Dorothy Stowe, Canadian and US ex-pat environmental activists. _____ states its goal is to "ensure the ability of the Earth to nurture life in all its diversity" and focuses its campaigning on worldwide issues such as climate change, deforestation, overfishing, commercial whaling, genetic engineering, and anti-nuclear issues. It uses direct action, lobbying, research, and ecotage to achieve its goals. The global organization does not accept funding from governments, corporations, or political parties, relying on three million individual supporters and foundation grants. _____ has a general consultative status with the United Nations Economic and Social Council and is a founding member of the INGO Accountability Charter, an international non-governmental organization that intends to foster accountability and transparency of non-governmental organizations.

Exam Probability: **Low**

11. *Answer choices:*
(see index for correct answer)

- a. surface-level diversity
- b. imperative
- c. interpersonal communication
- d. functional perspective

Guidance: level 1

:: Types of marketing ::

_____ is an advertisement strategy in which a company uses surprise and/or unconventional interactions in order to promote a product or service. It is a type of publicity. The term was popularized by Jay Conrad Levinson's 1984 book _____ .

Exam Probability: **Medium**

12. *Answer choices:*
(see index for correct answer)

- a. Share of voice
- b. Alliance marketing
- c. Guerrilla Marketing

- d. Megamarketing

Guidance: level 1

:: ::

Cannabis, also known as _____ among other names, is a psychoactive drug from the Cannabis plant used for medical or recreational purposes. The main psychoactive part of cannabis is tetrahydrocannabinol , one of 483 known compounds in the plant, including at least 65 other cannabinoids. Cannabis can be used by smoking, vaporizing, within food, or as an extract.

Exam Probability: **Medium**

13. *Answer choices:*
(see index for correct answer)

- a. Marijuana
- b. functional perspective
- c. information systems assessment
- d. Sarbanes-Oxley act of 2002

Guidance: level 1

:: ::

_____ is a cognitive process that elicits emotion and rational associations based on an individual's moral philosophy or value system. _____ stands in contrast to elicited emotion or thought due to associations based on immediate sensory perceptions and reflexive responses, as in sympathetic central nervous system responses. In common terms, _____ is often described as leading to feelings of remorse when a person commits an act that conflicts with their moral values. An individual's moral values and their dissonance with familial, social, cultural and historical interpretations of moral philosophy are considered in the examination of cultural relativity in both the practice and study of psychology. The extent to which _____ informs moral judgment before an action and whether such moral judgments are or should be based on reason has occasioned debate through much of modern history between theories of modern western philosophy in juxtaposition to the theories of romanticism and other reactionary movements after the end of the Middle Ages.

14. *Answer choices:*

(see index for correct answer)

- a. Conscience
- b. co-culture
- c. Character
- d. information systems assessment

Guidance: level 1

:: Commercial crimes ::

_____ is an agreement between participants on the same side in a market to buy or sell a product, service, or commodity only at a fixed price, or maintain the market conditions such that the price is maintained at a given level by controlling supply and demand.

Exam Probability: **Medium**

15. *Answer choices:*

(see index for correct answer)

- a. Price fixing
- b. Legal abuse
- c. Chiasso financial smuggling case
- d. Skimming

Guidance: level 1

:: ::

MCI, Inc. was an American telecommunication corporation, currently a subsidiary of Verizon Communications, with its main office in Ashburn, Virginia. The corporation was formed originally as a result of the merger of _____ and MCI Communications corporations, and used the name MCI _____ , succeeded by _____ , before changing its name to the present version on April 12, 2003, as part of the corporation's ending of its bankruptcy status. The company traded on NASDAQ as WCOM and MCIP . The corporation was purchased by Verizon Communications with the deal finalizing on January 6, 2006, and is now identified as that company's Verizon Enterprise Solutions division with the local residential divisions being integrated slowly into local Verizon subsidiaries.

Exam Probability: **Medium**

16. *Answer choices:*
(see index for correct answer)

- a. co-culture
- b. surface-level diversity
- c. WorldCom
- d. deep-level diversity

Guidance: level 1

:: Labour relations ::

_____ is a field of study that can have different meanings depending on the context in which it is used. In an international context, it is a subfield of labor history that studies the human relations with regard to work – in its broadest sense – and how this connects to questions of social inequality. It explicitly encompasses unregulated, historical, and non-Western forms of labor. Here, _____ define "for or with whom one works and under what rules. These rules determine the type of work, type and amount of remuneration, working hours, degrees of physical and psychological strain, as well as the degree of freedom and autonomy associated with the work."

Exam Probability: **High**

17. *Answer choices:*
(see index for correct answer)

- a. Global union federation
- b. Whipsaw strike

- c. United Students Against Sweatshops
- d. Labour council

Guidance: level 1

:: Workplace ::

In business management, _____ is a management style whereby a manager closely observes and/or controls the work of his/her subordinates or employees.

Exam Probability: **High**

18. *Answer choices:*
(see index for correct answer)

- a. Workplace conflict
- b. Workplace listening
- c. Work motivation
- d. Micromanagement

Guidance: level 1

:: ::

The _____ is an institution of the European Union, responsible for proposing legislation, implementing decisions, upholding the EU treaties and managing the day-to-day business of the EU. Commissioners swear an oath at the European Court of Justice in Luxembourg City, pledging to respect the treaties and to be completely independent in carrying out their duties during their mandate. Unlike in the Council of the European Union, where members are directly and indirectly elected, and the European Parliament, where members are directly elected, the Commissioners are proposed by the Council of the European Union, on the basis of suggestions made by the national governments, and then appointed by the European Council after the approval of the European Parliament.

Exam Probability: **High**

19. *Answer choices:*
(see index for correct answer)

- a. imperative
- b. empathy

- c. process perspective
- d. similarity-attraction theory

Guidance: level 1

:: ::

A _____ is an astronomical body orbiting a star or stellar remnant that is massive enough to be rounded by its own gravity, is not massive enough to cause thermonuclear fusion, and has cleared its neighbouring region of _____ esimals.

Exam Probability: **Medium**

20. *Answer choices:*
(see index for correct answer)

- a. Sarbanes-Oxley act of 2002
- b. open system
- c. Character
- d. information systems assessment

Guidance: level 1

:: ::

The _____ of 1977 is a United States federal law known primarily for two of its main provisions: one that addresses accounting transparency requirements under the Securities Exchange Act of 1934 and another concerning bribery of foreign officials. The Act was amended in 1988 and in 1998, and has been subject to continued congressional concerns, namely whether its enforcement discourages U.S. companies from investing abroad.

Exam Probability: **High**

21. *Answer choices:*
(see index for correct answer)

- a. Foreign Corrupt Practices Act
- b. information systems assessment
- c. imperative
- d. levels of analysis

Guidance: level 1

:: Electronic feedback ::

_____ occurs when outputs of a system are routed back as inputs as part of a chain of cause-and-effect that forms a circuit or loop. The system can then be said to feed back into itself. The notion of cause-and-effect has to be handled carefully when applied to _____ systems.

Exam Probability: **Medium**

22. *Answer choices:*
(see index for correct answer)

- a. feedback loop
- b. Feedback

Guidance: level 1

:: Culture ::

_____ is a society which is characterized by individualism, which is the prioritization or emphasis, of the individual over the entire group. _____ s are oriented around the self, being independent instead of identifying with a group mentality. They see each other as only loosely linked, and value personal goals over group interests. _____ s tend to have a more diverse population and are characterized with emphasis on personal achievements, and a rational assessment of both the beneficial and detrimental aspects of relationships with others. _____ s have such unique aspects of communication as being a low power-distance culture and having a low-context communication style. The United States, Australia, Great Britain, Canada, the Netherlands, and New Zealand have been identified as highly _____ s.

Exam Probability: **Medium**

23. *Answer choices:*
(see index for correct answer)

- a. Individualistic culture
- b. Low-context culture
- c. Intracultural
- d. cultural framework

Guidance: level 1

The Ethics & Compliance Initiative was formed in 2015 and consists of three nonprofit organizations: the Ethics Research Center, the Ethics & Compliance Association, and the Ethics & Compliance Certification Institute. Based in Arlington, Virginia, United States, ECI is devoted to the advancement of high ethical standards and practices in public and private institutions, and provides research about ethical standards, workplace integrity, and compliance practices and processes.

Exam Probability: **Low**

24. *Answer choices:*
(see index for correct answer)

- a. Ethics Resource Center
- b. levels of analysis
- c. hierarchical perspective
- d. co-culture

Guidance: level 1

:: Employment compensation ::

A _____ is the minimum income necessary for a worker to meet their basic needs. Needs are defined to include food, housing, and other essential needs such as clothing. The goal of a _____ is to allow a worker to afford a basic but decent standard of living. Due to the flexible nature of the term "needs", there is not one universally accepted measure of what a _____ is and as such it varies by location and household type.

Exam Probability: **Low**

25. *Answer choices:*
(see index for correct answer)

- a. Commission
- b. Dearness allowance
- c. Living wage
- d. Basic Income Earth Network

Guidance: level 1

:: Professional ethics ::

In the mental health field, a _____ is a situation where multiple roles exist between a therapist, or other mental health practitioner, and a client. _____ s are also referred to as multiple relationships, and these two terms are used interchangeably in the research literature. The American Psychological Association Ethical Principles of Psychologists and Code of Conduct is a resource that outlines ethical standards and principles to which practitioners are expected to adhere. Standard 3.05 of the APA ethics code outlines the definition of multiple relationships. Dual or multiple relationships occur when.

Exam Probability: **Medium**

26. *Answer choices:*
(see index for correct answer)

- a. ethical code
- b. professional conduct
- c. Continuous professional development

Guidance: level 1

:: ::

A _____ is a problem offering two possibilities, neither of which is unambiguously acceptable or preferable. The possibilities are termed the horns of the _____ , a clichéd usage, but distinguishing the _____ from other kinds of predicament as a matter of usage.

Exam Probability: **Low**

27. *Answer choices:*
(see index for correct answer)

- a. similarity-attraction theory
- b. surface-level diversity
- c. functional perspective
- d. process perspective

Guidance: level 1

:: Anti-capitalism ::

_____ is a range of economic and social systems characterised by social ownership of the means of production and workers' self-management, as well as the political theories and movements associated with them. Social ownership can be public, collective or cooperative ownership, or citizen ownership of equity. There are many varieties of _____ and there is no single definition encapsulating all of them, with social ownership being the common element shared by its various forms.

Exam Probability: **High**

28. *Answer choices:*
(see index for correct answer)

- a. Anticapitalist and Communist List
- b. Socialism
- c. Lesbian Nation
- d. Free association

Guidance: level 1

:: Renewable energy ::

_____ is the conversion of energy from sunlight into electricity, either directly using photovoltaics , indirectly using concentrated _____ , or a combination. Concentrated _____ systems use lenses or mirrors and tracking systems to focus a large area of sunlight into a small beam. Photovoltaic cells convert light into an electric current using the photovoltaic effect.

Exam Probability: **Low**

29. *Answer choices:*
(see index for correct answer)

- a. Passive solar building design
- b. Wind power
- c. Market transformation
- d. Micro combined heat and power

Guidance: level 1

:: ::

A _____ is a form of business network, for example, a local organization of businesses whose goal is to further the interests of businesses. Business owners in towns and cities form these local societies to advocate on behalf of the business community. Local businesses are members, and they elect a board of directors or executive council to set policy for the chamber. The board or council then hires a President, CEO or Executive Director, plus staffing appropriate to size, to run the organization.

Exam Probability: **High**

30. *Answer choices:*
(see index for correct answer)

- a. surface-level diversity
- b. Chamber of Commerce
- c. Character
- d. imperative

Guidance: level 1

:: ::

A _____ is an organization, usually a group of people or a company, authorized to act as a single entity and recognized as such in law. Early incorporated entities were established by charter . Most jurisdictions now allow the creation of new _____ s through registration.

Exam Probability: **Medium**

31. *Answer choices:*
(see index for correct answer)

- a. cultural
- b. information systems assessment
- c. similarity-attraction theory
- d. open system

Guidance: level 1

:: ::

_____ in the United States is a federal and state program that helps with medical costs for some people with limited income and resources. _____ also offers benefits not normally covered by Medicare, including nursing home care and personal care services. The Health Insurance Association of America describes _____ as "a government insurance program for persons of all ages whose income and resources are insufficient to pay for health care." _____ is the largest source of funding for medical and health-related services for people with low income in the United States, providing free health insurance to 74 million low-income and disabled people as of 2017. It is a means-tested program that is jointly funded by the state and federal governments and managed by the states, with each state currently having broad leeway to determine who is eligible for its implementation of the program. States are not required to participate in the program, although all have since 1982. _____ recipients must be U.S. citizens or qualified non-citizens, and may include low-income adults, their children, and people with certain disabilities. Poverty alone does not necessarily qualify someone for _____ .

Exam Probability: **Low**

32. *Answer choices:*
(see index for correct answer)

- a. empathy
- b. corporate values
- c. open system
- d. Medicaid

Guidance: level 1

:: ::

The _____ of 1906 was the first of a series of significant consumer protection laws which was enacted by Congress in the 20th century and led to the creation of the Food and Drug Administration. Its main purpose was to ban foreign and interstate traffic in adulterated or mislabeled food and drug products, and it directed the U.S. Bureau of Chemistry to inspect products and refer offenders to prosecutors. It required that active ingredients be placed on the label of a drug's packaging and that drugs could not fall below purity levels established by the United States Pharmacopeia or the National Formulary. The Jungle by Upton Sinclair with its graphic and revolting descriptions of unsanitary conditions and unscrupulous practices rampant in the meatpacking industry, was an inspirational piece that kept the public's attention on the important issue of unhygienic meat processing plants that later led to food inspection legislation. Sinclair quipped, "I aimed at the public's heart and by accident I hit it in the stomach," as outraged readers demanded and got the pure food law.

Exam Probability: **Medium**

33. *Answer choices:*

- a. co-culture
- b. empathy
- c. levels of analysis
- d. hierarchical

Guidance: level 1

:: Pyramid and Ponzi schemes ::

_____ was an Italian swindler and con artist in the U.S. and Canada. His aliases include Charles Ponci, Carlo, and Charles P. Bianchi. Born and raised in Italy, he became known in the early 1920s as a swindler in North America for his money-making scheme. He promised clients a 50% profit within 45 days or 100% profit within 90 days, by buying discounted postal reply coupons in other countries and redeeming them at face value in the United States as a form of arbitrage. In reality, Ponzi was paying earlier investors using the investments of later investors. While this type of fraudulent investment scheme was not originally invented by Ponzi, it became so identified with him that it now is referred to as a "Ponzi scheme". His scheme ran for over a year before it collapsed, costing his "investors" $20 million.

Exam Probability: **High**

34. *Answer choices:*
(see index for correct answer)

- a. High-yield investment program
- b. Charles Ponzi
- c. K1 fund
- d. Kevin Foster

Guidance: level 1

:: Anti-Revisionism ::

_____ , officially the German Democratic Republic , was a country that existed from 1949 to 1990, when the eastern portion of Germany was part of the Eastern Bloc during the Cold War. It described itself as a socialist "workers` and peasants` state", and the territory was administered and occupied by Soviet forces at the end of World War II — the Soviet Occupation Zone of the Potsdam Agreement, bounded on the east by the Oder–Neisse line. The Soviet zone surrounded West Berlin but did not include it; as a result, West Berlin remained outside the jurisdiction of the GDR.

Exam Probability: **Medium**

35. *Answer choices:*
(see index for correct answer)

- a. East Germany
- b. Chilean Communist Party
- c. New Communist Movement

- d. Party of Labour of Albania

Guidance: level 1

:: Business ethics ::

The _____ are the names of two corporate codes of conduct, developed by the African-American preacher Rev. Leon Sullivan, promoting corporate social responsibility.

Exam Probability: **Medium**

36. *Answer choices:*
(see index for correct answer)

- a. Proceedings of the International Association for Business and Society
- b. Anti-sweatshop movement
- c. Contingent work
- d. Sullivan principles

Guidance: level 1

:: ::

In ecology, a _____ is the type of natural environment in which a particular species of organism lives. It is characterized by both physical and biological features. A species' _____ is those places where it can find food, shelter, protection and mates for reproduction.

Exam Probability: **Medium**

37. *Answer choices:*
(see index for correct answer)

- a. functional perspective
- b. corporate values
- c. similarity-attraction theory
- d. Sarbanes-Oxley act of 2002

Guidance: level 1

:: Timber industry ::

The _____ is an international non-profit, multi-stakeholder organization established in 1993 to promote responsible management of the world's forests. The FSC does this by setting standards on forest products, along with certifying and labeling them as eco-friendly.

Exam Probability: **High**

38. *Answer choices:*
(see index for correct answer)

- a. Shingle weaver
- b. Lumber
- c. Lumber yard
- d. Firewood processor

Guidance: level 1

:: Criminal law ::

_____ is the body of law that relates to crime. It proscribes conduct perceived as threatening, harmful, or otherwise endangering to the property, health, safety, and moral welfare of people inclusive of one's self. Most _____ is established by statute, which is to say that the laws are enacted by a legislature. _____ includes the punishment and rehabilitation of people who violate such laws. _____ varies according to jurisdiction, and differs from civil law, where emphasis is more on dispute resolution and victim compensation, rather than on punishment or rehabilitation. Criminal procedure is a formalized official activity that authenticates the fact of commission of a crime and authorizes punitive or rehabilitative treatment of the offender.

Exam Probability: **Medium**

39. *Answer choices:*
(see index for correct answer)

- a. mitigating factor
- b. Criminal law
- c. Mala in se
- d. Self-incrimination

Guidance: level 1

:: Electronic waste ::

_____ or e-waste describes discarded electrical or electronic devices. Used electronics which are destined for refurbishment, reuse, resale, salvage, recycling through material recovery, or disposal are also considered e-waste. Informal processing of e-waste in developing countries can lead to adverse human health effects and environmental pollution.

Exam Probability: **Low**

40. *Answer choices:*

(see index for correct answer)

- a. Techreturns
- b. ReGlobe
- c. Computer liquidator
- d. Digger gold

Guidance: level 1

:: Private equity ::

In finance, a high-yield bond is a bond that is rated below investment grade. These bonds have a higher risk of default or other adverse credit events, but typically pay higher yields than better quality bonds in order to make them attractive to investors.

Exam Probability: **Low**

41. *Answer choices:*

(see index for correct answer)

- a. Management fee
- b. Airwide Solutions
- c. Angel investor
- d. Institutional Limited Partners Association

Guidance: level 1

:: ::

Oriental Nicety, formerly _____ , Exxon Mediterranean, SeaRiver Mediterranean, S/R Mediterranean, Mediterranean, and Dong Fang Ocean, was an oil tanker that gained notoriety after running aground in Prince William Sound spilling hundreds of thousands of barrels of crude oil in Alaska. On March 24, 1989, while owned by the former Exxon Shipping Company, and captained by Joseph Hazelwood and First Mate James Kunkel bound for Long Beach, California, the vessel ran aground on the Bligh Reef resulting in the second largest oil spill in United States history. The size of the spill is estimated to have been 40,900 to 120,000 m3 , or 257,000 to 750,000 barrels. In 1989, the _____ oil spill was listed as the 54th largest spill in history.

Exam Probability: **Medium**

42. *Answer choices:*
(see index for correct answer)

- a. Exxon Valdez
- b. hierarchical perspective
- c. imperative
- d. process perspective

Guidance: level 1

:: White-collar criminals ::

_____ refers to financially motivated, nonviolent crime committed by businesses and government professionals. It was first defined by the sociologist Edwin Sutherland in 1939 as "a crime committed by a person of respectability and high social status in the course of their occupation". Typical _____ s could include wage theft, fraud, bribery, Ponzi schemes, insider trading, labor racketeering, embezzlement, cybercrime, copyright infringement, money laundering, identity theft, and forgery. Lawyers can specialize in _____ .

Exam Probability: **Medium**

43. *Answer choices:*
(see index for correct answer)

- a. Tongsun Park
- b. Du Jun

Guidance: level 1

_____ , also known as reservation in India and Nepal, positive discrimination / action in the United Kingdom, and employment equity in Canada and South Africa, is the policy of promoting the education and employment of members of groups that are known to have previously suffered from discrimination. Historically and internationally, support for _____ has sought to achieve goals such as bridging inequalities in employment and pay, increasing access to education, promoting diversity, and redressing apparent past wrongs, harms, or hindrances.

Exam Probability: **Low**

44. *Answer choices:*
(see index for correct answer)

- a. cultural Relativism
- b. cultural dissonance
- c. Affirmative action

Guidance: level 1

_____ is a strategy for reducing the amount of waste created and released into the environment, particularly by industrial facilities, agriculture, or consumers. Many large corporations view P2 as a method of improving the efficiency and profitability of production processes by technology advancements. Legislative bodies have enacted P2 measures, such as the _____ Act of 1990 and the Clean Air Act Amendments of 1990 by the United States Congress.

Exam Probability: **Medium**

45. *Answer choices:*
(see index for correct answer)

- a. Regenerative design
- b. Design for the Environment
- c. Pollution Prevention
- d. Eco-costs value ratio

Guidance: level 1

The _____ of 1914 established the Federal Trade Commission. The Act, signed into law by Woodrow Wilson in 1914, outlaws unfair methods of competition and outlaws unfair acts or practices that affect commerce.

Exam Probability: **Low**

46. *Answer choices:*
(see index for correct answer)

- a. Federal Trade Commission Act
- b. Cuban Democracy Act
- c. Magnitsky Act
- d. Tariff of 1792

Guidance: level 1

:: ::

_____ Ltd. is the world's 2nd largest offshore drilling contractor and is based in Vernier, Switzerland. The company has offices in 20 countries, including Switzerland, Canada, United States, Norway, Scotland, India, Brazil, Singapore, Indonesia and Malaysia.

Exam Probability: **Low**

47. *Answer choices:*
(see index for correct answer)

- a. Transocean
- b. cultural
- c. Sarbanes-Oxley act of 2002
- d. interpersonal communication

Guidance: level 1

:: Cognitive biases ::

In personality psychology, _____ is the degree to which people believe that they have control over the outcome of events in their lives, as opposed to external forces beyond their control. Understanding of the concept was developed by Julian B. Rotter in 1954, and has since become an aspect of personality studies. A person's "locus" is conceptualized as internal or external .

Exam Probability: **Medium**

48. *Answer choices:*

(see index for correct answer)

- a. Ostrich effect
- b. Locus of control
- c. Publication bias
- d. Telescoping effect

Guidance: level 1

:: Social philosophy ::

The _____ describes the unintended social benefits of an individual's self-interested actions. Adam Smith first introduced the concept in The Theory of Moral Sentiments, written in 1759, invoking it in reference to income distribution. In this work, however, the idea of the market is not discussed, and the word "capitalism" is never used.

Exam Probability: **Medium**

49. *Answer choices:*

(see index for correct answer)

- a. vacancy chain
- b. Freedom to contract
- c. Invisible hand
- d. Societal attitudes towards abortion

Guidance: level 1

:: Data management ::

_____ is a form of intellectual property that grants the creator of an original creative work an exclusive legal right to determine whether and under what conditions this original work may be copied and used by others, usually for a limited term of years. The exclusive rights are not absolute but limited by limitations and exceptions to _____ law, including fair use. A major limitation on _____ on ideas is that _____ protects only the original expression of ideas, and not the underlying ideas themselves.

Exam Probability: **High**

50. *Answer choices:*
(see index for correct answer)

- a. Modular serializability
- b. CommVault Systems
- c. Copyright
- d. Data storage device

Guidance: level 1

:: Auditing ::

_____ , as defined by accounting and auditing, is a process for assuring of an organization's objectives in operational effectiveness and efficiency, reliable financial reporting, and compliance with laws, regulations and policies. A broad concept, _____ involves everything that controls risks to an organization.

Exam Probability: **High**

51. *Answer choices:*
(see index for correct answer)

- a. Chartered Institute of Internal Auditors
- b. OJD Morocco
- c. Internal control
- d. Auditing and Assurance Standards Board

Guidance: level 1

:: ::

The _____ , the Calvinist work ethic or the Puritan work ethic is a work ethic concept in theology, sociology, economics and history that emphasizes that hard work, discipline and frugality are a result of a person's subscription to the values espoused by the Protestant faith, particularly Calvinism. The phrase was initially coined in 1904–1905 by Max Weber in his book The Protestant Ethic and the Spirit of Capitalism.

Exam Probability: **Medium**

52. *Answer choices:*
(see index for correct answer)

- a. information systems assessment
- b. Protestant work ethic
- c. cultural
- d. corporate values

Guidance: level 1

:: United Kingdom labour law ::

The _____ was a series of programs, public work projects, financial reforms, and regulations enacted by President Franklin D. Roosevelt in the United States between 1933 and 1936. It responded to needs for relief, reform, and recovery from the Great Depression. Major federal programs included the Civilian Conservation Corps , the Civil Works Administration , the Farm Security Administration , the National Industrial Recovery Act of 1933 and the Social Security Administration . They provided support for farmers, the unemployed, youth and the elderly. The _____ included new constraints and safeguards on the banking industry and efforts to re-inflate the economy after prices had fallen sharply. _____ programs included both laws passed by Congress as well as presidential executive orders during the first term of the presidency of Franklin D. Roosevelt.

Exam Probability: **Low**

53. *Answer choices:*
(see index for correct answer)

- a. Coal Industry Commission Act 1919
- b. New Deal
- c. Truck Acts
- d. Collective laissez faire

:: Management ::

_____ is the identification, evaluation, and prioritization of risks followed by coordinated and economical application of resources to minimize, monitor, and control the probability or impact of unfortunate events or to maximize the realization of opportunities.

Exam Probability: **High**

54. *Answer choices:*
(see index for correct answer)

- a. Relevance paradox
- b. Public sector consulting
- c. Social business model
- d. Event chain diagram

:: Supply chain management terms ::

In business and finance, _____ is a system of organizations, people, activities, information, and resources involved inmoving a product or service from supplier to customer. _____ activities involve the transformation of natural resources, raw materials, and components into a finished product that is delivered to the end customer. In sophisticated _____ systems, used products may re-enter the _____ at any point where residual value is recyclable. _____ s link value chains.

Exam Probability: **High**

55. *Answer choices:*
(see index for correct answer)

- a. Will call
- b. Cool Chain Quality Indicator
- c. Direct shipment
- d. Capital spare

:: Human resource management ::

_____ is the ethics of an organization, and it is how an organization responds to an internal or external stimulus. _____ is interdependent with the organizational culture. Although it is akin to both organizational behavior and industrial and organizational psychology as well as business ethics on the micro and macro levels, _____ is neither OB or I/O psychology, nor is it solely business ethics . _____ express the values of an organization to its employees and/or other entities irrespective of governmental and/or regulatory laws.

Exam Probability: **Medium**

56. *Answer choices:*

- a. Enterprise architecture
- b. Skills management
- c. IDS HR in Practice
- d. Organizational ethics

Guidance: level 1

:: ::

A _____ is a proceeding by a party or parties against another in the civil court of law. The archaic term "suit in law" is found in only a small number of laws still in effect today. The term " _____ " is used in reference to a civil action brought in a court of law in which a plaintiff, a party who claims to have incurred loss as a result of a defendant's actions, demands a legal or equitable remedy. The defendant is required to respond to the plaintiff's complaint. If the plaintiff is successful, judgment is in the plaintiff's favor, and a variety of court orders may be issued to enforce a right, award damages, or impose a temporary or permanent injunction to prevent an act or compel an act. A declaratory judgment may be issued to prevent future legal disputes.

Exam Probability: **High**

57. *Answer choices:*

- a. Lawsuit
- b. cultural
- c. deep-level diversity

- d. hierarchical

:: Market-based policy instruments ::

Cause marketing is defined as a type of corporate social responsibility, in which a company's promotional campaign has the dual purpose of increasing profitability while bettering society.

Exam Probability: **Medium**

58. *Answer choices:*
(see index for correct answer)

- a. Fiscal localism
- b. Cobra effect
- c. Regional Clean Air Incentives Market
- d. Cause-related marketing

:: ::

_____ refers to a business initiative to increase the access between a company and their current and potential customers through the use of the Internet. The Internet allows the company to market themselves and attract new customers to their website where they can provide product information and better customer service. Customers can place orders electronically, therefore reducing expensive long distant phone calls and postage costs of placing orders, while saving time on behalf of the customer and company.

Exam Probability: **Low**

59. *Answer choices:*
(see index for correct answer)

- a. Global reach
- b. cultural
- c. similarity-attraction theory
- d. corporate values

Accounting

Accounting or accountancy is the measurement, processing, and communication of financial information about economic entities such as businesses and corporations. The modern field was established by the Italian mathematician Luca Pacioli in 1494. Accounting, which has been called the "language of business", measures the results of an organization's economic activities and conveys this information to a variety of users, including investors, creditors, management, and regulators.

:: Generally Accepted Accounting Principles ::

_____ is a small amount of discretionary funds in the form of cash used for expenditures where it is not sensible to make any disbursement by cheque, because of the inconvenience and costs of writing, signing, and then cashing the cheque.

Exam Probability: **High**

1. *Answer choices:*

(see index for correct answer)

- a. AICPA Statements of Position
- b. Indian Accounting Standards
- c. Generally Accepted Accounting Practice
- d. Net realizable value

Guidance: level 1

:: Business law ::

A _____ , also known as the sole trader, individual entrepreneurship or proprietorship, is a type of enterprise that is owned and run by one person and in which there is no legal distinction between the owner and the business entity. A sole trader does not necessarily work `alone`—it is possible for the sole trader to employ other people.

Exam Probability: **High**

2. *Answer choices:*
(see index for correct answer)

- a. Contract failure
- b. Sole proprietorship
- c. Consumer privacy
- d. Business courts

Guidance: level 1

:: Macroeconomics ::

_____ is a change in a price of a good or product, or especially of a currency, in which case it is specifically an official rise of the value of the currency in relation to a foreign currency in a fixed exchange rate system. Under floating exchange rates, by contrast, a rise in a currency's value is an appreciation. Altering the face value of a currency without changing its purchasing power is a redenomination, not a _____ .

Exam Probability: **Low**

3. *Answer choices:*
(see index for correct answer)

- a. Conference Board Leading Economic Index
- b. Rational expectations
- c. Depression
- d. Stockholm school

Guidance: level 1

:: Loans ::

In finance, a _____ is the lending of money by one or more individuals, organizations, or other entities to other individuals, organizations etc. The recipient incurs a debt, and is usually liable to pay interest on that debt until it is repaid, and also to repay the principal amount borrowed.

Exam Probability: **Medium**

4. *Answer choices:*

(see index for correct answer)

- a. Loan agreement
- b. Interest-only loan
- c. Installment loan
- d. Unpaid principal balance

Guidance: level 1

:: Finance ::

In accounting, _____ is the portion of a subsidiary corporation's stock that is not owned by the parent corporation. The magnitude of the _____ in the subsidiary company is generally less than 50% of outstanding shares, or the corporation would generally cease to be a subsidiary of the parent.

Exam Probability: **Medium**

5. *Answer choices:*

(see index for correct answer)

- a. Minority interest
- b. Cell Captive
- c. Portfolio optimization
- d. Treasury company

Guidance: level 1

:: Valuation (finance) ::

_____ refers to an assessment of the viability, stability, and profitability of a business, sub-business or project.

6. *Answer choices:*

- a. Member of the Appraisal Institute
- b. Financial analysis
- c. Appraisal Foundation
- d. Valuation using multiples

Guidance: level 1

:: Credit cards ::

The _____ Company, also known as Amex, is an American multinational financial services corporation headquartered in Three World Financial Center in New York City. The company was founded in 1850 and is one of the 30 components of the Dow Jones Industrial Average. The company is best known for its charge card, credit card, and traveler's cheque businesses.

7. *Answer choices:*

- a. Access
- b. American Express
- c. Negative database
- d. MPP Global Solutions

Guidance: level 1

:: Budgets ::

An _____ is the annual budget of an activity stated in terms of Budget Classification Code, functional/subfunctional categories and cost accounts. It contains estimates of the total value of resources required for the performance of the operation including reimbursable work or services for others. It also includes estimates of workload in terms of total work units identified by cost accounts.

8. *Answer choices:*

- a. Operating budget
- b. Budget set
- c. Budgeted cost of work scheduled
- d. Programme budgeting

Guidance: level 1

:: Legal terms ::

_____ or _____ interest, in law, is anything that functions contrary to a party's interest. This word should not be confused with averse.

Exam Probability: **Low**

9. *Answer choices:*
(see index for correct answer)

- a. Informed refusal
- b. Open verdict
- c. Adverse
- d. vacant possession

Guidance: level 1

:: Accounting source documents ::

A _____ or account statement is a summary of financial transactions which have occurred over a given period on a bank account held by a person or business with a financial institution.

Exam Probability: **High**

10. *Answer choices:*
(see index for correct answer)

- a. Bank statement
- b. Credit memorandum
- c. Banknote
- d. Superbill

Guidance: level 1

:: Commerce ::

A _____ , is a document acknowledging that a person has received money or property in payment following a sale or other transfer of goods or provision of a service. All _____ s must have the date of purchase on them. If the recipient of the payment is legally required to collect sales tax or VAT from the customer, the amount would be added to the _____ and the collection would be deemed to have been on behalf of the relevant tax authority. In many countries, a retailer is required to include the sales tax or VAT in the displayed price of goods sold, from which the tax amount would be calculated at point of sale and remitted to the tax authorities in due course. Similarly, amounts may be deducted from amounts payable, as in the case of wage withholding taxes. On the other hand, tips or other gratuities given by a customer, for example in a restaurant, would not form part of the payment amount or appear on the _____ .

Exam Probability: **Medium**

11. *Answer choices:*

(see index for correct answer)

- a. Receipt
- b. Group buying
- c. Gumball machine
- d. Hauls

Guidance: level 1

:: Accounting journals and ledgers ::

The subledger, or _____ , provides details behind entries in the general ledger used in accounting. The subledger shows detail for part of the accounting records such as property and equipment, prepaid expenses, etc. The detail would include such items as date the item was purchased or expense incurred, a description of the item, the original balance, and the net book value. The total of the subledger would match the line item amount on the general ledger. This corresponding line item in the general ledger is referred to as the controlling account. The _____ balance is compared with its controlling account balance as part of the process of preparing a trial balance.

Exam Probability: **High**

12. *Answer choices:*

- a. Cash receipts journal
- b. Subledger
- c. General journal
- d. Sales journal

Guidance: level 1

:: Generally Accepted Accounting Principles ::

_____ , or non-current liabilities, are liabilities that are due beyond a year or the normal operation period of the company. The normal operation period is the amount of time it takes for a company to turn inventory into cash. On a classified balance sheet, liabilities are separated between current and _____ to help users assess the company's financial standing in short-term and long-term periods. _____ give users more information about the long-term prosperity of the company, while current liabilities inform the user of debt that the company owes in the current period. On a balance sheet, accounts are listed in order of liquidity, so _____ come after current liabilities. In addition, the specific long-term liability accounts are listed on the balance sheet in order of liquidity. Therefore, an account due within eighteen months would be listed before an account due within twenty-four months. Examples of _____ are bonds payable, long-term loans, capital leases, pension liabilities, post-retirement healthcare liabilities, deferred compensation, deferred revenues, deferred income taxes, and derivative liabilities.

Exam Probability: **Medium**

13. *Answer choices:*

- a. Deferred income
- b. Standard Business Reporting
- c. Normal balance
- d. Long-term liabilities

Guidance: level 1

:: ::

An _____ , for United States federal income tax, is a closely held corporation that makes a valid election to be taxed under Subchapter S of Chapter 1 of the Internal Revenue Code. In general, _____ s do not pay any income taxes. Instead, the corporation's income or losses are divided among and passed through to its shareholders. The shareholders must then report the income or loss on their own individual income tax returns.

Exam Probability: **Medium**

14. *Answer choices:*
(see index for correct answer)

- a. open system
- b. S corporation
- c. empathy
- d. functional perspective

Guidance: level 1

:: Accounting terminology ::

_____ or capital expense is the money a company spends to buy, maintain, or improve its fixed assets, such as buildings, vehicles, equipment, or land. It is considered a _____ when the asset is newly purchased or when money is used towards extending the useful life of an existing asset, such as repairing the roof.

Exam Probability: **Medium**

15. *Answer choices:*
(see index for correct answer)

- a. Capital expenditure
- b. Accounting equation
- c. Accrued liabilities
- d. Absorption costing

Guidance: level 1

:: Management accounting ::

In economics, _____ s, indirect costs or overheads are business expenses that are not dependent on the level of goods or services produced by the business. They tend to be time-related, such as interest or rents being paid per month, and are often referred to as overhead costs. This is in contrast to variable costs, which are volume-related and unknown at the beginning of the accounting year. For a simple example, such as a bakery, the monthly rent for the baking facilities, and the monthly payments for the security system and basic phone line are _____ s, as they do not change according to how much bread the bakery produces and sells. On the other hand, the wage costs of the bakery are variable, as the bakery will have to hire more workers if the production of bread increases. Economists reckon _____ as a entry barrier for new entrepreneurs.

Exam Probability: **High**

16. *Answer choices:*

- a. Management accounting in supply chains
- b. Fixed cost
- c. Dual overhead rate
- d. Double counting

Guidance: level 1

:: Marketing ::

_____ or stock is the goods and materials that a business holds for the ultimate goal of resale .

Exam Probability: **Medium**

17. *Answer choices:*

- a. Chaotics
- b. Field marketing
- c. Postmodern branding
- d. Inventory

Guidance: level 1

:: Financial accounting ::

In macroeconomics and international finance, the _____ is one of two primary components of the balance of payments, the other being the current account. Whereas the current account reflects a nation's net income, the _____ reflects net change in ownership of national assets.

18. *Answer choices:*
(see index for correct answer)

- a. Capital account
- b. Financial Condition Report
- c. Valuation
- d. Holding gains

Guidance: level 1

:: Investment ::

In economics, _____ is spending which increases the availability of fixed capital goods or means of production and goods inventories. It is the total spending on newly produced physical capital and on inventories —that is, gross investment—minus replacement investment, which simply replaces depreciated capital goods. It is productive capital formation plus net additions to the stock of housing and the stock of inventories.

19. *Answer choices:*
(see index for correct answer)

- a. Guaranteed investment contract
- b. Net investment
- c. Shock absorber fee
- d. Qirad

Guidance: level 1

:: Generally Accepted Accounting Principles ::

_____ is, in accrual accounting, money received for goods or services which have not yet been delivered. According to the revenue recognition principle, it is recorded as a liability until delivery is made, at which time it is converted into revenue.

20. *Answer choices:*
(see index for correct answer)

- a. Treasury stock
- b. Historical cost
- c. Deferred income
- d. Gross profit

Guidance: level 1

:: ::

_____ is the field of accounting concerned with the summary, analysis and reporting of financial transactions related to a business. This involves the preparation of financial statements available for public use. Stockholders, suppliers, banks, employees, government agencies, business owners, and other stakeholders are examples of people interested in receiving such information for decision making purposes.

21. *Answer choices:*
(see index for correct answer)

- a. similarity-attraction theory
- b. Financial accounting
- c. interpersonal communication
- d. corporate values

Guidance: level 1

:: ::

Accounts _____ is a legally enforceable claim for payment held by a business for goods supplied and/or services rendered that customers/clients have ordered but not paid for. These are generally in the form of invoices raised by a business and delivered to the customer for payment within an agreed time frame. Accounts _____ is shown in a balance sheet as an asset. It is one of a series of accounting transactions dealing with the billing of a customer for goods and services that the customer has ordered. These may be distinguished from notes _____ , which are debts created through formal legal instruments called promissory notes.

Exam Probability: **High**

22. *Answer choices:*
(see index for correct answer)

- a. empathy
- b. hierarchical perspective
- c. functional perspective
- d. open system

Guidance: level 1

:: ::

_____ is a process whereby a person assumes the parenting of another, usually a child, from that person's biological or legal parent or parents. Legal _____ s permanently transfers all rights and responsibilities, along with filiation, from the biological parent or parents.

Exam Probability: **High**

23. *Answer choices:*
(see index for correct answer)

- a. Adoption
- b. deep-level diversity
- c. co-culture
- d. levels of analysis

Guidance: level 1

:: Real property law ::

A _____ or millage rate is an ad valorem tax on the value of a property, usually levied on real estate. The tax is levied by the governing authority of the jurisdiction in which the property is located. This can be a national government, a federated state, a county or geographical region or a municipality. Multiple jurisdictions may tax the same property. This tax can be contrasted to a rent tax which is based on rental income or imputed rent, and a land value tax, which is a levy on the value of land, excluding the value of buildings and other improvements.

Exam Probability: **Low**

24. *Answer choices:*
(see index for correct answer)

- a. Disseisor
- b. Good guy clause
- c. Property tax
- d. Atrisco Land Grant

Guidance: level 1

:: Accounting in the United States ::

The _____ was formed by the American Institute of Certified Public Accountants in 1972, and developed the Objective of Financial Statements. The committee's goal was to create financial statements that helped external users make decisions about the economics of companies. In 1978, the Financial Accounting Standards Board , whose purpose is to develop generally accepted accounting principles, adopted the key objectives established by the _____

.

Exam Probability: **Medium**

25. *Answer choices:*
(see index for correct answer)

- a. Institute of Internal Auditors
- b. Trueblood Committee
- c. Cotton Plantation Record and Account Book
- d. Governmental Accounting Standards Board

Guidance: level 1

:: Information systems ::

An accounting as an information system is a system of collecting, storing and processing financial and accounting data that are used by decision makers. An _____ is generally a computer-based method for tracking accounting activity in conjunction with information technology resources. The resulting financial reports can be used internally by management or externally by other interested parties including investors, creditors and tax authorities.

_____ s are designed to support all accounting functions and activities including auditing, financial accounting & reporting, managerial/ management accounting and tax. The most widely adopted accounting information systems are auditing and financial reporting modules.

Exam Probability: **High**

26. *Answer choices:*
(see index for correct answer)

- a. Joint Regional Information Exchange System
- b. Strategic information system
- c. Accounting information system
- d. Censhare

Guidance: level 1

:: Management accounting ::

_____ are costs that are not directly accountable to a cost object . _____ may be either fixed or variable. _____ include administration, personnel and security costs. These are those costs which are not directly related to production. Some _____ may be overhead. But some overhead costs can be directly attributed to a project and are direct costs.

Exam Probability: **Medium**

27. *Answer choices:*
(see index for correct answer)

- a. Dual overhead rate
- b. Extended cost
- c. Indirect costs
- d. Corporate travel management

Guidance: level 1

A _____ is a tax paid to a governing body for the sales of certain goods and services. Usually laws allow the seller to collect funds for the tax from the consumer at the point of purchase. When a tax on goods or services is paid to a governing body directly by a consumer, it is usually called a use tax. Often laws provide for the exemption of certain goods or services from sales and use tax.

Exam Probability: **High**

28. *Answer choices:*
(see index for correct answer)

- a. Sales tax
- b. empathy
- c. hierarchical
- d. Character

Guidance: level 1

:: Money ::

In economics, _____ is money in the physical form of currency, such as banknotes and coins. In bookkeeping and finance, _____ is current assets comprising currency or currency equivalents that can be accessed immediately or near-immediately . _____ is seen either as a reserve for payments, in case of a structural or incidental negative _____ flow or as a way to avoid a downturn on financial markets.

Exam Probability: **Low**

29. *Answer choices:*
(see index for correct answer)

- a. The Death of Money
- b. Plutus
- c. Key money
- d. Nominal money

Guidance: level 1

:: Password authentication ::

A _____ , or sometimes redundantly a PIN number, is a numeric or alpha-numeric password used in the process of authenticating a user accessing a system.

30. *Answer choices:*
(see index for correct answer)

- a. Microsoft Office password protection
- b. Default password
- c. PBKDF2
- d. Personal identification number

Guidance: level 1

:: Insurance terms ::

A _____ in the broadest sense is a natural person or other legal entity who receives money or other benefits from a benefactor. For example, the _____ of a life insurance policy is the person who receives the payment of the amount of insurance after the death of the insured.

31. *Answer choices:*
(see index for correct answer)

- a. Certified Insurance Counselor
- b. Self-revelation
- c. Bankassurer
- d. Contingent commissions

Guidance: level 1

:: United States Generally Accepted Accounting Principles ::

A _____ is a set of U.S. government financial statements comprising the financial report of a state, municipal or other governmental entity that complies with the accounting requirements promulgated by the Governmental Accounting Standards Board . GASB provides standards for the content of a CAFR in its annually updated publication Codification of Governmental Accounting and Financial Reporting Standards. The U.S. Federal Government adheres to standards determined by the Federal Accounting Standards Advisory Board .

Exam Probability: **Low**

32. *Answer choices:*
(see index for correct answer)

- a. Working Group on Financial Markets
- b. Cost segregation study
- c. Comprehensive annual financial report
- d. Permanent fund

Guidance: level 1

:: Accounting terminology ::

Accounts are typically defined by an identifier and a caption or header and are coded by account type. In computerized accounting systems with computable quantity accounting, the accounts can have a quantity measure definition.

Exam Probability: **Low**

33. *Answer choices:*
(see index for correct answer)

- a. Double-entry accounting
- b. Account
- c. Chart of accounts
- d. Internal auditing

Guidance: level 1

:: Commerce ::

Continuation of an entity as a _____ is presumed as the basis for financial reporting unless and until the entity`s liquidation becomes imminent. Preparation of financial statements under this presumption is commonly referred to as the _____ basis of accounting. If and when an entity`s liquidation becomes imminent, financial statements are prepared under the liquidation basis of accounting .

Exam Probability: **High**

34. *Answer choices:*
(see index for correct answer)

- a. Closed household economy
- b. Dumping
- c. Haul video
- d. Trade credit

Guidance: level 1

:: Accounting terminology ::

_____ of something is, in finance, the adding together of interest or different investments over a period of time. It holds specific meanings in accounting, where it can refer to accounts on a balance sheet that represent liabilities and non-cash-based assets used in _____ -based accounting. These types of accounts include, among others, accounts payable, accounts receivable, goodwill, deferred tax liability and future interest expense.

Exam Probability: **High**

35. *Answer choices:*
(see index for correct answer)

- a. Accounts payable
- b. Impairment cost
- c. Record to report
- d. Statement of financial position

Guidance: level 1

:: Management accounting ::

_____ is an accountancy practice, the aim of which is to provide an offset to the mark-to-market movement of the derivative in the profit and loss account. There are two types of hedge recognized. For a fair value hedge the offset is achieved either by marking-to-market an asset or a liability which offsets the P&L movement of the derivative. For a cash flow hedge some of the derivative volatility into a separate component of the entity's equity called the cash flow hedge reserve. Where a hedge relationship is effective , most of the mark-to-market derivative volatility will be offset in the profit and loss account. _____ entails much compliance - involving documenting the hedge relationship and both prospectively and retrospectively proving that the hedge relationship is effective.

36. *Answer choices:*
(see index for correct answer)

- a. Standard cost
- b. Fixed cost
- c. Hedge accounting
- d. activity based costing

Guidance: level 1

:: ::

_____ is the process of making predictions of the future based on past and present data and most commonly by analysis of trends. A commonplace example might be estimation of some variable of interest at some specified future date. Prediction is a similar, but more general term. Both might refer to formal statistical methods employing time series, cross-sectional or longitudinal data, or alternatively to less formal judgmental methods. Usage can differ between areas of application: for example, in hydrology the terms "forecast" and "_____" are sometimes reserved for estimates of values at certain specific future times, while the term "prediction" is used for more general estimates, such as the number of times floods will occur over a long period.

37. *Answer choices:*
(see index for correct answer)

- a. deep-level diversity
- b. Sarbanes-Oxley act of 2002
- c. interpersonal communication
- d. Forecasting

Guidance: level 1

:: ::

A _____ is a form of public administration which, in a majority of contexts, exists as the lowest tier of administration within a given state. The term is used to contrast with offices at state level, which are referred to as the central government, national government, or federal government and also to supranational government which deals with governing institutions between states. _____ s generally act within powers delegated to them by legislation or directives of the higher level of government. In federal states, _____ generally comprises the third tier of government, whereas in unitary states, _____ usually occupies the second or third tier of government, often with greater powers than higher-level administrative divisions.

Exam Probability: **Medium**

38. *Answer choices:*
(see index for correct answer)

- a. Local government
- b. similarity-attraction theory
- c. open system
- d. co-culture

Guidance: level 1

:: Finance ::

_____ is a notional asset or liability to reflect corporate income taxation on a basis that is the same or more similar to recognition of profits than the taxation treatment. _____ liabilities can arise as a result of corporate taxation treatment of capital expenditure being more rapid than the accounting depreciation treatment. _____ assets can arise due to net loss carry-overs, which are only recorded as asset if it is deemed more likely than not that the asset will be used in future fiscal periods. Different countries may also allow or require discounting of the assets or particularly liabilities. There are often disclosure requirements for potential liabilities and assets that are not actually recognised as an asset or liability.

Exam Probability: **Low**

39. *Answer choices:*
(see index for correct answer)

- a. Probability of default
- b. Deferred tax
- c. Creative industries
- d. Qontis

Guidance: level 1

:: Payment systems ::

An _____ is an electronic telecommunications device that enables customers of financial institutions to perform financial transactions, such as cash withdrawals, deposits, transfer funds, or obtaining account information, at any time and without the need for direct interaction with bank staff.

Exam Probability: **Low**

40. *Answer choices:*
(see index for correct answer)

- a. MM code
- b. Debit card cashback
- c. Interac
- d. Amazon Payments

Guidance: level 1

:: Accounting terminology ::

In accounting/accountancy, _____ are journal entries usually made at the end of an accounting period to allocate income and expenditure to the period in which they actually occurred. The revenue recognition principle is the basis of making _____ that pertain to unearned and accrued revenues under accrual-basis accounting. They are sometimes called Balance Day adjustments because they are made on balance day.

Exam Probability: **High**

41. *Answer choices:*
(see index for correct answer)

- a. Basis of accounting
- b. Account
- c. Record to report
- d. Mark-to-market

Guidance: level 1

:: Investment ::

In finance, the benefit from an _____ is called a return. The return may consist of a gain realised from the sale of property or an _____, unrealised capital appreciation, or _____ income such as dividends, interest, rental income etc., or a combination of capital gain and income. The return may also include currency gains or losses due to changes in foreign currency exchange rates.

Exam Probability: **Medium**

42. *Answer choices:*
(see index for correct answer)

- a. Investment
- b. Active management
- c. CAN SLIM
- d. Asian option

Guidance: level 1

:: Types of business entity ::

A _____ is a partnership in which some or all partners have limited liabilities. It therefore can exhibit elements of partnerships and corporations. In a LLP, each partner is not responsible or liable for another partner's misconduct or negligence. This is an important difference from the traditional partnership under the UK Partnership Act 1890, in which each partner has joint and several liability. In a LLP, some or all partners have a form of limited liability similar to that of the shareholders of a corporation. Unlike corporate shareholders, the partners have the right to manage the business directly. In contrast, corporate shareholders must elect a board of directors under the laws of various state charters. The board organizes itself and hires corporate officers who then have as "corporate" individuals the legal responsibility to manage the corporation in the corporation's best interest. A LLP also contains a different level of tax liability from that of a corporation.

Exam Probability: **High**

43. *Answer choices:*
(see index for correct answer)

- a. Numbered company
- b. Limited liability partnership
- c. Sole proprietor
- d. Hidden champions

Guidance: level 1

:: Taxation ::

A _____ is a person or organization subject to pay a tax. _____ s have an Identification Number, a reference number issued by a government to its citizens.

Exam Probability: **Medium**

44. *Answer choices:*
(see index for correct answer)

- a. Taxpayer
- b. Hotchpot
- c. Virtual tax
- d. Directorate-General for Taxation and Customs Union

Guidance: level 1

An _____ is a comprehensive report on a company's activities throughout the preceding year. _____ s are intended to give shareholders and other interested people information about the company's activities and financial performance. They may be considered as grey literature. Most jurisdictions require companies to prepare and disclose _____ s, and many require the _____ to be filed at the company's registry. Companies listed on a stock exchange are also required to report at more frequent intervals .

Exam Probability: **Medium**

45. *Answer choices:*
(see index for correct answer)

- a. corporate values
- b. Annual report
- c. levels of analysis
- d. co-culture

Guidance: level 1

:: Accounting software ::

_____ is a freely available and global framework for exchanging business information. _____ allows the expression of semantic meaning commonly required in business reporting. The language is XML-based and uses the XML syntax and related XML technologies such as XML Schema, XLink, XPath, and Namespaces. One use of _____ is to define and exchange financial information, such as a financial statement. The _____ Specification is developed and published by _____ International, Inc. .

Exam Probability: **Medium**

46. *Answer choices:*
(see index for correct answer)

- a. NewViews
- b. Cheqbook
- c. Unit4
- d. Sage 50 Accounting

Guidance: level 1

:: Real estate ::

An _____ is to, interest in, or legal liability on real property that does not prohibit passing title to the property but that may diminish its value. _____ s can be classified in several ways. They may be financial or non-financial . Alternatively, they may be divided into those that affect title or those that affect the use or physical condition of the encumbered property . _____ s include security interests, liens, servitudes , leases, restrictions, encroachments, and air and subsurface rights. Also, those considered as potentially making the title defeasible are _____ s, for example, charging orders, building orders and structure alteration. _____ : charge upon or claim against land arising out of private grant or a contract.

Exam Probability: **High**

47. *Answer choices:*
(see index for correct answer)

- a. Dockominium
- b. Land agent
- c. Encumbrance
- d. Originating application

Guidance: level 1

:: Supply chain management terms ::

In business and finance, _____ is a system of organizations, people, activities, information, and resources involved inmoving a product or service from supplier to customer. _____ activities involve the transformation of natural resources, raw materials, and components into a finished product that is delivered to the end customer. In sophisticated _____ systems, used products may re-enter the _____ at any point where residual value is recyclable. _____ s link value chains.

Exam Probability: **Medium**

48. *Answer choices:*
(see index for correct answer)

- a. Cool Chain Quality Indicator
- b. Stockout
- c. Supply chain
- d. Price look-up code

:: Generally Accepted Accounting Principles ::

Expenditure is an outflow of money to another person or group to pay for an item or service, or for a category of costs. For a tenant, rent is an _____ . For students or parents, tuition is an _____ . Buying food, clothing, furniture or an automobile is often referred to as an _____ . An _____ is a cost that is "paid" or "remitted", usually in exchange for something of value. Something that seems to cost a great deal is "expensive". Something that seems to cost little is "inexpensive". " _____ s of the table" are _____ s of dining, refreshments, a feast, etc.

Exam Probability: **Low**

49. *Answer choices:*
(see index for correct answer)

- a. Deferral
- b. Net realizable value
- c. Expense
- d. Cost pool

:: Accounting source documents ::

An _____ , bill or tab is a commercial document issued by a seller to a buyer, relating to a sale transaction and indicating the products, quantities, and agreed prices for products or services the seller had provided the buyer.

Exam Probability: **Low**

50. *Answer choices:*
(see index for correct answer)

- a. Parcel audit
- b. Credit memorandum
- c. Superbill
- d. Purchase order

:: International taxation ::

A _____ tax, or a retention tax, is an income tax to be paid to the government by the payer of the income rather than by the recipient of the income. The tax is thus withheld or deducted from the income due to the recipient. In most jurisdictions, _____ tax applies to employment income. Many jurisdictions also require _____ tax on payments of interest or dividends. In most jurisdictions, there are additional _____ tax obligations if the recipient of the income is resident in a different jurisdiction, and in those circumstances _____ tax sometimes applies to royalties, rent or even the sale of real estate. Governments use _____ tax as a means to combat tax evasion, and sometimes impose additional _____ tax requirements if the recipient has been delinquent in filing tax returns, or in industries where tax evasion is perceived to be common.

51. *Answer choices:*
(see index for correct answer)

- a. Expatriation tax
- b. Euromod
- c. Arm's-length transaction
- d. Withholding

Guidance: level 1

:: Options (finance) ::

A _____ bond is a type of bond that allows the issuer of the bond to retain the privilege of redeeming the bond at some point before the bond reaches its date of maturity. In other words, on the call date, the issuer has the right, but not the obligation, to buy back the bonds from the bond holders at a defined call price. Technically speaking, the bonds are not really bought and held by the issuer but are instead cancelled immediately.

52. *Answer choices:*
(see index for correct answer)

- a. LEAPS
- b. Cash or share option
- c. Mountain range
- d. Covered call

:: Generally Accepted Accounting Principles ::

A _____ or reacquired stock is stock which is bought back by the issuing company, reducing the amount of outstanding stock on the open market .

Exam Probability: **Medium**

53. *Answer choices:*
(see index for correct answer)

- a. Historical cost
- b. Statement of recommended practice
- c. Vendor-specific objective evidence
- d. Treasury stock

:: ::

A _____ is an entity that owes a debt to another entity. The entity may be an individual, a firm, a government, a company or other legal person. The counterparty is called a creditor. When the counterpart of this debt arrangement is a bank, the _____ is more often referred to as a borrower.

Exam Probability: **Low**

54. *Answer choices:*
(see index for correct answer)

- a. similarity-attraction theory
- b. levels of analysis
- c. hierarchical perspective
- d. Debtor

:: Management accounting ::

In finance, the _____ or net present worth applies to a series of cash flows occurring at different times. The present value of a cash flow depends on the interval of time between now and the cash flow. It also depends on the discount rate. NPV accounts for the time value of money. It provides a method for evaluating and comparing capital projects or financial products with cash flows spread over time, as in loans, investments, payouts from insurance contracts plus many other applications.

55. *Answer choices:*

(see index for correct answer)

- a. Backflush accounting
- b. Institute of Certified Management Accountants
- c. Extended cost
- d. Variable cost

Guidance: level 1

:: Stock market ::

A _____ , securities exchange or bourse, is a facility where stock brokers and traders can buy and sell securities, such as shares of stock and bonds and other financial instruments. _____ s may also provide for facilities the issue and redemption of such securities and instruments and capital events including the payment of income and dividends. Securities traded on a _____ include stock issued by listed companies, unit trusts, derivatives, pooled investment products and bonds. _____ s often function as "continuous auction" markets with buyers and sellers consummating transactions via open outcry at a central location such as the floor of the exchange or by using an electronic trading platform.

56. *Answer choices:*

(see index for correct answer)

- a. Stock Exchange
- b. Paper valuation
- c. Immediate or cancel
- d. Stock certificate

Guidance: level 1

A _____ is a payment made by a corporation to its shareholders, usually as a distribution of profits. When a corporation earns a profit or surplus, the corporation is able to re-invest the profit in the business and pay a proportion of the profit as a _____ to shareholders. Distribution to shareholders may be in cash or, if the corporation has a _____ reinvestment plan, the amount can be paid by the issue of further shares or share repurchase. When _____ s are paid, shareholders typically must pay income taxes, and the corporation does not receive a corporate income tax deduction for the _____ payments.

Exam Probability: **High**

57. *Answer choices:*
(see index for correct answer)

- a. Poison pill
- b. Dividend
- c. Stock dilution
- d. Shareholder Rights Directive

Guidance: level 1

In production, research, retail, and accounting, a _____ is the value of money that has been used up to produce something or deliver a service, and hence is not available for use anymore. In business, the _____ may be one of acquisition, in which case the amount of money expended to acquire it is counted as _____ . In this case, money is the input that is gone in order to acquire the thing. This acquisition _____ may be the sum of the _____ of production as incurred by the original producer, and further _____ s of transaction as incurred by the acquirer over and above the price paid to the producer. Usually, the price also includes a mark-up for profit over the _____ of production.

Exam Probability: **High**

58. *Answer choices:*
(see index for correct answer)

- a. deep-level diversity
- b. levels of analysis
- c. Character
- d. Cost

Guidance: level 1

:: Basic financial concepts ::

_____ is a sustained increase in the general price level of goods and services in an economy over a period of time. When the general price level rises, each unit of currency buys fewer goods and services; consequently, _____ reflects a reduction in the purchasing power per unit of money a loss of real value in the medium of exchange and unit of account within the economy. The measure of _____ is the _____ rate, the annualized percentage change in a general price index, usually the consumer price index, over time. The opposite of _____ is deflation.

Exam Probability: **Low**

59. *Answer choices:*
(see index for correct answer)

- a. Future-oriented
- b. Leverage cycle
- c. Base effect
- d. Inflation

Guidance: level 1

INDEX: Correct Answers

Foundations of Business

1. b: Image

2. : Utility

3. a: Balance sheet

4. c: Organizational culture

5. c: Money

6. b: Perception

7. b: Description

8. b: Supply chain

9. a: Recession

10. d: Procurement

11. c: Cooperative

12. c: Economic growth

13. : Arthur Andersen

14. d: Free trade

15. d: Patent

16. b: Purchasing

17. d: Information technology

18. c: Fixed cost

19. c: Preference

20. : Technology

21. c: Training

22. b: Property

23. b: Law

24. d: Capital market

25. c: American Express

26. : Insurance

27. b: Career

28. d: E-commerce

29. c: Restructuring

30. b: Decision-making

31. d: Political risk

32. c: Advertising

33. a: Office

34. : Strategic alliance

35. c: Entrepreneur

36. c: Resource management

37. b: Income statement

38. : Opportunity cost

39. b: Logistics

40. : Security

41. b: Comparative advantage

42. : Tool

43. b: Good

44. : Dividend

45. b: Regulation

46. a: Number

47. c: Bribery

48. : Protection

49. c: Selling

50. c: Management

51. a: Explanation

52. a: Demand

53. c: Tariff

54. : Sexual harassment

55. d: Competitive advantage

56. a: Revenue

57. b: Alliance

58. : Social security

59. d: Project management

Management

1. : Justice

2. : Business plan

3. c: Bottom line

4. d: Interaction

5. c: Human resources

6. d: Best practice

7. b: Organization chart

8. d: Raw material

9. : Expert

10. b: Balanced scorecard

11. b: Subsidiary

12. b: Brainstorming

13. c: Control chart

14. a: Competitive advantage

15. d: Human resource management

16. : Cross-functional team

17. d: Sexual harassment

18. b: SWOT analysis

19. c: Process control

20. b: Continuous improvement

21. a: Training and development

22. a: Leadership style

23. : Time management

24. a: Information

25. d: Scientific management

26. b: Chief executive

27. b: Environmental protection

28. c: Business process

29. b: Standardization

30. c: Grievance

31. : Interview

32. b: Collaboration

33. c: Compromise

34. a: Intellectual property

35. d: Scheduling

36. b: Overtime

37. b: Proactive

38. d: Training

39. : Statistical process control

40. b: Description

41. b: Warehouse

42. b: Dilemma

43. a: Enabling

44. c: Synergy

45. a: Glass ceiling

46. : Senior management

47. a: Crisis

48. b: Small business

49. b: Kaizen

50. d: Industry

51. b: Wage

52. b: Industrial Revolution

53. c: Checklist

54. b: Job design

55. c: Mission statement

56. d: Intranet

57. d: Strategy

58. d: Myers-Briggs type

59. a: Reinforcement

Business law

1. b: Clayton Act

2. : Insider trading

3. d: Perfection

4. a: Insurable interest

5. b: Lanham Act

6. : Voidable contract

7. c: Impossibility

8. c: Assumption of risk

9. c: Competitor

10. : Duty

11. c: Delegation

12. a: Anticipatory repudiation

13. c: Utility

14. d: Employment law

15. d: Trade

16. : Federal Trade Commission

17. : Accounting

18. : Estoppel

19. c: Foreign Corrupt Practices Act

20. b: Verdict

21. d: Administrative law

22. a: Petition

23. : Enron

24. : Board of directors

25. c: Indictment

26. b: Rescind

27. d: Merger

28. c: Assignee

29. d: Disclaimer

30. d: Affidavit

31. a: Consumer Good

32. d: Environmental Protection

33. a: Personal property

34. d: Supreme Court

35. d: Commerce Clause

36. : Consumer protection

37. a: Mens rea

38. a: Precedent

39. : Partnership

40. : Public policy

41. : Apparent authority

42. a: Inventory

43. c: Cause of action

44. d: Offeror

45. b: Categorical imperative

46. b: Real property

47. d: Revocation

48. c: Free trade

49. c: Antitrust

50. c: Subsidiary

51. a: Rehabilitation Act

52. a: Buyer

53. : Policy

54. c: Wage

55. a: Treaty

56. c: Executory contract

57. c: Tort

58. c: Trial

59. d: Accord and satisfaction

Finance

1. : Compounding

2. b: Pension fund

3. b: Forecasting

4. : Interest

5. b: Future value

6. c: Capital market

7. d: Asset management

8. d: Annuity

9. c: S corporation

10. d: Bank of America

11. d: Debit card

12. : Advertising

13. c: Monte Carlo

14. : Interest expense

15. a: Presentation

16. a: Choice

17. d: Debt-to-equity ratio

18. : Adjusting entries

19. d: Stock split

20. a: Property

21. c: Board of directors

22. c: Accrued interest

23. a: Tax expense

24. d: Cash flow

25. a: Cost object

26. c: Wall Street

27. a: Policy

28. a: Need

29. d: Capital expenditure

30. c: Financial management

31. d: Financial analysis

32. b: Financial instrument

33. a: Bank statement

34. a: Maturity date

35. : Going concern

36. c: Cost accounting

37. b: Treasury stock

38. c: Firm

39. a: Perpetual inventory

40. b: Finished good

41. d: Trade

42. d: Retained earnings

43. : Internal Revenue Service

44. a: Double taxation

45. : Management accounting

46. d: Marketing

47. c: Cost of goods sold

48. b: Technology

49. b: Ending inventory

50. c: Dividend yield

51. a: Mortgage

52. d: Chart of accounts

53. c: Debt ratio

54. d: Mutual fund

55. b: Capital stock

56. d: Factory

57. c: Liquidation

58. : Currency

59. : Arbitrage

Human resource management

1. c: Strategic planning

2. c: Offshoring

3. c: Enforcement

4. : Best practice

5. : National Labor Relations Act

6. a: Onboarding

7. c: Prevailing wage

8. a: Compa-ratio

9. a: Family violence

10. c: Emotional intelligence

11. a: National Institute for Occupational Safety and Health

12. c: Social media

13. d: Centralization

14. a: Social contract

15. c: Applicant tracking system

16. d: Human resource management

17. : Criterion validity

18. a: Fair Labor Standards Act

19. b: Control group

20. a: Intuition

21. d: Human resources

22. c: Social network

23. b: Interview

24. c: Job description

25. c: Mining

26. c: Background check

27. b: Seniority

28. b: Impression management

29. c: Glass ceiling

30. b: Goal setting

31. d: Discipline

32. b: Job security

33. : Task force

34. b: Skill

35. c: E-learning

36. d: Assessment center

37. b: Closed shop

38. d: Equal Employment Opportunity Commission

39. c: Talent management

40. a: Faragher v. City of Boca Raton

41. d: Needs assessment

42. : Survey research

43. a: Psychological contract

44. d: Job rotation

45. c: Person Analysis

46. b: Conformity

47. d: Alcoholism

48. c: Intellectual capital

49. a: E-HRM

50. c: Eustress

51. c: Evidence-based

52. c: Executive officer

53. a: Performance measurement

54. c: Physician

55. d: Executive search

56. d: Severance package

57. c: Open shop

58. b: Work ethic

59. : Employee retention

Information systems

1. : Data mart

2. c: Input device

3. c: Top-level domain

4. b: Read-only memory

5. d: Geocoding

6. b: Intranet

7. d: QR code

8. a: Facebook

9. : Consumer-to-business

10. : Metadata

11. b: Star

12. b: Business intelligence

13. d: Backup

14. c: Virtual reality

15. a: Yelp

16. c: System

17. b: Worm

18. d: Innovation

19. a: Payment card

20. a: Porter five forces analysis

21. a: Flash memory

22. c: Web page

23. : Disintermediation

24. : Google

25. a: Census

26. a: Data link

27. b: Second Life

28. c: Interaction

29. b: Gmail

30. a: Information ethics

31. b: Competitive advantage

32. b: Click fraud

33. b: Semantic Web

34. c: Database management system

35. c: Crowdsourcing

36. : Online analytical processing

37. d: Collision

38. : Data redundancy

39. : Master data management

40. : Dashboard

41. d: Strategic planning

42. c: Blogger

43. d: Fraud

44. d: Data analysis

45. d: PayPal

46. : Resource management

47. c: Business rule

48. d: Decision support system

49. b: Drill down

50. d: Online advertising

51. : Information flow

52. a: Cookie

53. b: Information systems

54. d: ITunes

55. c: Property

56. d: Computer-integrated manufacturing

57. c: Identity theft

58. b: Supplier relationship management

59. a: Netscape

Marketing

1. : Interview

2. : Retailing

3. a: Patent

4. a: Green marketing

5. c: Coupon

6. b: Economy

7. b: Testimonial

8. b: Social networking

9. d: Data analysis

10. d: Retail

11. c: Incentive

12. c: Respondent

13. d: North American Free Trade Agreement

14. d: Services marketing

15. d: Quantitative research

16. c: Convenience

17. b: Federal Trade Commission

18. : Census

19. c: Sherman Antitrust Act

20. : Direct marketing

21. b: Market segments

22. b: Insurance

23. : Trial

24. : Life

25. c: Leadership

26. : Small business

27. d: Loyalty program

28. c: Statistic

29. : Distribution channel

30. : Utility

31. c: Business-to-business

32. : Marketing management

33. d: Competitive intelligence

34. b: Warranty

35. c: Demand

36. d: Target market

37. d: Qualitative research

38. b: Return on investment

39. b: Marketing research

40. a: Brand awareness

41. d: Early adopter

42. b: Code

43. b: Investment

44. b: Marketing communications

45. b: Supply chain management

46. a: Database

47. c: Firm

48. a: Commercialization

49. c: Hearing

50. c: Sales promotion

51. c: Advertising campaign

52. : Purchasing

53. c: Reseller

54. d: Strategy

55. a: Performance

56. c: Cost-plus pricing

57. d: Complaint

58. d: Globalization

59. b: Auction

Manufacturing

1. : Authority

2. b: Planning

3. a: Quality audit

4. a: Solution

5. c: Ishikawa diagram

6. b: Inspection

7. b: Strategy

8. : DMAIC

9. c: Quality costs

10. c: Consortium

11. a: Change control

12. c: Total cost

13. : Raw material

14. : Economies of scope

15. d: Certification

16. a: Cost estimate

17. c: HEAT

18. : Manufacturing

19. : Quality control

20. d: Total cost of ownership

21. d: Purchasing manager

22. : Extended enterprise

23. a: Management process

24. c: Average cost

25. c: Strategic sourcing

26. a: Synergy

27. b: Dimension

28. a: American Society for Quality

29. d: Cash register

30. d: Initiative

31. c: Material requirements planning

32. : Pattern

33. b: Consensus

34. a: Sharing

35. b: Ball

36. : Performance

37. c: Service quality

38. a: Workflow

39. a: Purchase order

40. c: Credit

41. a: Cost reduction

42. c: Product differentiation

43. b: Process management

44. a: Six Sigma

45. d: Purchasing

46. d: Indirect costs

47. a: Metal

48. c: Voice of the customer

49. a: Time management

50. d: Sony

51. : Histogram

52. : Purchasing process

53. b: Asset

54. b: Root cause

55. d: Sunk costs

56. : Durability

57. a: Quality function deployment

58. : Paper

59. c: Malcolm Baldrige National Quality Award

Commerce

1. b: Marketing mix

2. b: Bankruptcy

3. b: Encryption

4. d: Customs

5. c: Automated Clearing House

6. c: Industrial Revolution

7. a: Management team

8. a: Welfare

9. c: Competitor

10. b: Risk management

11. a: Game

12. a: Case study

13. d: Disintermediation

14. a: Budget

15. d: Collaborative filtering

16. a: Logistics

17. : Inventory

18. b: Expense

19. d: Basket

20. b: Customer satisfaction

21. d: Commodity

22. : Statutory law

23. a: Supply chain management

24. a: Merger

25. b: Teamwork

26. : Authority

27. b: Policy

28. b: Incentive

29. b: Regulation

30. b: Leadership

31. : Short run

32. : Consortium

33. d: E-commerce

34. d: Electronic data interchange

35. b: Quality control

36. d: Market segmentation

37. c: Anticipation

38. a: Personnel

39. d: Overtime

40. b: Forward auction

41. b: Utility

42. a: Consignee

43. : Wage

44. c: Accounting

45. c: Automation

46. d: Payment card

47. b: Quality management

48. d: Preference

49. d: E-procurement

50. d: Performance

51. b: Consultant

52. a: Inventory control

53. a: English auction

54. a: Regulatory agency

55. c: Firm

56. d: Charter

57. c: Yield management

58. d: WebSphere Commerce

59. a: Purchasing

Business ethics

1. b: Employee Polygraph Protection Act

2. c: Wall Street

3. c: Sustainability

4. a: Working poor

5. d: Corporate structure

6. : Coal

7. a: Community development financial institution

8. c: Corporate citizenship

9. c: Real estate

10. a: Financial Stability Oversight Council

11. : Greenpeace

12. c: Guerrilla Marketing

13. a: Marijuana

14. a: Conscience

15. a: Price fixing

16. c: WorldCom

17. : Labor relations

18. d: Micromanagement

19. : European Commission

20. : Planet

21. a: Foreign Corrupt Practices Act

22. b: Feedback

23. a: Individualistic culture

24. a: Ethics Resource Center

25. c: Living wage

26. d: Dual relationship

27. : Dilemma

28. b: Socialism

29. : Solar power

30. b: Chamber of Commerce

31. : Corporation

32. d: Medicaid

33. : Pure Food and Drug Act

34. b: Charles Ponzi

35. a: East Germany

36. d: Sullivan principles

37. : Habitat

38. : Forest Stewardship Council

39. b: Criminal law

40. : Electronic waste

41. : Junk bond

42. a: Exxon Valdez

43. c: White-collar crime

44. c: Affirmative action

45. c: Pollution Prevention

46. a: Federal Trade Commission Act

47. a: Transocean

48. b: Locus of control

49. c: Invisible hand

50. c: Copyright

51. c: Internal control

52. b: Protestant work ethic

53. b: New Deal

54. : Risk management

55. : Supply Chain

56. d: Organizational ethics

57. a: Lawsuit

58. d: Cause-related marketing

59. a: Global reach

Accounting

1. : Petty cash

2. b: Sole proprietorship

3. : Revaluation

4. : Loan

5. a: Minority interest

6. b: Financial analysis

7. b: American Express

8. a: Operating budget

9. c: Adverse

10. a: Bank statement

11. a: Receipt

12. : Subsidiary ledger

13. d: Long-term liabilities

14. b: S corporation

15. a: Capital expenditure

16. b: Fixed cost

17. d: Inventory

18. a: Capital account

19. b: Net investment

20. c: Deferred income

21. b: Financial accounting

22. : Receivable

23. a: Adoption

24. c: Property tax

25. b: Trueblood Committee

26. c: Accounting information system

27. c: Indirect costs

28. a: Sales tax

29. : Cash

30. d: Personal identification number

31. : Beneficiary

32. c: Comprehensive annual financial report

33. c: Chart of accounts

34. : Going concern

35. : Accrual

36. c: Hedge accounting

37. d: Forecasting

38. a: Local government

39. b: Deferred tax

40. : Automated teller machine

41. : Adjusting entries

42. a: Investment

43. b: Limited liability partnership

44. a: Taxpayer

45. b: Annual report

46. : XBRL

47. c: Encumbrance

48. c: Supply chain

49. c: Expense

50. : Invoice

51. d: Withholding

52. : Callable

53. d: Treasury stock

54. d: Debtor

55. : Net present value

56. a: Stock Exchange

57. b: Dividend

58. d: Cost

59. d: Inflation

CPSIA information can be obtained
at www.ICGtesting.com
Printed in the USA
LVHW041329301019
635717LV00008B/1014/P